S0-BYW-213

For they know not what they do

PHRONESIS

A series from Verso edited by
Ernesto Laclau and Chantal Mouffe

There is today wide agreement that the left-wing project is in crisis. New antagonisms have emerged – not only in advanced capitalist societies but also in the Eastern bloc and in the Third World – that require the reformulation of the socialist ideal in terms of an extension and deepening of democracy. However, serious disagreements exist as to the theoretical strategy needed to carry out such a task. There are those for whom the current critique of rationalism and universalism puts into jeopardy the very basis of the democratic project. Others argue that the critique of essentialism – a point of convergence of the most important trends in contemporary theory: post-structuralism, philosophy of language after the later Wittgenstein, post-Heideggerian hermeneutics – is the necessary condition for understanding the widening of the field of social struggles characteristic of the present stage of democratic politics. *Phronesis* clearly locates itself among the latter. Our objective is to establish a dialogue between these theoretical developments and left-wing politics. We believe that an anti-essentialist theoretical stand is the sine qua non of a new vision for the Left conceived in terms of a radical and plural democracy.

For they know not what they do

Enjoyment as a Political Factor

SLAVOJ ŽIŽEK

VERSO
London · New York

First published by Verso 1991
© Slavoj Žižek 1991
Reprinted 1994
All rights reserved

Verso
UK: 6 Meard Street, London W1V 3HR
USA: 29 West 35th Street, New York, NY 10001-2291

Verso is the imprint of New Left Books

British Library Cataloguing in Publication Data

Žižek, Slavoj
For they know not what they do: enjoyment
as a political factor. – (Phronesis)
320.5019

ISBN 0-86091-355-4
ISBN 0-86091-563-8 pbk

Library of Congress Cataloging-in-Publication Data

Žižek, Slavoj.
[Ils ne savent pas ce qu'ils font. English]
For they know not what they do: enjoyment as a political factor/
Slavoj Žižek.
p. cm. – (Phronesis)
Translation of : Ils ne savent pas ce qu'ils font.
Includes index.
ISBN 0-86091-355-4: £32.95
ISBN 0-86091-563-8 (pbk): £11.95
1. Ideology. 2. Psychoanalysis—Social aspects. 3. Social problems—Psychological aspects. 4. Civilization. Modern—20th century—Psychological aspects. I. Title. II. Series: Phronesis (London, England)
B823.3.Z5813 1991
140—dc20

Typeset by York House Typographic Ltd, London
Printed and bound in
Finland by Werner Söderström Oy

For Kostja, my son

Contents

PART II Dialectics and its Discontents

PART III Cum Grano Praxis

INTRODUCTION

Destiny of a Joke

The background of the present book is best illustrated by the well-known Soviet joke about Rabinovitch, a Jew who wants to emigrate. The bureaucrat at the emigration office asks him why. Rabinovitch answers: "There are two reasons why. The first is that I'm afraid that the Communists will lose power in the Soviet Union, and the new forces will blame us Jews for the Communist crimes . . . " "But", interrupts the bureaucrat, "this is pure nonsense, the power of the Communists will last for ever!" "Well," responds Rabinovitch calmly, "that's my second reason."

In *The Sublime Object of Ideology*, published in 1989,[1] it was still possible to count on the efficacy of this joke, while according to the latest data, the main reason which Jews who emigrate from the Soviet Union cite is Rabinovitch's *first* reason. They effectively fear that, with the disintegration of Communism and the emergence of nationalistic forces openly advocating anti-Semitism, the blame will be again put on them, so that today we can easily imagine the reversal of the joke, with Rabinovitch answering the bureaucrat's question: "There are two reasons why. The first is that I know that Communism in Russia will last for ever, nothing will really change here, and this prospect is unbearable for me . . . " "But", interrupts the bureaucrat, "this is pure nonsense, Communism is disintegrating all around! All those responsible for the Communist crimes will be severely punished!" "That's my second reason!" responds Rabinovitch.

Retaining from the good old times the idea that the impetus of progress in socialism is self-criticism, the present book supplements the analyses of *The Sublime Object of Ideology* by endeavouring to articulate the theoretical apparatus which enables us to grasp the historical shift indicated by the strange destiny of the Rabinovitch joke: the eruption of enjoyment in the form of the re-emergence of the aggressive nationalism and racism that accompany the disintegration of "actually existing socialism" in Eastern Europe. This is what the book's title aims at – psychoanalysis is much more severe than Christianity: ignorance is *not* a sufficient reason for forgiveness since it conveys a hidden dimension of *enjoyment*. Where one doesn't (want to) know, in the blanks of one's symbolic universe, one enjoys, and there is no Father to forgive, since these blanks escape the authority of the Name-of-the-Father.

As with *The Sublime Object of Ideology*, the theoretical space of the present book is moulded by three centres of gravity: Hegelian dialectics, Lacanian psychoanalytic theory, and contemporary criticism of ideology. These three circles form a Borromeian knot: each of them connects the other two; the place that they all encircle, the "symptom" in their midst, is of course the author's (and, as the author hopes, also the reader's) enjoyment of what one depreciatingly calls "popular culture": detective and horror movies, Hollywood melodramas . . . . The three theoretical circles are not, however, of the same weight: it is their middle term, the theory of Jacques Lacan, which is – as Marx would say – "the general illumination which bathes all the other colours and modifies their particularity", "the particular ether which determines the specific gravity of every being which has materialized within it". In other words, as the "deconstructivists" would put it, the very theoretical frame of the present book is enframed by the (Lacanian) part of its content. In contrast to the false "anti-dogmatic spirit" which maintains a "critical distance" towards every theoretical *enunciated* in order to maintain the steady and full identity of its position of *enunciation*, it is the author's conviction that only by unreservedly assuming a determinate theoretical position does one effectively expose oneself to possible criticism.

In what precise sense, then, is the present book Lacanian? In his *Pragmatism*, William James develops the idea, taken up again by Freud, of the three necessary stages in the acceptance of a new theory: first, it is dismissed as nonsense; then, someone claims that the new theory, although not without its merits, ultimately just puts into new words things already said elsewhere; finally, the new theory is recognized in its novelty. It is easy, for a Lacanian, to discern in this succession the three moments of "logical time" as articulated by Lacan:[2] the *instant of looking* ("I can see immediately that this is nothing"), the *time* for *understanding* ("let us try to understand what the author is trying to say" – that is, let us try to reduce it to what is already known), the *moment for concluding* (the decision to have done with hesitation and accept the new theory in its novelty, in fear of being too late to attach oneself to the new doxa). The same three moments, of course, also determine the reception of the Lacanian theory itself: (1) "Lacan is simply bluffing, his so-called theory is a totally worthless sophism";[3] (2) "Lacan just formulates in obscure jargon what has already been said in a much clearer way by Freud himself and others"; (3) "I affirm myself to be a Lacanian, for fear of being convinced by others that I am not a Lacanian".

What the present book endeavours to accomplish, however, is precisely a break with this logic of *recognition*, its replacement with the process of *cognition*, of theoretical work: Lacan's theoretical apparatus is simply *put to work*. The book elaborates the contours of a Lacanian theory of ideology, moving step by step, via ever new detours, towards its main object, the status of enjoyment in ideological discourse, delaying this encounter in the same way as one delays the climactic reunion with a Lady in courtly love. The accent shifts slowly from Hegel through Lacan to the present politico-ideological deadlocks.

What gives the book its "specific flavour", however, is not so much its content as its *place of enunciation*. It conveys the text of lectures delivered on six consecutive Mondays in the winter semester of 1989–90 in Ljubljana, Yugoslavia. The lectures served as an introductory course to Lacan, organized by the Slovene Society for Theoretical Psychoanalysis and aimed at the "benevolently neutral" public of intellectuals who were the moving force of the drive for democracy; in other words, far from assuming the position of a Master "supposed to know", the lecturer acted as the analysand addressing the analyst composed of his public. The lectures were delivered in the unique atmosphere of those months: a time of intense political ferment, with "free elections" only weeks ahead, when all options still seemed open, the time of a "short circuit" blending together political activism, the "highest" theory (Hegel, Lacan) and unrestrained enjoyment in the "lowest" popular culture – a unique utopian moment which is now, after the electoral victory of the nationalist–populist coalition and the advent of a new "scoundrel time", not only over but even more and more *invisible*, erased from the memory like a "vanishing mediator".

Each lecture is composed of two parts, since it took three hours to deliver it – from seven to ten, with a break in the middle; it was, to use an expression from cinema, a theoretical double bill. Although the lectures are now "put in order", rewritten and edited with proper references, and so on, there is still in them more than a trace of the chaotic circumstances of their origins. These traces have been preserved deliberately, as a kind of monument to the unique moment of their enunciation.

Notes

1. Slavoj Žižek, *The Sublime Object of Ideology*, London: Verso 1989, pp. 175–6.
2. Jacques Lacan, "Logical Time and the Assertion of Anticipated Certainty", *Newsletter of the Freudian Field*, vol. 2, no. 2, Columbia: University of Missouri 1988.
3. To avoid the notion that this possibility is purely fictional, let us quote from a recent interview with Noam Chomsky: " . . . my frank opinion is that [Lacan] was a conscious charlatan, and was simply playing games with the Paris intellectual community to see how much absurdity he could produce and still be taken seriously"(Noam Chomsky, "An Interview", *Radical Philosophy* 53, Autumn 1989, p. 32).

PART I

E Pluribus Unum

1

On the One

I The Birth of a Master-Signifier

The non-analysable Slovene

Let us begin with our place of enunciation – Slovenia. What does it mean, psychoanalytically speaking, to be a Slovene?

There is only one mention of a "Slovene" in Freud's entire opus, and that is in a letter to the Trieste psychoanalyst Edoardo Weiss on 28 May 1922; however, this one mention is itself more than enough, since it condenses within it a whole series of key questions of psychoanalytic theory and practice, from the ambiguity of the superego to the problem of the mother as the bearer of the Law/Prohibition in Slovene tradition. So it's worth taking a closer look at it.

Weiss, who practised psychoanalysis in the twenties (he emigrated to America in the thirties, when political conditions in Italy made his practice impossible), corresponded regularly with Freud. Their correspondence revolved mainly on Weiss's cases: Weiss reported to Freud on the course of analysis and asked him for his advice. So he appealed for Freud's view on two patients at the beginning of the twenties, who both suffered from the same symptom – impotence. Let us look at Weiss's own presentation of the two cases:

> I have been treating two patients in 1922, who both suffer from impotence. The first is a highly cultured man, around forty years old, so some ten years older than I. His wife, whom he loved very much, had died a few years earlier. He experienced full sexual vigour during the time of the marriage. The wife fell into a heavy depression, attempts to cure her by

> some Viennese analyst produced no results at all. She committed suicide. My patient reacted to the suicide with heavy melancholy . . . .
>
> The second patient, a Slovene, was a young man. He had served in the army in the first world war and had only shortly prior to this been demobilized. In the sexual field he was completely impotent. A number of people had fallen prey to his deception and he had a thoroughly immoral Ego.[1]

What strikes the eye in this presentation is the almost total symmetry of the two cases: the first patient is ten years older than Weiss, the second some ten years younger; the first is a highly cultured and moral man, the second extremely immoral – and in both cases we are dealing with the same effect, impotence. (Strictly speaking, the symmetry is not complete: the Italian was capable of occasional sexual contact with prostitutes – to a man of "high culture and mores" this does not, of course, count as real sexual contact, contact with an equal – while the Slovene was completely impotent.) Freud's answer in the letter of 28 May 1922 took up this duality: he opined that the Italian warranted further treatment, since one was dealing with a man of "high culture and mores"; in his case it was simply exaggerated remorse, his impotence was the result of a pathological guilt complex; the solution for him – a man of refined sensitivity – was acceptance of his wife's suicide. About the Slovene, Freud remarked:

> The second case, the Slovene, is obviously a good-for-nothing who does not warrant your efforts. Our analytical art fails when faced with such people, our perspicacity alone cannot break through to the dynamic relation which controls them.[2]

It is not difficult to detect a basic deadlock in Freud's answer – it shows primarily in the contradictory nature of it, his oscillation between two positions. He first presents the Slovene as someone unworthy of psychoanalytic care, with the implication that it is a simple case of direct, superficial evil, immorality, without any kind of "depth" that pertains to our unconscious psychic dynamic; then, in the following sentence, his case is contrarily defined as such that it cannot be analysed; the barrier here is thus not "ethical" (unworthy of analysis) but of an epistemological nature (it is in itself non-analysable, an analytic attempt at it fails). The paradox with which we are dealing here corresponds precisely to the logical paradox of the "prohibition of incest": what is prohibited is something already in itself impossible, and the enigmatic character of the prohibition of incest is precisely in this redundancy – if something is in itself impossible, why is it necessary further to forbid it?

Wherein consists, then, the paradox of the Slovene's impotence? Nothing is easier than to explain this impotence as a result of excessive obedience, remorse, as a result of a "feeling of guilt" resulting from excessive discipline and rigid "moral sensitivity", and so on. This is the habitual, everyday concept of psychoanalysis: against the excessive discipline of superego, this agency of "internalized social repression", it is necessary to reaffirm the subject's capacity for relaxed fruition; it is necessary for the subject to free the "internal inhibition" which blocks his access to enjoyment.

Freud's Slovene exhibits clearly the insufficiency of such a logic of "freeing desire from the restraint of internal repression": he is, in Weiss's words, "very immoral", he exploits his neighbours and deceives with no kind of moral scruple – yet in all this he is far from able to achieve relaxed fruition in sex, without any kind of "internal obstruction"; he is "completely impotent", enjoyment is entirely forbidden to him. Or, in the words of Lacan against Dostoevsky, against his famous position "If there is no God, all is permitted": if there is no God – the Name-of-the-Father as an instance of the Law/Prohibition – everything is forbidden. And is it too much to suggest that this is precisely the logic of "totalitarian" political discourse? The "impediment" of the subject, produced by this discourse, results from a similar absence, suspension, of the Law/Prohibition. However, to return to our Slovene: on the basis of the fact that it was only Lacan who elaborated this logical paradox of "impediment", of universalized prohibition, brought about by the very absence of the Law/Prohibition, we could venture some wild speculation and say that we Slovenes – "unanalysable" according to Freud – had to wait for Lacan to find a meeting with psychoanalysis; only with Lacan did psychoanalysis itself achieve a level of sophistication on which it is capable of tackling such foul apparitions as the Slovenes.[3]

How do we account for this paradox that the absence of Law universalizes Prohibition? There is only one possible explanation: *enjoyment itself, which we experience as "transgression", is in its innermost status something imposed, ordered* – when we enjoy, we never do it "spontaneously", we always follow a certain injunction. The psychoanalytic name for this obscene injunction, for this obscene call,

"Enjoy!", is superego. This paradox of the superego is staged in its pure form in *Monty Python's Meaning of Life*, in the episode about sexual education: bored schoolboys yawn in the classroom, awaiting their teacher's arrival; when one of them shouts "He is coming!", all of a sudden they start to make a noise, shout and throw things at each other – the entire spectacle of wild uproar is here exclusively to impress the teacher's gaze. After quietening them, the teacher begins to examine them on how to arouse the vagina; caught in their ignorance, the embarrassed pupils avoid his gaze and stammer half-articulated answers, while the teacher reprimands them severely for not practising the subject at home. With his wife's assistance, he thereupon demonstrates to them the penetration of penis into vagina; bored by the subject, one of the schoolboys casts a furtive glance through the window, and the teacher asks him sarcastically: "Would you be kind enough to tell us what is so attractive out there in the courtyard?" Things are here brought to extreme: the reason this inverted presentation of the "normal", everyday relationship between Law (authority) and pleasure produces such an uncanny effect is of course that it exhibits in broad daylight the usually concealed truth about the "normal" state of things where enjoyment is sustained by a severe superego imperative.

The crucial theoretical point not to be missed here is that such mirror-inversion cannot be reduced to the domain of the Imaginary. That is to say, when one deals with the opposition of the Imaginary (captivation by the mirror-image, recognition in a fellow-creature) and the Symbolic (the purely formal order of differential features), one usually fails to notice how the specific dimension of the Symbolic emerges from the very imaginary mirroring: namely, from its *doubling*, by means of which – as Lacan puts it succinctly – the real image is substituted by a virtual one. The Imaginary and the Symbolic are therefore not simply opposed as two external entities or levels: within the Imaginary itself, there is always a point of double reflection at which the Imaginary is, so to speak, hooked on the Symbolic.

Hegel demonstrates the mechanism of this passage in the dialectic of the "topsy-turvy world" [*die verkehrte Welt*] which concludes the section on Consciousness in his *Phenomenology of Spirit*. After exposing the Christian notion of the Beyond as the inversion of the terrestrial life (here, injustice and violence reign, while There, goodness will be rewarded, etc.) he points out how inversion is always double – how, on a closer look, it becomes manifest that the "first" world whose inverted image is the topsy-turvy world is already in itself inverted. Therein consists the rationale of caricature – let us just recall Swift's procedure in *Gulliver's Travels*: the reader is confronted with a series of mocking inversions of our "normal" human universe (the island populated by dwarfs two inches tall; a country where "normal" relations between humans and horses are reversed – where humans live in stables and serve horses . . .). Swift's true targets are, of course, our own weaknesses and stupidities: by means of a fantasy-world which presents its inverted image, he endeavours to turn into ridicule the follies – the *invertedness* – of our own allegedly "normal" world. The image of humans who serve horses should arouse us to the vanity of the human species as compared with the simple dignity of horses; the null disputes of the Lilliputians are there to remind us of the conceit of human customs, and so on.[4]

Here, we can clearly discern the function of the Ego-Ideal – that is, of symbolic identification – from its imaginary counterpart: symbolic identification is identification with the ideal ("virtual") point *from which* the subject looks upon himself when his own actual life appears to him as a vain and repulsive spectacle. That is to say, Swift, like Monty Python, belongs to the "misanthropic" lineage of English humour based on an aversion to life as the substance of enjoyment, and the Ego-Ideal is precisely the viewpoint assumed by the subject when he perceives his very "normal" everyday life as something inverted. This point is *virtual*, since it figures nowhere in reality: it differs from "actual" life as well as from its inverted caricature – that is to say, it cannot be located within the mirror-relationship between reality and its inverted image – as such, it is of a strictly *symbolic* nature.

Let the Emperor have his clothes!

Another way of arriving at the same point is via the gesture of stating that the Emperor has no clothes. The child from Andersen's tale who with disarming innocence states the obvious is usually taken as an exemplar of the word which delivers us from stuffy hypocrisy and forces us to confront the actual state of things. What one prefers to pass over in silence are the catastrophic consequences of such a liberating gesture for its environs, for the intersubjective network within which it takes place: by stating openly that the Emperor has no clothes, we intend only to get rid of the unnecessary hypocrisy and pretence. After the deed, when it is already too late, we suddenly notice that we got more than we bargained for – that the very community of which we were a member has disintegrated. This is why, perhaps, the time has come to abandon the usual praise of the child's gesture and rather conceive it as the prototype of the innocent chatterbox who – by blurting out what should remain unspoken if the existing intersubjective network is to retain its consistency – unknowingly and involuntarily sets off the catastrophe.

Ring Lardner's little masterpiece "Who dealt?"[5] tells the story of such a prattler. There is nothing special in its plot line as such: two friendly couples – the narrator and her husband Tom; Helen and Arthur – spend an evening together playing bridge. The narrator, who is only recently married to Tom, knows nothing about his stormy past: years ago, he and Helen were passionately in love; because of a petty misunderstanding they split up; broken and helpless, Helen married their reliable friend Arthur, while Tom struggled to pull himself out of despair and took comfort in writing poems which, in a half-concealed way, tell the story of his lost love. The narrator has found Tom's literary efforts among his papers; unaware of their impact, she recites them during the game to amuse the company. The story ends at the precise moment when the catastrophe comes to light: when the narrator becomes aware of saying something terribly wrong . . .[6]

So far, nothing special. The effect of the story hinges exclusively on its *narrative perspective*: it is written entirely as the narrator's monologue, as her confused prattle accompanying the game – we are strictly limited to her perspective, to what she says and sees. It would be easy to imagine the same story retold from another perspective: that of her husband Tom, for example, who trembles with anxiety as he observes his prattling wife approaching the "dangerous ground". Lardner wisely preferred the viewpoint of the person who unknowingly acted as the *cause* of catastrophe: instead of presenting the catastrophe immediately, he evokes it "off champ" (to use this term from cinema theory) – that is, *as it is mirrored in the face of its cause*. Therein consists his narrative mastery: although strictly limited to the viewpoint of the innocent chatterbox, we – the readers – simultaneously occupy the position of the Hitchcockian "man who knows too much" – who knows that the prattler's words inscribe themselves in a framework within which they mean catastrophe. Our horror is strictly co-dependent on the radical limitation of our perspective to that of the ignorant prattler who, until the very end, has no presentiment of the effect of her words.

This is what Lacan means when he ascertains that the subject of the signifier is constitutively *split*: the speaking subject is split into the ignorance of her imaginary experience (the narrator imagines that she is pursuing the usual light table conversation) and the weight her words assume within the field of the big Other, the way they affect the intersubjective network – the "truth" of innocent prattle can well be intersubjective catastrophe. Lacan's point is simply that these two levels never fully cohere: the gap separating them is constitutive; the subject, by definition, cannot master the effects of his speech, since the big Other is in charge.

This limitation to the viewpoint of the narrator as cause of the catastrophe implies again the structure of double mirroring: our view is not confined to the way her words are mirrored in the eyes of those affected by them, but even more radically to the way the effect of her words upon her environs – the mirroring of her words in her environs – *is mirrored back in herself*. Here, again, this double reflection produces a symbolic point the nature of which is purely virtual: neither what I immediately see ("reality" itself) nor the way others see me (the "real" inverted image of reality) but *the way I see the others seeing me*. If we do not add this third, purely virtual viewpoint of the Ego-Ideal, then it remains totally incomprehensible how the inverted representation of our "normal" world can act as an ironic refusal of the invertedness that pertains to our "normal" world itself – that is, how the depiction of a strange world opposed to ours can give rise to the radical estrangement from our own. The key to the efficacy of Lardner's story is that, by means of such a double mirroring, *we – its readers – are set up in the position of the narrator's Ego-Ideal*: we are capable of locating her self-infatuated prattle in its intersubjective context and thus taking notice of its catastrophic effects. In Hegelese: we, the readers, are her "In-itself or For-us".

This is also the point at which all attempts to define the "invertedness" of the modern world reach an impasse: the double inversion calls into question the very standard of "normality" which they make use of to measure the invertedness; what we have in mind here are formulations based upon the "instead-of" logic, like those which abound in the works of young Marx ("instead of recognizing in the product of my work the actualization of my essential forces, this product appears to me as an independent power oppressing me . . . ").

Let us just recall the famous research on authoritarian personality from the late forties where Adorno and his collaborators endeavoured to define the "authoritarian syndrome" – the Weberian ideal-type of the authoritarian psychic disposition. How did they construct their initial hypothesis, the coherent series of features which constitute the "authoritarian type"? Martin Jay, in his *Dialectical Imagination*,[7] makes a sarcastic remark on how they arrived at the "authoritarian syndrome" by simply inverting the features that define the (ideological) image of the liberal bourgeois individual. The ambiguity consists in the non-explicated status of this "positive" counterpart to the "authoritarian personality": is it effectively its positive counterpart for the realization of which we should strive, or is the "authoritarian personality" the reverse of the "liberal personality" in the sense of its inherent dark side?

In the first case, "liberal personality" is conceived as a kind of "essential possibility" the realization of which turned into its opposite because of the Fascist "regression"; their relationship is therefore that of the ideal paradigm ("liberal personality") and its perverted realization ("authoritarian personality") – as such, it could easily be described by means of the young-Marxian rhetorics ("instead of tolerating difference and accepting non-violent dialogue as the only means to arrive at a common decision, the subject advocates violent intolerance and distrust in free dialogue"; "instead of critically examining every authority, the subject uncritically obeys those in power", etc.).

In the second case, "authoritarian personality" has a strict symptomatic value: in it, the "repressed truth" of the liberal, "open" personality emerges – that is, the liberal personality is confronted with its "totalitarian" foundation.[8] The same ambiguity pertains to Marx's formulation of the "topsy-turvy world" of commodity-fetishism as the inversion of the "normal" transparent relations between individuals – as, for example, when he compares the inversion proper to commodity-fetishism with the idealist inversion of the relationship between the Universal and the Particular:

> If I say: Roman law and German law are both laws, it is something which stands by itself. But if, on the contrary, I say: THE Law, this abstract thing realizes itself in Roman law and in German law, i.e. in these concrete laws, the interconnection becomes mystical.[9]

How do common-sense nominalism (Roman law and German law as two laws) and speculative idealism (THE Law realizes itself in Roman law and in German law) relate? Is the latter a simple inversion of the first, and as such the theoretical expression of the invertedness ("alienation") of the actual social life itself, or is the "topsy-turvy world" of dialectical speculation the hidden "truth" of our very "normal", everyday, commonsensical universe? What is at stake here is the very notion of "alienation" in Marx: the moment invertedness is redoubled – the moment the inversion attests to the invertedness of the "normal" state itself – the very standard by means of which we measure alienation is called in to question.

We could further posit that with Lacan, the status of the subject itself (the subject of the signifier) is that of just such a "virtual image": it exists only as a virtual point in the self-relating of the signifier's dyads; as something that "will have been", that is never present in reality or its "real" (actual) image. It is always-already "past", although it never appeared "in the past itself"; it is constituted by means of a double reflection, as the result of the way the past's mirroring in the future is mirrored back in the present. We all remember from our youth the sublime dialectical materialist formulas of the "subjective mirroring–reflection of the objective reality"; all we have to do to arrive at the Lacanian notion of the subject is to redouble the reflection: *the subject designates that virtual point in which reflection itself is reflected back into "reality"* – in which, for example, (my perception of) the possible future outcome of my present acts determines what I will do now. What we call "subjectivity" is at its most elementary this self-referential "short circuit" which ultimately invalidates every prognosis in intersubjective relations: the prognosis itself, as soon as it is uttered, bears upon the predicted outcome, and it is never able to take into account this effect of its own act of enunciation. And the same goes for Hegelian reflection: far from being reducible to the imaginary mirror-relationship between the subject and its other, it is always redoubled in the above-described way; it implies a non-imaginary "virtual" point.[10]

The basic lesson of the double reflection is therefore that the symbolic truth emerges via the "imitation of imitation" – this is what Plato found unbearable in the illusion of painting, this is why he wanted to expel painters from his ideal state: "The picture does not compete with appearance, it competes with what Plato designates for us beyond appearance as being the Idea."[11] Here, one has only to recall the resort to "theatre within theatre" in order to stage a concealed truth (this is how the king-murderer is unmasked in *Hamlet*, for example), or the resort to "painting within painting" in order to indicate the dimension excluded from the painting. And is not the lesson of Hitchcock's *Vertigo* precisely the same: the hour of truth arrives for Scottie, the film's hero, when he discovers that the copy he was trying to re-create (i.e. Judy, whom he was trying to remodel into a perfect copy of Madeleine, his lost great love) actually *is* the girl whom he knew as "Madeleine", and that he was therefore busy at making a *copy of a copy*? Gavin Elster, the film's evil spirit, has already used Judy as a substitute for his wife – that is, remodelled her after the "true" Madeleine. In other words, Scottie's fury at the end is an authentic *Platonic* fury: he is furious at discovering that he was *imitating the imitation*.

The "quilting point"

At the level of the semiotic process, the Ego-Ideal that emerges from the double reflection equals what Lacan called *le point de capiton* (the "quilting point", literally: the "upholstery button").[12] Lacan introduces this concept in Chapter XXI of his seminar *Les Psychoses*,[13] with regard to the first act of Jean Racine's play *Athalie*: to Abner's lamentations about the sad fate which awaits the partisans of God under the reign of Athaliah, Jehoiada replies with the famous lines:

> The one who puts a stop to the fury of the waves
> Knows also of the evil men how to stop the plots.
> Subservient with respect to his holy will,
> I fear God, dear Abner, and have no other fear.

This "*Je crains Dieu, cher Abner, et n'ai point d'autre crainte*" brings about an instant conversion of Abner: from an impatient, fervent – and precisely for this reason unreliable – *zealot* it creates a firm, faithful *adherent*, sure of himself and of divine power. How does this evocation of the "fear of God" succeed in effecting the miraculous conversion? Previous to it, Abner sees in the earthly world only a multitude of dangers which fill him with fear, and he waits for the opposite pole, that of God and His representatives, to lend him their help and allow him to conquer the many difficulties of this world. However, faced with this opposition between the earthly realm of dangers, uncertainty, fears, and so on, and the divine realm of peace, love and assurance, Jehoiada does not simply try to convince Abner that divine forces are, despite everything, powerful enough to gain the upper hand over earthly disarray; he appeases his fears in a quite different way: by presenting their very opposite – God – as a thing more frightening than all earthly fears. And – that is the "miracle" of the *point de capiton* – this supplemental fear, fear of God, retroactively changes the character of all other fears; it

> accomplishes the magical trick of transforming, from one minute to another, all fears into a perfect courage. All fears – *I have no other fear* – are exchanged against what is called the fear of God.[14]

The common Marxist formula of religious consolation as compensation for – or, more precisely, an "imaginary supplement" to – earthly misery is based upon a dual, imaginary relation between the earthly below and the celestial Beyond: according to this conception, the religious operation consists in compensating us for earthly horrors and uncertainties by the promise of beatitude which awaits us in the other world – one has only to recall all the famous formulas of Ludwig Feuerbach on the divine Beyond as a specular, reversed image of earthly misery. Yet for this operation to work, a third, properly *symbolic* moment must intervene which somehow "mediates" between the two opposite poles of the *imaginary* dyad (the fearful earthly below versus the blissful divine Beyond): the fear of God – that is, the horrifying reverse of the celestial Beyond itself. The only way effectively to cancel earthly misery is to know that behind the multitude of earthly horrors, the infinitely more frightening horror of God's wrath must show through, so that earthly horrors undergo a kind of "transubstantiation" and become so many manifestations of divine anger. This is one of the ways to draw the line that divides the Imaginary from the Symbolic: on the imaginary level, we react to earthly fears by "have patience, eternal bliss is waiting for you in the Beyond . . . "; whereas on the symbolic level, what delivers us from earthly fears is the assurance that the only thing we have to fear is God Himself – an *additional* fear that retroactively cancels all the others.

One can discern the same operation in Fascist anti-Semitism: what does Hitler do in *Mein Kampf* to explain to the Germans the misfortunes of the epoch, economic crisis, social disintegration, moral "decadence", and so on? He constructs a new terrifying subject, a unique cause of Evil who "pulls the strings" behind the scene and is the sole precipitator of the series of evils: the Jew. The simple evocation of the "Jewish plot" *explains everything*: all of a sudden "things become clear", perplexity is replaced by a firm sense of orientation, all the diversity of earthly miseries is conceived as the manifestation of the "Jewish plot". In other words, the Jew is Hitler's *point de capiton*; the fascinating figure of the Jew is the product of a purely formal inversion; it is based upon a kind of "optical illusion" the mechanism of which was elaborated by Victor Schklovsky and, more recently, by Fredric Jameson:

> Don Quixote is not really a character at all, but rather an organizational device that permits Cervantes to write his book, serving as a thread that holds a number of different types of anecdotes together in a single form.[15]

Henry James designated this kind of narrative character whose actual function is to represent within the diegetic space its own process of enunciation – the discursive structure of the work itself – by the term *ficelle* (Maria Gostrey in *The Ambassadors*, for example, is a *ficelle*). Therein consists also the function of the Jew in anti-Semitic ideology: in so far as an ideological edifice gains consistency from organizing its heterogeneous "raw material" into a coherent narrative, the entity called "Jew" is a device enabling us to unify in a single large narrative the experiences of economic crisis, "moral decadence" and loss of values, political frustration and "national humiliation", and so on. As soon as we perceive as their common thread the "Jewish plot", they became part of the same (narrative) *plot*.

What we have here is an inversion by means of which what is effectively an *immanent*, purely textual operation – the "quilting" of the heterogeneous material into a unified ideological field – is perceived and experienced as an unfathomable, *transcendent*, stable point of reference concealed behind the flow of appearances and acting as its hidden cause. This inversion is best epitomized by the difference between the traditional and the modern notions of *allegory*: within the traditional space, the immediate diegetic content of a work personifies transcendent values or ideas (concrete individuals stand for Evil,

Wisdom, Love, Lust, and so on); whereas in the modern space, the diegetic content is conceived as an allegory of its own immanent process of enunciation, of writing and reading. Let us take, for example, Hitchcock's *Psycho*: the two opposed allegorical readings of this film are those of Jean Douchet (who reads it as a traditional allegory: the patrolman as Angel trying to save Marion from destruction, and so forth) and William Rothmann (who reads the diegetic content of *Psycho* as an allegory of the very relationship between Hitchcock and the viewer of his film: the aggression in the shower scene epitomizes Hitchcock's sadistic punishment of the viewer for his inquisitiveness, and so on).

In this precise sense, the "criticism of ideology" consists in unmasking traditional allegory as an "optical illusion" concealing the mechanism of modern allegory: the figure of the Jew as an allegory of Evil conceals the fact that it represents within the space of ideological narration the pure immanence of the textual operation that "quilts" it.[16] The real questions, however, are: How is this purely formal inversion possible? On what does it rely? More precisely: How is it possible that the result of a purely formal inversion acquires enough substantiality to be perceived as a flesh-and-blood personality? The psychoanalytic answer is, of course, *enjoyment* – the only substance acknowledged by psychoanalysis, according to Lacan. The "Jew" cannot be reduced to a purely formal organizational device; the efficacy of this figure cannot be explained by reference to the textual mechanism of "quilting"; the surplus on which this mechanism relies is the fact that we impute to the "Jew" an impossible, unfathomable enjoyment, allegedly stolen from us.

Conceived in this way, the *point de capiton* enables us to locate the misreading of the notion of "suture" in Anglo-Saxon "deconstructivism" – namely, its use as a synonym for ideological closure, for the gesture by means of which a given ideological field encloses itself, effaces the traces of the material process which generated it; the traces of externality in its interior, the traces of senseless contingency in its immanent necessity. Let us recall how the King – this exemplar of *point de capiton*, this individual who "quilts" the social edifice – was conceptualized by Hegel: the King is undoubtedly the point of the "suture" of social totality, the point whose intervention transforms a contingent collection of individuals into a rational totality – *yet precisely as such*, as the point which "sutures" Nature and Culture, as the point at which a cultural–symbolic function (that of being a king) immediately coincides with a natural determination (who will be king is determined by nature, by biological lineage), *the King radically "de-sutures" all other subjects*; makes them lose their roots in some pre-ordained organic social body that would fix their place in society in advance and forces them to acquire their social status by means of hard labour. It is therefore not sufficient to define the King as the only immediate junction of Nature and Culture – the point is rather that this very gesture by means of which the King is posited as their "suture" de-sutures all other subjects, makes them lose their footing; throws them into a void where they must, so to speak, create themselves.

Therein consists the accent of the Lacanian notion of "suture", passed over in silence in Anglo-Saxon "deconstructivism" (in "deconstructivist" cinema theory, for example): to put it succinctly, *the only thing that actually de-sutures is suture itself.* This paradox comes to light in a palpable way apropos of the ambiguous and contradictory nature of the modern *nation*. On the one hand, "nation" of course designates modern community delivered of the traditional "organic" ties, a community in which the pre-modern links tying down the individual to a particular estate, family, religious group, and so on, are broken – the traditional corporate community is replaced by the modern nation-state whose constituents are "citizens": people as abstract individuals, not as members of particular estates, and so forth. On the other hand, "nation" can never be reduced to a network of purely symbolic ties: there is always a kind of "surplus of the Real" that sticks to it – to define itself, "national identity" must appeal to the contingent materiality of the "common roots", of "blood and soil", and so on. In short, "nation" designates at one and the same time the instance by means of reference to which traditional "organic" links are dissolved *and* the "remainder of the pre-modern in modernity": the form "organic inveteracy" acquires within the modern, post-traditional universe; the form organic substance acquires within the universe of the substanceless Cartesian subjectivity. The crucial point is again to conceive both aspects in their interconnection: it is precisely the new "suture" effected by the Nation which renders possible the "de-suturing", the disengagement from traditional organic ties. "Nation" is a pre-modern leftover which functions as an inner condition of modernity itself, as an inherent impetus of its progress.

"A signifier represents the subject for another signifier"

An attentive reader of Lacan will have noted how, apropos of the "fear of God" as "quilting point", he produces the formula of *general equivalent*: the "fear of God" springs up as the general equivalent of all fears – all fears "are exchanged against what is called the fear of God". Do we not consequently encounter here the very logic which is at work in the dialectic of the commodity-form, when Marx infers the appearance of money, the general equivalent of all commodities? The moment all commodities are exchangeable against money – the moment their value, their universal dimension, is incarnated in a sole commodity – all other commodities undergo a "transubstantiation" and start to function as the appearance of the universal Value embodied in money; as with religion, where all fears start to function as the appearance of the fear of God.

We mention this homology since the succession of the "forms of value" in the Marxian analysis of commodity provides the conceptual tools enabling us to clarify what – at first sight, at least – cannot but appear as a confusion, a contradiction even, in the Lacanian formula of the signifier ("that which represents the subject for another signifier"). Which of these two signifiers is namely S1 (the "Master-Signifier") and which S2 (the chain of knowledge)? If we rely on the doxa, the answer seems clear: S1 represents the subject for S2, for the chain of signifiers which includes it. Yet in a passage of what is probably the crucial text of *Écrits*, "Subversion of the Subject and Dialectic of Desire", Lacan univocally avers the exact opposite:

> . . . a signifier is that which represents the subject for another signifier. This signifier will therefore be the signifier for which all the other signifiers represent the subject: that is to say, in the absence of this signifier, all the other signifiers do not represent anything, since something is represented only for something else.[17]

It would follow from this that S1, the Master-Signifier, the One, is the signifier *for which* all the others represent the subject. A further complication is involved in the play of singular and plural in the different versions of the formula of the signifier: at times a signifier represents the subject for "all the others", whereas at other times it represents the subject simply for "another signifier". Are what we have here really meaningless variations that one can get rid of by simply ascertaining that "another signifier" stands for "all the others" in a given signifier's chain?

How, then, are we to disentangle this mess? Let us begin at the most elementary: in what does the "differential" nature of the signifier consist? S1 and S2, the terms of the signifier's dyad, are not simply two terms that appear at the same level, against the background of their common genus, and are held apart by a specific difference. "Differentiality" designates a more precise relationship: in it, the opposite of one term, of its *presence*, is not immediately the other term but the *absence* of the first term, the *void* at the place of its inscription (the void which *coincides* with its place of inscription) and the presence of the other, opposite, term *fills out* this void of the first term's absence – this is how one has to read the well-known "structuralist" thesis according to which, in a paradigmatic opposition, the presence of a term means (equals) the absence of its opposite. The signifier's opposition of "day" to "night", for example, does not convey a simple alteration of day and night as two complementary terms which, together, would form a Whole ("there is no day without night, and vice versa"); the point is rather that

> the human being posits the day as such, whereby the day is present as day – against a background which is not the concrete background of night but the possible absence of day whereinto night is located, and vice versa, of course.[18]

Within a signifier's dyad, a signifier thus always appears against the background of its possible absence which is materialized – which assumes positive existence – in the presence of its opposite. The Lacanian matheme for this absence is of course $\mathrm{S}\!\!\!/$, the "barred", "crossed-out" signifier: a signifier fills out the absence of its opposite – that is, it "represents", holds the place of, its opposite . . . . We have already thus produced the formula of the signifier, so we can understand why $\mathrm{S}\!\!\!/$ is for Lacan also the matheme for the *subject*: a signifier (S1) represents for another signifier (S2) its absence, its lack $\mathrm{S}\!\!\!/$, which is the subject. The crucial point here is that in a signifier's dyad, a signifier is never a direct complement to its opposite but always represents (gives body to) its possible absence: the two signifiers enter a "differential" relationship only via the third term, the void of their possible absence – to say that signifier is differential means that there is no signifier which does not represent the subject.

At this point, however, things start to get complicated: the same goes for *every* signifier with which the first signifier is "accoupled" – that is to say, *each of them* represents for the first signifier the void of its possible absence (the subject). In other words, at the beginning there is no master-signifier, since "any signifier can assume the role of the master-signifier if its eventual function becomes to represent a subject for another signifier".[19] One can ascribe to every signifier a never-ending series of "equivalences", of signifiers which represent for it the void of its place of inscription; we find ourselves in a kind of dispersed, non-totalized network of links, every signifier enters into a series of particular relationships with other signifiers. The only possible way out of this impasse is that we simply *reverse* the series of equivalences and ascribe to *one* signifier the function of representing the subject (the place of inscription) for all the others (which thereby become "all" – that is, are totalized): in this way, the proper *Master-Signifier* is produced.

The parallel with the articulation of the value-form from the first chapter of *Capital* strikes the eye: first, in the "simple, isolated or accidental form of value", a commodity B appears as the expression of value of a commodity A; thereupon, in the "total or expanded form of value", equivalences are multiplied – commodity A finds its equivalents in a series of commodities, B, C, D, E, which give expression to its value; finally, in the "general form of value", we reach the level of the "general equivalent" by simply *reversing* the "total or expanded form" – it is now commodity A itself which gives expression to the value of all other commodities, B, C, D, E . . . . In both cases, the starting point consists in a radical contradiction (use-value and (exchange-)value of a commodity; a signifier and the void-place of its inscription, i.e. S/$) because of which the first aspect of the contradiction (use-value, signifier) must from the very beginning be posited as a dyad: a commodity can express its (exchange-)value only in the use-value of *another* commodity; for a signifier, its place of inscription – its possible absence ($) – can be represented only in the presence of another *signifier*. The play of singular and plural, as well as the exchange of places between S1 and S2 in the different versions of the Lacanian formula of the signifier, can thus be accounted for by means of reference to the succession of the three forms of value:

1. The simple form: "for *a* signifier, *another* signifier represents the subject" (i.e. "*a* signifier represents the subject for *another* signifier");
2. The expanded form: "for *a* signifier, *any* of the other signifiers can represent the subject";
3. The general form: "*a* (one) signifier represents the subject for *all the other* signifiers".

The turning point is of course the passage from 2 to 3, from "expanded" to "general" form: apparently, it only reverses the relationship (instead of *any* signifier representing the subject for *one* signifier, we obtain *one* signifier representing the subject for *all* others), whereas it actually shifts the entire economy of representation by introducing an additional "reflective" dimension.

To discern this dimension, let us return to the above-quoted passage from *L'Envers de la psychanalyse*: in its continuation, Lacan says that the subject "is simultaneously represented and not represented since at this level" (that is, in our "Marxian" reading, at the level of the "expanded form" where there is as yet no Master-Signifier *stricto sensu*) "something remains concealed in the relationship to this same signifier" – this oscillation between representation and non-representation points towards the ultimate *failure* of the subject's signifying representation: the subject has no "proper" signifier which would "fully" represent it, every signifying representation is a misrepresentation which, however imperceptibly, always-already displaces, distorts, the subject . . . . And it is precisely this irreducible failure of the signifying representation which elicits the passage from "simple" into "expanded" form: since every signifier *mis*represents the subject, the movement of representation goes on to the next signifier in search of an ultimate "proper" signifier, the result of which is a non-totalized "bad infinity" of signifying representations. The crucial point, however, is that the signifier which, with the emergence of the "general form", is posited as the "general equivalent" representing the subject for "all the others" is *not* the finally found "proper" signifier, a representation which is not a misrepresentation: it does not represent the subject at the same level, within the same logical space, as the others (the "any of the others" from form 2). This signifier is, on the contrary, a "reflective" one: in it, the very failure, the very impossibility of the signifier's representation is reflected into this representation itself. In other words, this paradoxical signifier represents (gives body to) the very impossibility of the subject's signifying representation – to resort to the worn-out Lacanian formula, it functions as the "signifier of the lack of the signifier", as the place of the reflective inversion of the lacking signifier into the signifier of the lack.

This "reflective" signifier "totalizes" the battery of "all others" – makes out of them a totality of "*all* the others": we could say that all signifiers represent the subject for the signifier which in advance represents for them their own ultimate failure and is precisely as such – as the representation of the failure of representation – "closer" to the subject than all the others (since the Lacanian "subject of the signifier" is not a positive, substantial entity persisting outside the series of its representations: it coincides with its own impossibility; it "is" nothing but the void opened up by the failure of its representations). The logic of this vicious circle is actually that of the old theological formula "you would not be looking for me if you had not already found me": all signifiers are in search of the subject for a signifier which has already found it for them.

The logic of this "reflective" signifier – designated by Lacan also as "phallic" signifier – comes out in its purest in the paradox of *bodhisattva* in Mahayana Buddhism: the general conception of *bodhisattva* is that of one who has attained enlightenment and can pass over into Nirvana; yet the *bodhisattva* alone cannot actually pass over into Nirvana:

> because, were he to do so he would exhibit a selfishness that a *bodhisattva* cannot have. If he has the selfishness, he is not a *bodhisattva*, and so cannot enter Nirvana. If he lacks the selfishness, again, he cannot enter Nirvana, for that would be a selfish act. . . . So no one can reach Nirvana: we cannot because we are not *bodhisattvas* and the *bodhisattva* cannot because he is a *bodhisattva*.[20]

In Lacanian theory, mysticism is usually located on the feminine side of his "formulae of sexuation": the mystical experience as a boundless and therefore "not-all", non-phallic enjoyment; the paradox of *bodhisattva* provides the contours of a "masculine", "phallic" mystical subjective position.

The difference may be grasped clearly by confronting *bodhisattva* with the Taoist sage: in Taoism, the choice is ultimately a simple one: we either persist in the world of illusions or "follow the Way" [*Tao*] – leave behind us the world of false oppositions – whereas the basic experience of *bodhisattva* concerns precisely the *impossibility* of such an immediate withdrawal of the individual from the world of illusions – if an individual accomplishes it, he thereby ascertains his difference from other human beings and thus falls prey to his selfishness in the very gesture of leaving it behind. The only escape from this deadlock is for the *bodhisattva* to postpone his own bliss until all mankind has reached the same point as he; this way, the Taoist sage's *indifference* passes over into *ethical heroism*: the *bodhisattva* performs the act of supreme sacrifice by postponing his own entry into Nirvana for the sake of the salvation of mankind. In relation to other, ordinary humans who are still victims of the veil of illusions, the *bodhisattva* functions as a "reflective", "phallic" element: he does represent Liberation, stepping out of the world of illusions – but not immediately, like the Taoist sage; rather, he embodies the very *impossibility* of the individual's immediate Liberation. In opposition to other, ordinary human beings, Liberation (the passage into Nirvana) is already present in him, but as *a pure possibility which must forever remain postponed*.

The parallel with the Marxian analysis of the "value-form" can be prolonged a step further: with Marx, the "general form" itself has two stages – first, the commodity which serves as "general equivalent" is the one which is most often exchanged, which has the greatest use-value (furs, corn, and so on); then, the relationship is inverted and the role of "general equivalent" is taken over by a commodity with no use-value (or at least with negligible use-value) – *money* (the "money form").[21] Following the same logic, the "general form" of the signifying equivalence ("a signifier represents the subject for *all of the other* signifiers") could be supplemented by its inversion – precisely that found in the above-quoted passage from "Subversion of the Subject":

4. the money form: "*a (one)* signifier *for which all the other* signifiers represent the subject"

– where the crucial point is the difference between this form and the "expanded" (2) form: the multitude of others which represent the subject for a signifier is here no longer "*any* of the others" – that is, the non-totalized collection of "others" – but the totality of "*all* the others": the multitude is totalized through the exceptional position of the One which embodies the moment of impossibility. On the other hand, the co-dependence of the two stages of "general form" ("one for all the others" and then "all the others for the one") pertains to the different level of representation: "all" represent for the One the subject, whereas the One represents for "all" the very impossibility of representation. We can see how the One of a "pure" signifier again emerges from a movement of *double reflection*: a simple inversion of the "expanded" form into the "general" form – the "reflection-into-itself" of the reflection of the value of A into B – accomplishes the miracle of transforming the amorphous network of particular links into a consistent field totalized by the One's exceptional position. In other words, the One "quilts" the field of the multitude.[22]

Why is morality the darkest of conspiracies?

The "Dreyfus Affair" unfolds this "miraculous inversion" of the discursive field, produced by the intervention of the *point de capiton*, in a paradigmatic fashion. Its role in French and European political history already resembles that of a *point de capiton*: it restructured the entire field and released, directly or indirectly, a series of displacements which even today determine the political scene: the separation of Church and State in bourgeois democracies, socialist collaboration in bourgeois governments and the split of social democracy into Socialists and Communists that ensued from it, up to the birth of Zionism and the elevation of anti-Semitism to the key moment of right-wing populism.

Here, however, one will try only to locate the decisive turn in its development: the intervention which made a judiciary quarrel bearing on the equity and legality of a verdict the stake of a political battle which shook the very foundations of national life. This turning point is not to be sought, as one usually presumes, in the famous *J'accuse* that appeared in *Aurore* on 13 January 1898, where Émile Zola took up once again all the arguments for Dreyfus's defence and denounced the corruption of official circles. Zola's intervention remained in the realm of bourgeois liberalism, that of the defence of the liberties and rights of the citizen, and so on. The real upset took place in the second half of that year. On 30 August, Lieutenant Colonel Henry, new Chief of the Second Bureau (the French intelligence service) was arrested: he was suspected of having forged one of the secret documents on the basis of which Dreyfus had been condemned for high treason. The next day Henry committed suicide with a razor in his cell. This news provoked a shock in public opinion: if Henry had confessed his guilt – and what other meaning could one give to his suicide? – the accusation against Dreyfus must, in its entirety, lack solidity. Everyone expected a retrial and the acquittal of Dreyfus. Then:

> Then in the midst of the confusion and consternation, a newspaper article appeared which altered the situation. Its author was Maurras, a thirty-year-old writer hitherto known only in limited circles. The article was entitled "The first blood". It looked at things in a way no one had thought or dared to look.[23]

What did Charles Maurras do? He did not present any supplementary evidence, he did not refute any fact. He simply made a global reinterpretation by means of which the whole "affair" appeared in a different light. Out of Lieutenant Colonel Henry he made a heroic victim who had preferred patriotic duty to abstract "justice". That is to say, having seen how the Jewish "Syndicate of Treason" had exploited a little judiciary error in order to undermine the foundation of French life and to break the backbone of the army, Henry did not hesitate to commit a small patriotic crime to stop this race towards the precipice. The true stake in the "affair" was no longer the fairness of a sentence but the degeneration of the vital French power orchestrated by the Jewish financiers who hid behind corrupt liberalism, freedom of the press (which they controlled), autonomy of justice, and so on. As a result, its true victim was not Dreyfus but Henry himself, the solitary patriot who risked everything for the salvation of France and on whom his superiors, at the decisive moment, turned their backs: the "first blood" spilled by the Jewish plot.

That intervention by Maurras changed everything: the Right united its forces, and "patriotic" unity rapidly took the upper hand over disarray. Maurras provoked this reversal by *creating the triumph, the myth of the "first victim", from the very elements which, before his intervention, roused disorientation and amazement* (the falsification of documents, the inequity of the sentence, and so on), and which he was far from contesting. It is not surprising that right up to his death he considered this article his finest achievement.

The elementary operation of the *point de capiton* should be sought in this "miraculous" turn, in this *quid pro quo* by means of which what immediately before was the very source of disarray becomes proof of a triumph – as in the first act of *Athalie*, where the intervention of the "supplementary fear", that of God, momentarily changes all the other fears into their opposite. Here one is dealing with the act of "creation" *stricto sensu*: the act which turns chaos into a "new harmony" and suddenly makes "comprehensible" what was up to then a meaningless and even terrifying disturbance. It is impossible not to recall Christianity – less the act of God which made an ordered world out of chaos than the decisive turning from which the definitive form of the Christian religion, the form which has shown its worth in the tradition which is ours, resulted: the Pauline break, of course.

Saint Paul centred the whole Christian edifice precisely on the point which up to then appeared, to the disciples of Christ, as a horrifying trauma, "impossible", non-symbolizable, non-integrable in their field of meaning: Christ's shameful death on the cross between two robbers. Saint Paul made of this final defeat of Christ's earthly mission (which was, of course, the deliverance of the Jews from Roman domination) the very act of salvation: by means of his death, Christ has redeemed humankind.

One can cast another light on the logic of this "magical inversion" of defeat into triumph by a small detour through the detective story. What is its principal charm concerning the relationship between law and its transgression, the criminal adventure? We have on one side the reign of law, tranquillity, certainty, but also the triteness, the boredom of everyday life; and on the other side crime as – to quote Brecht – the only possible adventure in the bourgeois world. Detective stories, however, operate a radical turnround of this relation between law and its transgression:

> While it is the constant tendency of the Old Adam to rebel against so universal and automatic a thing as civilization, to preach departure and rebellion, the romance of police activity keeps in some sense before the mind the fact that civilization itself is the most sensational of departures and the most romantic of rebellions. . . . When the detective in a police romance stands alone, and somewhat fatuously fearless amid the knives and fists of a thieves' kitchen, it does certainly serve to make us remember that it is the agent of social justice who is the original and poetic figure, while the burglars and footpads are merely placid old cosmic conservatives, happy in the immemorial respectability of apes and wolves. The romance of the police force is thus the whole romance of man. It is based on the fact that morality is the most dark and daring of conspiracies.[24]

The fundamental operation of the detective story then consists in presenting the detective himself – the one who works for the defence of the law, in the name of the law, in order to restore the reign of the law – as the greatest adventurer and law-breaker, as a person in comparison to which it is the criminals themselves who appear like indolent petty bourgeois, careful conservators. . . . There are, of course, a great number of transgressions of the law, crimes, adventures which break the monotony of everyday loyal and tranquil life, yet the only true transgression, the only true adventure, the one which changes all other adventures into bourgeois pettiness, is the adventure of civilization, of the defence of the law itself – again, as if all other crimes are exchanged against the crime that pertains to the law itself, which accomplishes the magical trick of turning all other crimes into perfect triteness.

And it is the same with Lacan. For him also, the greatest transgression, the most traumatic, the most senseless thing, is *law itself*: the "mad" superegotistical law which inflicts enjoyment. One does not have on one side a multitude of transgressions, perversions, aggressivenesses, and so on, and on the other side a universal law which regulates, normalizes, the cul-de-sac of transgressions, thereby making possible the pacific coexistence of subjects. The maddest thing is the reverse of the appeasing law itself, the law as a misunderstood, dumb injunction to enjoyment. One can say that law divides itself necessarily into an "appeasing" law and a "mad" law: the opposition between the law and its transgressions repeats itself inside (in Hegelese: is "reflected into") the law itself. Thus one has here the same operation as that in *Athalie*: confronted with ordinary criminal transgressions, law appears as the only true transgression, as in *Athalie* where God appears, in the face of earthly fears, as the only thing which is really to be feared. God thus divides Himself into an appeasing God, a God of love, tranquillity and grace, and a fierce, enraged God, He who provokes in man the most terrible fear.

This turnround, this point of reversal at which the law itself appears as the only true transgression, corresponds exactly to what Hegel designated as the "negation of the negation". First, we have the simple opposition between the position and its negation – in our case, between the positive, appeasing law and the multitude of its particular transgressions, crimes; the "negation of the negation" occurs when one notices that the only true transgression, the only true negativity, is that of the law itself which changes all the ordinary criminal transgressions into an indolent positivity. In this precise sense, "negation of the negation" designates "self-relating negativity": the moment when the external negative relationship between law and crime turns into law's internal self-negation – when law appears as the sole true transgression.

That is why Lacanian theory is irreducible to any variant of transgressism, of anti-Oedipism,and so on: the only true anti-Oedipus is Oedipus itself, its superegotistical reverse. . . . One can follow this "Hegelian" economy of Lacan up to his purely organizational decisions: the dissolution of the *École freudienne de Paris* and the constitution of the *Cause freudienne* in 1980 could have given the impression of a liberating act – Cause instead of School; an end to bureaucratization and regimentation of the school. . . . Yet a couple of months later, the new organization was rebaptized *École de la Cause freudienne*: the School of the Cause itself, incomparably more severe than all other schools, just as the surpassing of earthly fears by divine love presupposes the intervention of the fear of God Himself, incomparably more horrifying than all earthly fears.

II How to Count Zero for One?

Derrida as a reader of Hegel

In defence of Derrida against the traditional philosophical criticism – represented, for example, by Habermas in his *Philosophical Discourse of Modernity* – it should be pointed out that Derridean "deconstruction" has nothing in common with the assertion of an all-embracing "textuality" or "writing" in which the frontiers separating literature from science, metaphor from literal sense, myth from *logos*, rhetoric from truth, and so on, are abolished – that is to say, in which science is reduced to a species of literature, literal sense to a special case of metaphor, *logos* (rational thinking) to the "mythology of the Western man", truth to a special rhetorical effect, and so forth. Derrida's line of argument is here far more refined. Apropos of the difference between truth and rhetoric, for example, what Derrida endeavours to demonstrate is how the very opposition of truth and "mere rhetoric" – the establishment of truth as something which is prior to and independent of "secondary" rhetorical effects and figures – *is founded upon a radical rhetorical gesture.*[25] It is the same with all other couples we have mentioned: philosophical *logos* implies an inverted "white mythology" [*mythologie blanche*], and so on.

The crucial aspect not to be missed is how Derrida is here *thoroughly "Hegelian"*, whereby "Hegelian" is the inversion by means of which the moment which negates the point of departure coincides with this point of departure brought to its extreme. "Truth" as opposed to "mere rhetoric" is nothing but rhetoric brought to its extreme, to the point of its self-negation; literal sense is nothing but metaphor brought to self-negation; *logos* nothing but myth brought to self-negation, and so forth. In other words, the difference between rhetoric and truth *falls within the very field of rhetoric*; the difference *mythos/logos* is inherent to the field of myth; the difference metaphor/literal sense depends upon self-differentiation of metaphoricity. In the course of the dialectical process, the moment which, at first sight, appeared as the external limit of the point of departure proves to be nothing but the extreme of its negative self-relationship; and the perspicacity of a dialectical analysis is demonstrated precisely by its ability to recognize the supreme rhetorical gesture in a reference to Truth which haughtily depreciates rhetoric; to discern in *logos* which treats the "mythical way of thinking" condescendingly its concealed mythical foundation – or, as regards the relationship of law and crime, to identify "law" as *universalized crime*. The external opposition of particular crimes and universal law has to be dissolved in the "inner" antagonism of crime: what we call "law" is nothing but universalized crime – that is, law results from the negative self-relationship of crime.

The problem with the Derridean approach is that it systematically overlooks the Hegelian character of its own basic operation and reduces Hegelian dialectics to the teleological circle of the Notion's self-mediation whereby – to refer again to the examples already mentioned – crime is nothing but a "sublated" moment of the law's self-mediation, whereby the teleological movement of Truth subordinates rhetoric to itself, literal sense encompasses metaphor, and so on. Law needs crime to affirm its own reign by means of the crime's "sublation" . . . . It is apropos of the dialectic of law and crime that the contours of the two opposed readings of Hegelian dialectics come to light most clearly:

- the traditional reading (followed also by Derrida) according to which negative particularity (crime as particular negation of the universal law, for example) is just a passing moment of the law's mediated identity-with-itself;

- the reading according to which universal law itself is nothing but universalized crime, crime brought to its extreme, to the point of self-negation, whereby the difference crime/law falls within crime. Law "dominates" crime when some "absolute crime" particularizes all other crimes, converts them into "mere particular crimes" – and this gesture of universalization by means of which an entity turns into its opposite is, of course, precisely that of *point de capiton*.

Identity as "reflective determination"

Hereby, we are in the very heart of the problem of identity. That is to say, these two readings point towards two different approaches to the Hegelian notion of self-identity:

- The first reading implies the commonplace opposition of "abstract" identity which excludes difference, and "concrete" identity *qua* "identity of identity and non-identity": identity which includes all the wealth of difference, since, ultimately, it consists in the identity of the very process of mediation between differences. To return again to the example of law – law as the agency which excludes crime, which is abstractly opposed to it, is an abstract identity, in so far as it is a dead scheme – all actual, effective life remains out of its reach; it lies within the particular content provided by crime. The concrete identity is, on the contrary, that of the law which is "mediated" by the particularity of crime; which includes crime as a sublated moment of the wealth of its content. Such a conception is usually expressed by means of well-known textbook phrases: "Identity is not a dead, rigid identity-with-itself of an entity, excluding all change, but identity which preserves itself through the very dynamics of change, identity of the life-process itself" . . . .

- Within the frame of the second reading, identity-with-itself is another name for "absolute contradiction". For the coincidence between law and universalized crime, for example, the identity-with-itself of the law *means that* the law coincides with its opposite, with universalized crime. In other words, the law in its "abstract identity" – opposed to crimes, exclusive of their particular content – is in itself supreme crime. This is how the tautology "law is law" has to be read. The first law ("law is . . . ") is the universal law in so far as it is abstractly opposed to crime, whereas the second law (" . . . law") reveals the concealed truth of the first: the obscene violence, the absolute, universalized crime as its hidden reverse. (We can sense this concealed dimension of violence already apropos of the everyday, "spontaneous" reading of the proposition "law is law" – is not this phrase usually evoked precisely when we are confronted with the "unfair", "incomprehensible" constraint that pertains to the law? In other words, what does this tautology effectively mean if not the cynical wisdom that law remains in its most fundamental dimension a form of radical violence which must be obeyed regardless of our subjective appreciation?) In "The Class Struggles in France", in the midst of a concrete analysis of the revolutionary process, Marx articulated an exemplary case of such a doubling of the Universal when it is confronted with its particular content. He discusses the role of the "party of Order" in the brisk events after the 1848 revolution:

> the secret of its existence [was] the *coalition of Orleanists and Legitimists into one party* . . . the *nameless realm of the republic* was the only one in which both factions could maintain with equal power the common class interest without giving up their mutual rivalry. . . . if each of their factions, regarded separately, by itself, was royalist, the product of their chemical combination had necessarily to be *republican.*[26]

"Republican" is thus, in this logic, a species of the genus royalism; within the level of species, it holds the place of the genus itself – in it, the universal genus of royalism is represented, acquires particular existence, in the form of its opposite. In other words, the genus of royalism is divided into three species: Orleanists, Legitimists and republicans. We could also grasp this paradoxical conjunction as a question of choice. A royalist is forced to choose between Orleanism and Legitimism – can he avoid the choice by choosing royalism in general, the very medium of the choice? Yes – by choosing to be republican, by placing himself at the point of intersection of the two sets of Orleanists and Legitimists.

This paradoxical element, the *tertium datur*, the excluded third of the choice, is the uncanny point at which the universal genus *encounters itself* within its own particular species – that is to say, the proposition

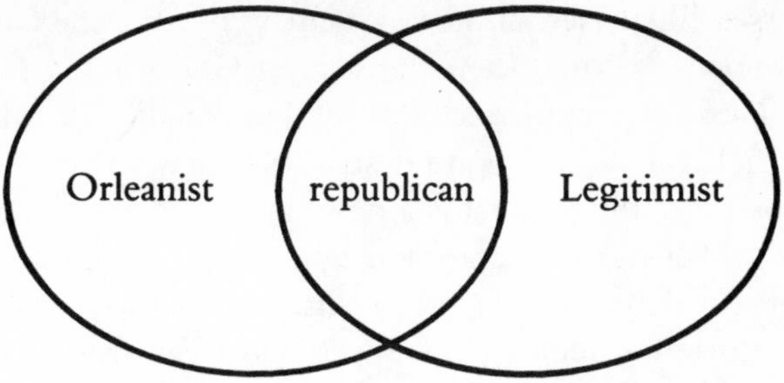

"A royalist is a republican" is a tautology whose structure corresponds perfectly to that of the proposition "God is God", unmasked by Hegel as pure contradiction:

> If anyone opens his mouth and promises to state what God is, namely God is – God, expectation is cheated, for what was expected was a *different determination* . . . . Looking more closely at this tedious effect produced by such truth, we see that the beginning, "The plant is – ", sets out to say *something*, to bring forward a further determination. But since only the same thing is repeated, the opposite has happened, *nothing* has emerged. Such *identical* talk therefore *contradicts itself*. Identity, instead of being in its own self truth and absolute truth, is consequently the very opposite; instead of being the unmoved simple, it is the passage beyond itself into the dissolution of itself.[27]

As Hegel himself points out in the next paragraph, the key to this paradox consists in the tension between form and content: in the fact that we are concerned with the "*form of the proposition*". It is this form which produces the "expectation" of the specific determination of the initial neutral, abstract universality to be brought about by the second part of the proposition. Contrary to the usual conception, it is the form of the proposition which conveys *difference*, whereas the content remains stuck within inert identity. The form demands that the second part of the equation should procure a *species* of the genus, a *determination* of the abstract universality, a *mark* inscribed into the place, an *element* of the set . . . . What do we get instead? *Identity*, this tedious point at which a set encounters itself among its elements, at which a genus encounters itself in the shape of its own species.

More precisely, instead of encountering itself, the initial moment comes across *its own absence*, the set comes across itself as *empty set*. If the first God ("God is . . . ") is the positive God, the genus which encompasses all species, all His particular content, the God of peace, reconciliation and love, then the second God (" . . . God") is the negative God, He who excludes all His predicates, all particular content, the God of hatred and destructive fury, the mad God – as in the proposition "the royalist is a republican", in which "republican" embodies royalism in general by means of excluding all its particular content (the different species of royalism). This is what Hegel means by the notorious "identity of opposites". Far from implying the nonsensical identification of mutually exclusive predicates ("this rose is simultaneously red and blue"), this identity designates the above-mentioned *self-reference of the Universal* – the Universal is the opposite to itself in so far as it relates to itself in the Particular; in so far as it arrives at its being-for-itself in the form of its opposite.

This effect of contradiction can take place only within the framework of a dialogical economy. The first part ("God is . . . ") provokes in the interlocutor the *expectation* determined by the very form of the proposition (one *awaits* a predicate *different* from the subject, a specific determination of the divine universality: God is . . . omnipotent, infinitely good and wise, and so on). The expectation thus provoked is then *disappointed* by the second part (" . . . God") in which the *same* term recurs. This dialogical economy therefore implies a purely logical *temporality*: a temporal scansion between the moment of expectation and the moment of its disappointment, a minimal *delay* of the second part of the tautology. Without this minimal temporality, the proposition A = A remains a simple affirmation of identity and cannot produce the effect of pure contradiction.

"God is . . . "

Therein consists, in short, the Hegelian conception of identity: identity of an entity with itself equals the coincidence of this entity with the empty place of its "inscription". We come across identity when predicates fail. Identity is the surplus which cannot be captured by predicates – more precisely (and this precision is crucial if we want to avoid a misconception of Hegel), identity-with-itself is *nothing but* this impossibility of predicates, *nothing but* this confrontation of an entity with the void at the point where we expect a predicate, a determination of its positive content ("law is . . . "). Identity-with-itself is thus another name for absolute (self-referential) negativity, for the negative relationship towards all predicates that define one's – what? – *identity*. In so far as, in Hegel, absolute negativity constitutes the fundamental feature of subjectivity, we could add that "A = A" offers us the shortest possible formulation of the identity of substance and subject: subject is substance reduced to the pure point of negative relationship towards its predicates; substance in so far as it excludes all the wealth of its contents. In other words, it is a totally "desubstantialized" substance whose entire consistency lies in the refusal of its predicates.[28]

And – to return to Derrida – *this* is the step that the Derridean "deconstruction" seems unable to accomplish. That is to say, Derrida incessantly varies the motif of how full identity-with-itself is impossible; how it is always, constitutively, deferred, split; how the condition of its possibility is the condition of its impossibility; how there is no identity without reference to an outside which always-already truncates it, and so on, and so on. Yet what eludes him is the Hegelian inversion of *identity qua impossible* into *identity itself as a name for a certain radical impossibility*. The impossibility unearthed by Derrida through the hard work of deconstructive reading supposed to subvert identity constitutes the very definition of identity. It is here that we should recall the proposition from Hegel's *Logic*: "By way of reconciliation, the negative force recognizes in what it fights against its own force" – by way of reconciliation, the "deconstruction" recognizes in identity that it endeavours to subvert via the hard-working symptomal reading "its own essence": the name for the impossibility that hinders the constitution of a full identity-with-itself. The same proposition applies also to the relation of law and crime: by way of reconciliation, the negative force of crime recognizes in the law it fights against its own essence – universalized crime.[29]

This very logic of identity was at work in the fantasy-image of Margaret Thatcher. Within a "deconstructivist" approach, it is easy to locate the paradoxical Outside by reference to which Thatcherism constructed its identity. The invasion of "alien" powers ("maladjusted" immigrants, IRA terrorism, Scargill's NUM as the "enemy within", and so on) threatens to undermine "British character", the attitude of self-reliance, law and order, respect for values and industrious work; and thus to overflow and dissolve British identity. It is therefore highly significant that in her description of the adversary

Thatcher has often resorted to the metaphor of an alien Monster eroding and corrupting the fabric of "our way of life". Here, the "deconstructivist" approach would point out the fundamental ambiguity of this "alien" element, its double status: it is simultaneously *within* the structure as its subordinated, contained element (the immigrant who accepts the superiority of the British way of life) and *outside* it (the threatening, cancerous foreign body).

This ambiguity forces us to reverse the spontaneous ideological perception of Thatcherism: it is not sufficient to say that Thatcherism was obsessed by the fear of the "alien" intruder supposed to undermine our identity; what must be added is that the very identity of the "British character" constitutes itself by reference to this intruder, not only in sense of a simple differential opposition whereby an identity can assert itself only via its difference to its Other, but in a far more radical way. Our identity is in itself always-already "truncated", impossible, mutilated, "antagonistic", and the threatening intruder is nothing but an outside-projection, an embodiment of our own inherent antagonism . . . . From the Hegelian–Lacanian perspective, however, a further crucial step is necessary, indicated already by Jacqueline Rose in her analysis of Thatcherism's appeal.[30]

The starting point of Rose's analysis is the uncanny resemblance between Thatcher, the "cold-blooded" defender of "tough" measures, the Iron Lady, and Ruth Ellis, a mythical figure of English crime history, a murderess who irritated the public by not accomplishing the crime in the usual "feminine" way (outburst of passions, hysterical breakdown, and so on) – until the very end, she kept her composure, did not show any remorse, attended the trial impeccably dressed . . . . The "secret" of Thatcher consists in the same "impossible" conjunction of femininity with the resolute and calculating "male" attitude: although she acts as a male criminal, she can get away with it in so far as she is a woman . . . . Are we not again at the Hegelian formula of identity? Is the equation "Thatcher = Ellis" not a new version of the tautology "God is God" or "royalist is republican"? The point is not only that Thatcher's identity is constituted by reference to a constitutive Outside; this identity itself consists in an "impossible" coincidence of caring, law-and-order woman with the toughest possible criminal attitude. When the critics of Thatcher drew attention to her "darker" side (cold-blooded spirit of revenge, and so on) they unwittingly *consolidated* her identity.

x the tautology is actually a marriage of opposites: Law is law = law is crime; Thatcher is Thatcher = Thatcher is Ellis

A "chiasmic exchange of properties"

Umberto Eco's *Foucault's Pendulum* contains an ironic digression that enables us to grasp clearly this crucial difference between *transgression* of an identity and the conception of *identity itself as the result of a certain "transgression"*. With regard to some great literary classic, a "transgression" of its identity would consist in treating it sacrilegiously. One would be expected to imitate it ironically, to introduce arbitrary changes of details into it, to demonstrate how it does not constitute a closed, harmonious Whole but is full of flaws (and elements which fill out these flaws) . . . in short, our aim would be to "deconstruct" the classic's identity-with-itself. What Eco accomplishes in the ironic digression apropos of Shakespeare's *Hamlet*, however, is of quite another nature. He does not "deconstruct" the identity of *Hamlet*. On the contrary, he *(re)constructs* it, but in such a way that its identity appears as the result of a series of contingent, incoherent operations. To use Hegelian terminology: instead of subverting the positive consistency of *Hamlet* by setting free the deconstructive "power of the negative", he lets us see the very positivity of *Hamlet* as something that results from the self-referential activity of the "power of the negative". This digression consists in an imagined conversation between Shakespeare and his publisher:

> "I've looked at your work. Not bad. It has tension, imagination. Is this the first piece you've written?"
>
> "No. I wrote another tragedy. It's the story of two lovers in Verona who . . . "
>
> "Let's talk about this piece first, Mr. S. I was wondering why you set it in France. May I suggest – Denmark? It wouldn't require much work. If you just change two or three names, and turn the chateau of Chalons-sur-Marne into, say, the castle of Elsinore . . . . In a Nordic, Protestant atmosphere, in the shadow of Kierkegaard, so to speak, all these existential overtones . . . "
>
> "Perhaps you're right."
>
> "I think I am. The work might need a little touching up stylistically. Nothing drastic; the barber's snips before he holds up the mirror for you, so to speak. The father's ghost, for example. Why at the end? I'd put him at the beginning. That way the father's warning helps motivate the young prince's behavior, and it establishes the conflict with the mother."
>
> "Hmm, good idea. I'd only have to move one scene."
>
> "Exactly. Now, style. This passage here, where the prince turns to the

audience and begins his monologue on action and inaction. It's a nice speech, but he doesn't sound, well, troubled enough. 'To act or not to act? This is my problem.' I would say not 'my problem' but 'the question'. 'That is the question.' You see what I mean? It's not so much his individual problem as it is the whole question of existence. The question whether to be or not to be . . . "[31]

The effect thus achieved in a way inverts the Brechtian *Verfremdung*: it does not simply "estrange", "denaturalize", a most familiar classic – it rather allows us to see negativity at work in the very constitution of this classic; it procures an answer to the question "How did the classic become a classic?" By displaying the intertwinement of contingent encounters that brought about the classic, it "generates" the familiar classic from the Strange. To refer again to Hegelian terms: it exhibits how the Familiar *results* from the *double* "estrangement" – from the estrangement's self-reference. Our starting point is the Unfamiliar: by varying it, by estranging it from itself, we find ourselves all of a sudden in the midst of the Familiar – this is what Hegel has in mind when he defines identity as "reflective determination", as a result of the self-referential movement of negativity.

Let us return for the last time to the dialectic of law, and crime as its transgression. "Law" in its positive identity results from the negative self-relationship of crime by means of its universalization, from an "absolute" criminal gesture which excludes all other, particular crimes – in other words, from the self-estrangement of the crime as "strange" to the law's "normality". This reversal, the dialectical "generatrix" of identity, is homologous to what Andrzej Warminski concisely called "an (chiasmic) exchange of properties",[32] although he also falls prey to the error common among perspicacious critics of Hegel and formulates as a *reproach* to Hegel what is actually a basic feature of Hegel's thought.

Warminski develops this "exchange of properties" apropos of the example of *example itself*; apropos of the way Hegel conceives the difference between example [*Beispiel*] and its meaning, pure thought. At first sight, things seem clear: an example is just an external, passive resource which enables us to give plastic expression to our thought; although thought needs it to achieve its clear comprehension, we must be careful to avoid being seduced by its literality, by the excess of its external, particular content – an example is ultimately "just an example", it should "sublate" itself by directing our attention towards its notional kernel. What we have here is thus, at first sight, a pure case of the classical metaphysics of meaning: we must prevent the inner presence-to-itself of the thought from getting lost and dispersing itself in the false, deceptive wealth of its example – the inner content must dominate and penetrate the false immediacy of the example.

However, as Warminski demonstrates by means of a detailed analysis of the way Hegel treats the classical Aristotelian wax/ring example (just as wax takes in only the sign of the golden signet ring, not the gold itself, rather purely its form, so in sensation only the form of the perceived object comes to the soul, without the matter), there is always some point at which this opposition of the inner/active thought and of its external/passive example breaks down – is inverted: at the point, namely, at which Hegel endeavours to explain by means of an example *the very difference between literal and proper (theoretical) readings of an example.* At this point, a kind of paradoxical short circuit occurs: the difference between example and the notional content it is supposed to exemplify *is inscribed into example itself* – the very example "provides an example" of how we should treat it as a "mere example". In short: true, there is a danger that we will be seduced by the excessive wealth of the example's immediate content, but the only way to avoid it is *to rely on a "good example".* This uncanny inversion is Warminski's "(chiasmic) exchange of properties" between the interior of thought and the exterior of its example. Here, on the contrary, it is the example which is "active", which generates the difference between itself and the thought, whereas the inner thought remains a passive medium that arrives at its content with the aid of its example . . . .

The homology between this "exchange of properties" and the dialectical genesis of law via the universalization of crime is striking: if the genesis of law brings forward the point at which law coincides with universalized crime, the exchange of properties between thought and its example brings about the point at which the "example" becomes indiscernible from its thought, in so far as it founds itself on its own difference from thought. In both cases, the difference between the "higher" and the "lower" moment – between law and crime, between thought and example – is contained within the "lower" moment itself; is generated through its self-differentiation, through its negative self-relationship.

Therein consists ultimately Hegel's conception of Jesus Christ. All human individuals are, of course, "exemplifications" of the divine Idea. This Idea, however, reaches its being-for-itself, fully actualizes itself, only by means of its embodiment in Christ, who is thus "the most sublime example", the reflective "example of the example", the exemplification of the very principle of example (of the Christian truth that God Himself becomes Man, that this "exemplification" of God in Man is part of the very notion of God). The crucial point not to be overlooked here is that the "example of the example" *coincides with Truth itself* (in contrast to the Platonic deprecation of the "imitation of imitation"): Christ is a point at which (human) example and (divine) Idea become indistinguishable, a point of "chiasmic exchange of properties" at which the exterior (of Jesus Christ, this miserable, wretched individual) is "active" in relation to the interior of the divine Idea. We could even say that this "chiasmic exchange of properties" defines the very status of subject in Hegel's philosophy: "substance becomes subject" by means of such an exchange of their respective "properties" – the subject which is at first caught in its substantial presuppositions, "embedded" in them – which is their passive attribute – retroactively "posits" them, subordinates them to its form, makes them its own passive object.

The "logic of the signifier"

Confronted with the multitude of particular crimes, the universal Law reveals itself as the absolute, universalized crime; confronted with the multitude of earthly horrors, God Himself, the beatitude of peace and love, reveals Himself as the absolute Horror . . . . This triad, this ternary structure in which the Universal, confronted with its particular content, redoubles into positive and negative, encompassing and exclusive, "pacifying" and "destructive" – in other words: in which the initial position, confronted ("mediated") with the multitude of its particular negations, is retroactively trans-coded into pure, self-relating negativity – furnishes the elementary matrix of the dialectical process. Such a self-referring logical space where the universal genus *encounters itself in the form of its opposite* within its own species (where, for example, the God of Love encounters Himself in the form of absolute Horror and destructive rage) – that is to say, where a set comes across itself within its own elements – is based on the possibility of reducing the structure of the set to a limit-case:

> that of a set with one sole element: the element has to differ only from the

> empty set, from the set which is nothing but the lack of the element itself (or from its place as such, or from the mark of its place – which amounts to saying that it is split). The element has to come out for the set to exist, it has to exclude itself, to except itself, to occur as deficient or in surplus.[33]

Within this logical space, the specific difference no longer functions as the difference between the elements against the background of the neutral-universal set: it coincides with the difference between the universal set itself and its particular element – *the set is positioned at the same level as its elements*, it operates as one of its own elements, as the paradoxical element which "is" the absence itself, the element-lack (that is, as one knows from the fundamentals of set theory, each set comprises as one of its elements the empty set). This paradox is founded in the differential character of the signifier's set: as soon as one is dealing with a differential set, one has to comprise in the network of differences the difference between an element and its own absence. In other words, *one has to consider as a part of the signifier its own absence* – one has to posit the existence of a signifier which positivizes, "represents", "gives body to" the very lack of the signifier – that is to say, coincides with the place of inscription of the signifier. This difference is in a way "self-reflective": the paradoxical, "impossible" yet necessary point at which the signifier differs not only from another (positive) signifier but *from itself as signifier*.

Abstract and nugatory as they may seem, these ruminations place us at the very heart of the Hegelian dialectics in which the universal genus has only one particular species; in which the specific difference coincides with the difference between the genus itself and its species. In the beginning, one has the abstract Universal; one arrives at the Particular not by way of complementing it with its particular counterpart but by way of apprehending how *the Universal is already in itself particular*: it is not "all" – what escapes it (in so far as it is *abstract*, that is to say: in so far as one obtains it through the process of abstracting common features from a set of particular entities) is the Particular itself.

For this reason, the discord between the Universal and the Particular is *constitutive*: their encounter is always "missed" – the impetus of the dialectical process is precisely this "contradiction" between the Universal and its Particular. The Particular is always deficient and/or in excess with regard to its Universal: in excess, since it eludes the Universal; since the Universal – in so far as it is "abstract" – cannot encompass it; deficient, since – and this is the reverse of the same predicament – there is never enough of the Particular to "fill out" the Universal frame. This discord between the Universal and the Particular would be "resolved" were it to attain the repose of the fortunate encounter, when the disjunction, the division of the universal genus into particular species, is *exhaustive*, when it is *without remainder*; yet the disjunction/division of a signifier's set is never exhaustive, there always remains an empty place occupied by the surplus element which is the set itself in the form of its opposite – that is, as empty set. This is how the signifying classification differs from the usual, commonsensical one: next to "normal" species, one always comes across a supplementary species which holds the place of the genus itself.

This, then, is the basic paradox of the Lacanian logic of "non-all" [*pas-tout*]: in order to transform a collection of particular elements into a consistent totality, one has to add (or to subtract, which amounts to the same thing: to posit as an exception) a paradoxical element which, in its very particularity, embodies the universality of the genus in the form of its opposite. To recall the Marxian example of royalism: the universal genus of "royalism" is totalized when one adds to it "republicanism" as the immediate embodiment of royalism in general, as such – the universality of the "royalist" function presupposes the existence of "at least one" which acts as exception. The radical consequence of it is that *the split, the division, is located on the side of the Universal*, not on the side of the Particular. That is to say, contrary to the usual notion according to which the diversity of particular content introduces division, specific difference, into the neutral frame of the Universal, it is the Universal itself which is constituted by way of subtracting from a set some Particular designed to embody the Universal as such: the Universal arises – in Hegelese: it is posited as such, in its being-for-itself – in the act of radical split between the wealth of particular diversity and the element which, in the midst of it, "gives body" to the Universal.

Therein consists the logic of sexual difference: the set of women is a particular, non-totalized, non-universal set; its multitude acquires the dimension of *universality* (that, precisely, of "humankind") as soon as one *excludes* from it an element which thereby embodies humankind as such: man. The opposition of man and woman is thus not symmetrical: *the genus of "man" has one species, woman*. The universality of "humankind" is not (logically) prior to the sexual difference, it is posited as such through the inscription of that difference. It is a commonplace of feminist theory to quote the ambiguity of the term "man" (human being as such, male or female; male) as a proof of the "male chauvinist" bias of our everyday language; what, however, one usually overlooks apropos of this ambiguity is the dialectical tension between its two aspects: true, man *qua* male "gives body" to the universality of man *qua* human being – yet it does it *in the form of its opposite* (as in Racine's *Athalie*, where God *qua* source of unspeakable Horror "gives body" to God *qua* Love and Beatitude) – in other words, precisely in so far as it immediately embodies humankind, man *qua* male is radically, constitutively, more "inhuman" than woman.[34]

Non-Hegelian idealism as well as materialist nominalism misrecognize the status of such a paradoxical Difference, which is constitutive of the Universal itself and therefore cannot be reduced to an ordinary specific difference against the neutral background of a universal genus. Although one usually conceives the category of *overdetermination* as "anti-Hegelian" (Althusser *et al.*), it actually designates precisely this inherently Hegelian paradox of a *totality which always comprises a particular element embodying its universal structuring principle* – as is the case with production in Marx:

> In all forms of society there is one specific kind of production which predominates over the rest, whose relations thus assign rank and influence to the others. It is a general illumination which bathes all the other colours and modifies their particularity. It is a particular ether which determines the specific gravity of every being which has materialized within it.[35]

That is "overdetermination": a determination of the Whole by one of its elements which, according to the order of classification, should be just a subordinated part – a part of the structure "envelops" its whole. When, in the totality of production, distribution, exchange and consumption, Marx accords this place to production, he resorts to the Hegelian category of "antithetical determination" [*gegensätzliche Bestimmung*]: "Production predominates not only over itself, in the antithetical determination of production, but over the other moments as well."[36] This "antithetical determination" designates the form in which the Universal comes across *itself* within its particularities: production encounters itself within its species; or: production is a species which encompasses its own genus (the totality of production, distribution, exchange and consumption) – as in theology, where God *qua* Love predominates over Himself in the antithetical determination, i.e. *qua* unspeakable Horror and Rage. The Hegelian *motto* "the True is the Whole" is therefore deeply misleading if one interprets it in the sense of traditional "holism" according to which the particular content is nothing but a passing, subordinated moment of the integral Totality; the Hegelian "holism" is, on the contrary, of a "self-referential" kind: the Whole is always-already *part of itself*, comprised within its own elements. Dialectical "progress" thus had nothing whatsoever to do with the gradual ramification of some initially non-differentiated totality into a network of concrete determinations; its mechanism is rather that of a Whole adding itself again and again to its own parts, as in the well-known witticism often quoted by Lacan: "I have three brothers, Paul, Ernest and myself" – "myself" is here exactly the "antithetical determination" of the "I".

The subjectivized structure

It is by way of this surplus element which embodies the Universal in its negative form, by way of this point at which the Universal comes across itself in its "antithetical determination", that the signifier's structure *subjectivizes* itself: subject exists only within this "failed encounter" between the Universal and the Particular – it is ultimately nothing but a name for their constitutive discord. The Particular is always deficient, there is not enough of it to "fill out" the extension of the Universal, yet simultaneously, it comes in surplus since it adds itself to the series of particular elements as the One which embodies Genus itself. As soon as we abolish this short circuit between the Universal and the Particular, this spacing of the Moebius band where the Universal and the Particular are located on the same surface – in other words, as soon as we arrive at a classification where the Universal is divided into species without the paradoxical remainder of its "antithetical determination" – we have an "objective" structure, a structure which does not stage the representation of the subject.

Did we not thereby reach the Lacanian formula of the signifier? Is this "antithetical determination", this paradoxical Particular which, within the series of Particulars, holds the place of, stands for, the Universal itself, not the signifier which represents the subject for the other signifiers? As, for example, in the Marxian example of the logic of royalism, whereby republicanism represents royalism in general for the (other) species of royalism? The answer is definitely negative: what such a simplistic reading fails to take into account is the dialectic of lack and excess. The surplus Particular embodies the Universal *in the form of its opposite*, it comes in excess precisely in so far as it fills out the *lack* of the Particular with regard to the Universal. The surplus is thus *the form of appearance of the lack*; the One (the Lacanian "plus-One") is the form of appearance of Zero, and it is only at this point that the formula of the signifier can legitimately be introduced: the excess, the surplus One which fills out the lack, is the signifier which represents the subject (the void, Zero, the empty set of the structure). To clarify this crucial point, let us recall the following passage from the third book of Hegel's *Science of Logic*:

> True, I *have* notions, that is to say, determinate notions; but the *I* is the pure Notion itself which, as Notion, has come into *existence*.[37]

The I (for Hegel, synonymous with the subject) is thus located at the crossing point of "being" and "having". The universal notion which only *has* predicates is still a substantial Universal lacking the self-referentiality that pertains to the subject. On the one hand, subject is pure negative universality: an identity-with-itself which "repels", makes abstraction of, all its determinate content ("I" am not any of my determinations but the universality which simultaneously encompasses and negates them); yet on the other hand, "I" is this abstract power of negativity *which has come into existence in the very domain of its determinations*; which has acquired "determinate-being". As such, it is the very opposite of universal self-identity: a vanishing point, the "other-of-itself" eluding every determination – in other words, a point of pure singularity. It is precisely this oscillation between abstract-negative universality (abstraction of all determinate content) and the vanishing point of pure singularity, this "absolute *universality* which is also immediately an absolute *individualization*", that constitutes, according to Hegel, "the nature of the *I* as well as of the Notion"[38] – the ultimate identity of the I and the Notion. Far from occupying the opposite pole of the universality, the Hegelian *individuality* designates the point at which the vanishing self-sublating content coincides with the abstract form of universal receptacle which is indifferent to all determinate content.

The three terms – the positive Universal (royalism as genus), the Particular (its different species: Orleanism, Legitimism . . .) and the Exception which embodies the Universal in the form of its opposite (republicanism as the only way to be "royalist in general") – are thus to be supplemented by a fourth – the void itself filled out by the Exception. This void comes into sight in the Hegelian subversion of the "principle of identity": the identity-with-itself as expressed in tautology ("God is God", for example) is in itself the purest, absolute contradiction, the lack of any particular determination – where one expects a specific determination, a predicate ("God is . . . ") one obtains nothing, the absence of determination. Far from exhibiting a kind of self-sufficient plenitude, tautology thus opens up a void in the Substance which is then filled out by the Exception: this void is the subject, and the Exception represents it for all other elements of the Substance. "God is God" is therefore the most succinct way of saying "Substance is Subject": the repetition of the same adds to the divine predicates (wisdom, goodness, omnipotence . . .) a certain "nothing", an empty place, a lack of determination which subjectivizes it – this is why only the Judaic-Christian God, the one of the tautology "I am what I am", can be said to be subject.

The starting point of the dialectical process is not the plenitude of a self-sufficient substance, identical with itself, but the absolute contradiction: *the pure difference is always-already the impossible "predicate" of identity-with-itself* – or, to put it in Lacanian terms, the identity of a signifier's mark (S) always-already represents the subject ($). This absolute contradiction is "resolved" by way of excluding from the substantial set an element charged with representing the void, the lack of determination that pertains to a tautology; by way of excluding from a series of signifier's marks "at least One" which thereby re-marks the void of their very space of inscription. *The subject is this void, this lack in the series of the predicates of the universal Substance*: it is the "nothing" implied in the Substance's tautological self-relationship – the mediating fourth term which vanishes in the final Result, in the accomplished Triad.

The "metaphor of the subject"

These paradoxes of the "logic of the signifier" enable us to locate properly Lacan's thesis on the "metaphor of the subject", his assertion that the very status of the subject is linked to a metaphor, to a metaphoric substitution. In a first approach, there are two complementary readings of this thesis:

• the first would be simply to conceive the subject as the last, ever-elusive Signified of the signifying chain: there is no "proper" signifier to the subject, every signifier can serve only as its metaphor; in it, the subject is always (mis)represented, simultaneously disclosed and concealed, given and withdrawn, indicated, hinted at between the lines . . .

• the opposite reading would insist that a signifying chain is "subjectivized" precisely by way of its metaphoricity: what we call "subject" is not the unfathomable X, the ultimate reference point of its meaning, but rather a name for the very gap that prevents human language from becoming a neutral tool for designation of some objective state of things, a name for the different ways the described state of things is always-already presented from some partial, biased position of enunciation. In other words, our speech is "subjectivized" precisely in so far as it never "says directly what it wants to say" – instead of "vagina", one can say "blossom of femininity", where the second expression, repulsively exuberant as it may be, is no less "objective" than the first.[39]

The interesting point about these two readings is that, although opposed, they both possess a kind of "primary", "common-sense" self-evidence: we somehow "feel" that no words can adequately represent our innermost subjectivity, that its proper content can only be alluded to; yet simultaneously we "feel" that a speech which functions as pure, transparent medium of designation is in a way "subjectless"; that one can detect the presence of a subject through the elements of style, metaphoric devices, and so on – in short: through all the elements which, from the viewpoint of transmitting information, present a superfluous "noise". How do we account for this opposition? The key to it is contained precisely in the paradoxical logic of the Exception, of the "reflective" term in the form of which the universal genus comes across itself within its species. To recall again the Marxian logic of royalism: republicanism in which royalism encounters itself in the form of its opposite is a *metaphoric substitution* for royalism:

$$\frac{\text{republicanism}}{\text{royalism}}$$

– that is, republicanism taking over the place of royalism-in-general.

Yet, as we have just seen, this Exception (the "pure" signifier) is a Janus-like entity with two faces:

- on the one hand, it entertains a *metonymic* relationship towards the universal genus: in it, a part functions as a metonymic substitute for the Whole, as in the Marxian example of production, where production as a term in the tetrad production–distribution–exchange–consumption simultaneously stands for the Whole;
- on the other hand, it entertains a *metaphoric* relationship towards the void, the lack in the substantial Universal: the Exception fills out the void in the midst of the Substance.

This duality is precisely what Lacan means when he speaks of the signifier as the "metonymy of the object" and the "metaphor of the subject": the Exception entertains a metonymic relationship towards the substantial Object and a metaphoric relationship towards the substanceless void which is the subject. The metaphor, in its most radical dimension, is this latter substitution of One for Zero, this act by means of which the One (the signifier's feature) "stands for" the Zero, the void which "is" the subject – in short, the act by means of which *Zero is counted as One*. This would be the most elementary Lacanian definition of the subject: a Nothing which is not pure nothingness but already "counted as One", re-marked by the Exception, the plus-One in the series of marks – in other words: a Nothing which appears in (is represented by) the form of its opposite, of One. The "original metaphor" is not a substitution of "something for something-else" but a substitution of *something for nothing*: the act by means of which "there is something instead of nothing" – which is why *metonymy is a species of metaphor*: the metonymic sliding from one (partial) object to another is set in motion by the metaphoric substitution constitutive of the subject: the "one for another" presupposes the "one for nothing".

From here we can return to the two ways to read the formula of the "metaphor of the subject": it is clear, now, that in the first reading (the subject as the last, ever-elusive point of reference) the subject is still conceived as substance, as a transcendent substantial entity, whereas the second reading (the subject as the gap preventing our speech from becoming a neutral medium of designation) indicates the proper dimension of the subject. In other words, these two readings express, on the level of commonsensical intuition, the very duality of Substance and Subject.

The Hegelian "one One"

Hegel articulates this paradoxical relationship between Zero and One where One counts as the very inscription of Zero in one of the crucial "knots" of his *Logic*, the passage of determinate-being [*Dasein*] into being-for-self [*Fürsichsein*] and being-for-one [*Sein-für-Eines*] as its specification. He starts by bringing to mind the German expression for inquiring about the quality of a thing: *Was für ein Ding ist das*? (What for a thing is this?, meaning "What kind of a thing is this?"). Relying on the double meaning of the German *ein* (the indeterminate article "a" and the number "one"), he reads it as the "one" of unity, as the "one" which is opposed to the others ("other-ones") – "What for *one* thing is this?" – and asks the obvious question: which is this One *for which* something (the thing) is?

He first points out that this One cannot coincide with Something [*Etwas*]: the correlate of Something is Something-else [*ein Anderes*]; here we are on the level of finitude, of finite reality, of its network of reciprocal determinations where something is always linked to something else, limited, defined, "mediated" by other "somethings". The being of Something is therefore always a being-for-other [*Sein-für-Anderes*]; one attains the One only when this other, something-other for which something is, is reflected into the (some)thing itself as its own ideal unity – that is to say, when something is no more for something-else but *for itself*; in this way, we pass from being-for-other into being-for-self. The One denotes the ideal unity of a thing beyond the multitude of its real properties: the thing as element of reality is sublated [*aufgehoben*] in the One. The passage of Something into One thus coincides with the passage of reality into ideality: the One for which the thing *qua* real is ("What for *one* thing is this?") is this thing itself in its ideality.

This passage clearly implies the intervention of the symbolic order: it can take place only when the One, the ideal unity of a thing beyond its real properties, is again embodied, materialized, externalized in its *signifier*. The thing as element of reality is "murdered", abolished, and at the same preserved in its ideal content – in short: sublated – in its symbol which posits it as One: reduces it to a unitary feature designated by its signifying mark. In other words, the passage of being-for-other into being-for-self entails a radical decentring of the thing with regard to itself: this "self" of "for-self", the most intimate kernel of its identity, is "posited", acquires actual existence, only in so far as it is again externalized in an arbitrary signifying mark. *Being-for-self equals the being of a thing for its symbol*: the thing is "more itself" in its external, arbitrary symbol than in its immediate reality.

If the correlate of Something is Something-else, which then is the correlate of One? What must be borne in mind is that, as to the inherent order of the categories of Hegel's *Logic*, we are here still at the level of *quality*: the One we are dealing with is not yet the One of quantity, the First-One to which can be added the Second, the Third, and so on. It is for this reason that the correlate of One is not the Other but *the void* [*das Leere*]: it cannot be the (something-)other since the One is already the unity of itself with its Other, the reflection-into-self of the Other, its own Other – the One is precisely the "inherent" Other for which the thing is, in which it persists as sublated. If, consequently, the One is Something reflected-into-self, posited as its own ideal unity, then the Void is precisely *the reflection-into-self* of the *Otherness* – that is to say, a "pure" Otherness which is no longer *Something*-other.

There is, however, an ambiguity which still persists here: the relationship between the One and the Void is usually conceived as an external coexistence like, for example, atoms and the empty space around them. Although this conception may seem to be confirmed by Hegel himself, for whom the category of being-for-self assumes historical existence in Democritus' philosophy of atoms, it is none the less misleading: the Void is not external to One, it dwells in its very heart – the One itself is "void"; the Void is its only "content". A reference to the "logic of the signifier" may help here: the One is what Lacan calls "pure signifier", the signifier "without signified", the signifier which does not designate any positive properties of the object since it refers only to its pure notional Unity brought about performatively by this signifier itself (the exemplary case of it is, of course, proper names) – and the Void: is it not precisely *the signified of this pure signifier*? This Void, the signified of the One, is the *subject* of the signifier: the One represents the Void (the subject) for the other signifiers – which others? Only on the basis of this One of quality can one arrive at the One of quantity; at the One as the first in a series of counting – no wonder, then, that the same paradoxical expression "the one One" [*das eine Eins; l'un Un*] occurs in Hegel as well as in Lacan: we have to have the One of quality, the "unitary feature" [*le trait unaire*] in order to count them and say, "here is one One, here is the second One, here the third . . . ". With this passage of One of quality into One of quantity, the Void changes into Zero.

On another level, the same goes for the infamous first couple of Hegel's *Logic*, Being and Nothing. As to the "content", there is no difference between them – what, then, maintains the gap separating them; why do they not coincide immediately? "Being" is the first (the emptiest, the most immediate) determination-of-form [*Formbestimmtheit*] the "truth" (the "content") of which is "nothing" – pure lack of any determinate content. It is precisely because of this immediate coincidence of their respective "contents" that the contradiction between Being and Nothing is absolute: it is not a simple incompatibility of two positive "contents" but the contradiction between "content" and "form" at its purest. That is to say, as to its *form*, Being already possesses a determination of "something", yet its content is "nothing" – it is therefore "nothing in the form of something", Nothing counted as Something. Without this absolute tension, Being and Nothing would coincide immediately and the dialectical process would not be "set in motion". Precisely in so far as this contradiction is absolute, "real-impossible", it is "repressed", "pushed away" into a timeless past (like the primordial antagonism of drives with Schelling): Hegel repeats again and again that Being "does not pass over but has passed over"[40] into Nothing, which is why the first category that can be used in the present is determinate being [*Dasein*] or Something, the unity of Being and Nothing that "came to be". In other words, it is only with Something that we actually start to think; Being and Nothing are the absence of determination conceived from within the field of notional determination and as such condemned to the shadowy realm of eternal, timeless past.[41]

The role played by the unique German expression *Was für ein Ding* . . . in the passage of being-for-other into being-for-self cannot but evoke cynical remarks on how "according to Hegel, the Absolute speaks German". Furthermore, this is not the only instance: a whole series of notional "passages" in Hegel's *Logic* rely on wordplays or ambiguities proper to German: the three meanings of *Aufhebung* (annihilate, maintain, elevate), the way the category of *Grund* (Reason–Ground) is deduced from reading the German verb *zugrundegehen* (decompose, disintegrate) as *zu-Grunde-gehen* (reaching one's ground), and so on. Yet Hegel in no way conceives these features as a kind of writ of privilege of German (as Heidegger does for Greek and German): for him, they remain felicitous encounters where, totally by chance, the meaning of some word (more precisely: the split of its meaning) comes to exhibit a speculative dimension. The usual, everyday meanings of words move on the level of Understanding, and the "exact" scientific definitions only harden the non-dialectical inclosure; the speculative meaning which, in principle, eludes words (notions) as well as propositions, since it comes through only in the completed movement of syllogism – this meaning can sometimes, due to a contingent fortunate encounter, emerge at the level of words alone.

We can see how far Hegel is from the standard picture of the "panlogicism" attributed to him: "speculative truth", expression of the Absolute itself, has to rely on such frivolous resources as wordplays and contingent ambiguities! Here, Hegel undermines Plato's opposition (from *Cratyle*) of the "natural" and "arbitrary" characters of language, the opposition which later, in modern thought, evolved into the two fundamentally divergent notions of language: the "rationalist" one (reduction of language to a system of arbitrary, available signs, the meaning of which is conventional and which, consequently, carry no intrinsic Truth) versus the "romantic" one (according to which language cannot be reduced to an external tool or medium since, deep in itself, it carries an original Sense forgotten by the progress of history). Hegel's position with regard to this alternative is paradoxical: language does contain an intrinsic Truth, yet it is not to be sought in obscure Origins, in an original inveteracy dissipated by progressive instrumentalization; this Truth rather results from contingent encounters which occur afterwards. *In principle*, language "lies", it renders invisible the dialectical movement of notions, yet sometimes, by means of some felicitous accident, the speculative content can emerge. Contrary to the Platonic tradition, Truth is not contained in the Universal as such: its emergence is strictly a matter of particular conjunctures.

NOTES

1. Sigmund Freud/Edoardo Weiss, *Lettres sur la pratique psychanalytique*, Toulouse: Privat 1975, p. 55.
2. Ibid., p. 57.

3. The "immoral" Slovene mentioned does not just embody the paradoxical way enjoyment and the Law are linked, but hides yet another surprise, which leads to the key to the Slovene national fantasy, to the theme of the "maternal superego", to the theme of the mother (not the father) as the bearer of the Law/Prohibition. Freud's Slovene tried to profit from the analytic process in a unique way. The role of the patient's payment to the analyst is well known – by accepting the patient's money, a distance is maintained between the analyst and the patient-analysand; the analyst can keep himself outside the intersubjective circuit of desire in which the analysand is caught (payment of the symbolic debt, and so on). Our Slovene overturned this basic analytic condition in a unique way, so that he even profited financially from his analysis. Weiss writes:

> Some days ago I learned that he had quoted to his father as my fee a total somewhat higher than that for which I had asked. His father had the habit of settling such accounts in cash. He gave the money intended for me to the patient, who retained the surplus himself. (Ibid., pp. 55–6)

In so far as the Name-of-the-Father – the Law whose bearer is the Father – did not have any kind of authority over this Slovene, the only question which remains open is: How was it possible for this Slovene to evade psychosis? Because we are concerned with a Slovene, it is probably not too risky to propose a hypothesis that somewhere in the background is hiding the ubiquitous figure of the mother – in other words, that it was the mother (not the father) who embodied Law for him – so firmly and severely that she blocked the very possibility of a "normal" sexual relationship. When the Name-of-the-Father is replaced by the Name-of-the-Mother, an additional "turn of the screw" invigorates the pressure of the symbolic debt upon the subject.

4. This viewpoint could perhaps be designated as that of the Persian ambassador (from Montesquieu's famous *Persian Letters*): a strange look upon our world destined to bring about our own estrangement from it.

5. Ring Lardner, "Who dealt?", in *The Penguin Book of American Short Stories*, Harmondsworth: Penguin 1969, pp. 295–305.

6. The paranoiac interpretation of the story would of course ascertain that the narrator played the part of the innocent prattler who ruins the life of her companions *on purpose*: in order to take revenge on her husband for his lack of true love for her.

7. Martin Jay, *The Dialectical Imagination*, London: Heinemann 1974, Chapter 7.

8. "Authoritarian Syndrome" is also symptomatic in the sense of *sinthome*, of a signifying formation that structures our innermost kernel of enjoyment – witness the fascination with authority which is a crucial component of its exercise, the enjoyment which accompanies the subject's subordination to the authoritarian call: in the "authoritarian syndrome", the liberal personality locates and organizes its enjoyment.

9. Paul-Dominique Dognin, *Les 'sentiers escarpés' de Karl Marx* I, Paris: CERF 1977, p. 132.

10. The ultimate proof that Marx *did* master the Hegelian double reflection is his deduction of the capitalist from the notion of capital: the relationship of the subject (work force) and the object (objective conditions of the process of production) necessarily reflects itself *within* the subjectivity of the work force and thus duly complicates the logic of "reification" ("relations between things instead of relations between people"). It is not sufficient to ascertain that in capitalism, relations between

individuals appear in a reified form, as relations between things; the crucial point is that the relationship of individuals towards "things" is reflected back in the relationship between individuals, which is why the necessary reverse of "reification" is "personification", the process by means of which "things" themselves assume the shape of "persons" (capital becomes the capitalist). This second, "squared" reflection where the first reflection – "reification" ("things instead of people") – is reflected back into "people" themselves constitutes the specificity of the dialectical self-relationship.

11. Jacques Lacan, *The Four Fundamental Concepts of Psycho-Analysis*, London: Hogarth 1977, p. 112.

12. For a detailed introduction to this notion, see Slavoj Žižek, *The Sublime Object of Ideology*, London: Verso 1989, Chapter 3.

13. Jacques Lacan, *Le Séminaire, livre III: Les Psychoses*, Paris: Éditions du Seuil 1981, pp. 281–306.

14. Ibid., p. 303.

15. Fredric Jameson, *The Ideologies of Theory*, vol. 1, Minneapolis: University of Minnesota Press 1988, p. 7.

16. Here we can also see why – if we apply this logic of the figure of Jew as an "optical illusion" to the King's charisma – the reproach according to which the King *de facto* never functions as an "empty" signifier – that is, according to which subjects obey him because and only in so far as they believe in his "substantial" kingliness – *misses the point*: what appears as a reproach is actually the basic implication of the criticized theory itself. It is of course a condition of the King's charisma that the subjects "believe" in its kingliness (as with anti-Semitism, where it is a condition of its efficacy that the subject perceives the Jew as a substantial, positive entity, not as the materialization of a purely formal textual operation) – the moment the mechanism is exposed, it loses its power.

In other words, precisely in so far as it is misrecognized, the purely formal textual operation determines the way we perceive the Jew or the King in their very material positivity: in the absence of this formal operation, the Jew would be perceived as a person like others, not as a bearer of some inherent, mysterious Evil; as somebody whose very existence is deceitful. And it is homologous with the King: why are we so fascinated by the everyday details about royal families (has Princess Diana a lover? is Prince Andrew gay? is it true that Queen Elizabeth often gets drunk?) – that is to say, by details which, in other, ordinary families, we definitely would not find noticeable? Because, as a result of the above-mentioned *purely formal* operation, these everyday features undergo a kind of "transubstantiation" and start to function as the emanation of kingliness.

17. Jacques Lacan, *Écrits: A Selection*, London: Tavistock 1977, p. 316 (translation amended).

18. Lacan, *Le Séminaire, livre III: Les Psychoses*, p. 169.

19. Jacques Lacan, *Le Séminaire, livre XVII: L'Envers de la psychanalyse* (1969–70), unauthorized manuscript.

20. Arthur Danto, *Mysticism and Morality*, Harmondsworth: Penguin 1976, p. 82.

21. For a historical-materialist analysis, the points of special interest are those phenomena where money is not yet reduced to a neutral "general equivalent", which bear witness to the material weight of a concrete social relationship. An obvious example here is the seemingly "irrational" and "superfluous" distinction between *pound* and *guinea* ("a pound and a shilling") – where does this mysterious 5 per cent

surplus come from? A guinea served as payment for doctors, lawyers and the like: it was a pound plus a tip for those whose social position was considered too dignified to allow them to accept the tip. In the Kantian division of Faculties, these professions belong to the Faculties which are grounded in the "discourse of the Master" and not in the "discourse of the University": they concern Belief and Power (Belief as the foundation of Power), not "powerless" Knowledge – theological faculty, faculty of law, medical faculty.

22. A further analysis should deal with *labour force*, a special commodity whose "use-value", labour itself, is a source of value and thereby produces a surplus-value over its own value as commodity. It is here, at this point of self-reference where *the force which produces value exchanges itself for value*, that we come across the other aspect of money: not only S1, the master-signifier, the general equivalent, but also the *object*. The Lacanian correlative of surplus-value is surplus-enjoyment embodied in *objet petit a*, the object-cause of desire. The exchange of the labour force for money thus posits an "impossible" equivalence *labour force = money*, a kind of Hegelian "infinite judgement" whose terms are radically incompatible.

When Marx determines proletariat as pure, substanceless subjectivity – as pure possibility the actualization of which turns against itself (the more a worker produces, the less he possesses, since the product of his work assumes the shape of a foreign power directed against him) – he brings out his own version of the Hegelian formula "the Spirit is a Bone" (Hegel himself proposes the version "Wealth is the Self", which already prefigures Marx): proletariat is a subject without substance, a void of pure potentiality without any positive content, delivered from all substantial links with the objective conditions of production, *and* an entity that is for sale on the market and is thus posited as equal to a dead piece of metal – $\$ \Diamond a$, the junction of the empty, barred subjectivity and money (the object-cause of desire in capitalism). The point of Marx, a pupil of Hegel, is of course that there is no $\$$ without its support in *a*: the subject can arrive at its being-for-itself, can free itself from all substantial ties and appear as the point of pure negativity, only by being posited as equivalent to its absolute antipode, money, that inert piece of metal that one can hold in one's hands and manipulate freely . . .

23. Ernst Nolte, *Three Faces of Fascism*, New York: Mentor 1969, p. 85.

24. G.K. Chesterton, "A Defence of Detective Stories", in H. Haycraft, ed., *The Art of the Mystery Story*, New York: The Universal Library 1946, pp. 5–6.

25. Incidentally, this was already Adorno's thesis – in his *Negative Dialectics* (New York: Continuum 1973) he pointed out how the traditional philosophical depreciation of rhetoric as a secondary tool which does nothing but disturb the direct approach to Truth is itself dependent on rhetoric. The supreme rhetorical gesture is that of renouncing itself – of referring to itself in a negative way ("What I will say now is not mere rhetoric, I mean it seriously . . . ").

26. Karl Marx/Friedrich Engels, *Collected Works*, vol. 10, London: Lawrence & Wishart 1978, p. 95. Incidentally, this paradox of the "nameless realm of the republic" also serves as a perfect example of what Hegelian "reconciliation" means. The party of Order believed in Restoration, but postponed it indefinitely, "preserving the republican form with foaming rage and deadly invective against it" (ibid., p. 96). In short: by continuing to be captivated by the spectre of the Monarchy to be restored, by treating Restoration as an Ideal whose realization is indefinitely postponed, they overlooked the

fact that *this ideal was already fully realized in the "nameless realm of the republic"*. They already had in their hands what they were looking for, the "republican form" was the form of appearance of its opposite, Royalism as such.

27. *Hegel's Science of Logic*, London: Allen & Unwin 1969, p. 415.

28. A perfect example of this Hegelian inversion – passage of subject into predicate – is offered by the theory of relativity. As is well known, Einstein's revolution in the conception of the relationship between space and matter occurred in two steps. First, he refuted the Newtonian idea of a homogeneous, "uniform" space by demonstrating that matter "curves" space. It is because of matter that the shortest way between two points in space is not necessarily a straight line – if the space is "bent" by matter, the shortest way is a curve. This, however, is only the first of Einstein's steps; it still implies the notion of matter as a substantial entity, as an agent independent of space which acts upon it: bends it. The crucial breakthrough is brought about by Einstein's next step, his thesis according to which *matter itself is nothing but curved space*.

Already on the level of style, this inversion (of matter *qua* cause curving space into matter *qua* the very curvature of space) is deeply Hegelian. It repeats the figure that occurs again and again in Hegel, the general form of which is best exemplified by the dialectic of essence and appearance. It is not sufficient to say that the (hidden) essence appears in a distorted way – that the appearance is never adequate to the essence. What we should add is that *the very essence is nothing but this distortion of the appearance, this non-adequacy of the appearance to itself, its self-fissure*. (To refer to the terms of the logic of reflection: essence reflects itself in appearance, since it is nothing but the reflection-into-itself of the appearance.) This is what is at stake in the Hegelian "passage of the subject into predicate". When Hegel says that in opposition to the judgement of Understanding in which the subject *qua* solid, substantial, given entity is supplemented by predicates – attributes – the speculative judgement is characterized by the "passage" of subject into predicate, the structure of this paradoxical passage corresponds perfectly to the above-mentioned example from Einstein.

First, the curvature of space is posited as a "predicate" of the matter *qua* substantial entity; then "the subject passes into the predicate"; it becomes manifest that the actual subject of this process is the very "curvature of space" – in other words, what previously appeared as predicate. Even the very fundamental Hegelian thesis on "Substance as Subject" has to be grasped against the background of this passage of subject into predicate. Substance is the "Subject" in so far as it remains a solid, self-identical support of its "predicates", whereas the Hegelian subject is the (substantial) subject which has "passed into predicate".

According to the well-known nominalist criticism of Hegel found (among others) in early Marx, the basic mystification of the Hegelian speculation consists in the way predicate starts to function as subject ("instead of conceiving the universal idea as a predicate of the individual subjects, we conceive these individual subjects that exist concretely as mere moments-predicates of the universal Idea, the true subject of the dialectical process"). This criticism unwittingly tells the truth. Its only problem is that it imputes to Hegel the Platonic substantialism of ideas – as if the Hegelian Idea is a Platonic substantial Universal, penetrating and animating the sphere of particular, material reality. In other words, what it overlooks is that the fundamental "matrix" of Hegelian dialectics consists in the very mechanism it puts forward as the "secret of the speculative construction", as the hidden mechanism of dialectical "mystification" –

that is, the "inversion" of subject and predicate. In the course of the dialectical process, what was at the beginning presupposed as subject transforms itself retroactively into something posited by its own "predicate".

This reversal could be further specified as the inversion of the "otherness of consciousness" into the "consciousness itself in its otherness". Let us take the well-known Lévi-Straussian thesis that the (ethnological) description of the "wild thought" is a wild description of our own thought – what appears as a property of the "object" is actually a property of our own interpretative procedure apropos of the object. What appears as the "otherness of consciousness" (the exotic "wild thought", foreign to us) is "consciousness itself in its otherness" (our own thought in its "wild" state). In other words, what we have here is again the inversion of subject into predicate: the substantial subject opposed to "consciousness", appearing as a positively given entity ("wild thought"), passes into a "predicate", into a determination of this very observing "consciousness" (the "wildness" of its descriptive procedure).

29. It is almost superfluous to point out the applicability of such a notion of identity for the analysis of *social* identity. The triad of Law as opposed to crime, particular crimes and Law as universalized crime – the way Law itself, when confronted with the particular content of crimes, splits into itself and its own obscene, perverse reverse – has already been used by Lilian Zac to analyse the ideological discourse of the Argentinian military dictatorship (see her unpublished manuscript "Logical Resources and the Argentinian Military Discourse", Colchester: University of Essex 1989).

In its confrontation with the "terrorist" subversive threat, the official discourse split into public and secret discourse. On the public level it organized itself around the values of National Unity, Law and Order, the assurance of public peace, and so on against the threat of the all-present subversive enemy. This public discourse, however, was always accompanied by its shadowy double, a secret discourse in which the "enemy" is reduced to an impotent object of torture, a discourse which talks about the "disappeared", the discourse of the so-called "dirty war" where, in the name of national salvation, one is allowed to break even the most elementary legal norms and rights of man, a discourse in which emerges an obscene enjoyment procured by the fact that the *raison d'état* changes our indulgence in sadistic drives into fulfilment of patriotic Duty . . .

This hidden reverse of the official discourse, which encompasses what "everybody knows" although one isn't supposed to speak about it publicly (the "public secrets" about who was taken away last night, about where the torture chambers and mass graves are, and so on), is not a kind of external stain on the public discourse's immaculate surface, but its necessary reverse: the condition of its efficiency. The public discourse which legitimizes itself by means of a reference to social peace and stability, and so on, remains "efficacious" only in so far as it is redoubled by a hidden discourse which spreads an all-pervasive, indefinable terror and a paralysing horror.

30. Jacqueline Rose, "Margaret Thatcher and Ruth Ellis", *New Formations* 6, London: Routledge 1989.

31. Umberto Eco, *Foucault's Pendulum*, New York: Harcourt Brace Jovanovich 1989, p. 69.

32. Andrzej Warminski, *Readings in Interpretation*, Minneapolis: University of Minnesota Press 1987, p. 110.

33. Jacques-Alain Miller, "Matrice", *Ornicar?* 4, Paris 1975, p. 6.

34. In Lacan's infamous proposition "Woman doesn't exist", "existence" is therefore to be conceived in the strict Hegelian sense, not as simply synonymous with "being". In Hegel's *Logic*, the category of existence has its place towards the end of the second part, which deals with "essence"; yet its correlative term is not "essence" itself (which is accoupled with "appearance" – "essence" is being in so far as it "appears", in so far as it is posited as "mere appearance") but "ground" [das Grund]: existence is being in so far as it is "grounded", founded in a unique, universal Ground acting as its "sufficient Reason". In this precise sense "Woman doesn't exist": she does not possess a unique Ground, she cannot be totalized with reference to some encompassing Principle. One can see, consequently, how this Lacanian thesis radically *precludes* the "male chauvinist" idea that Man is the proper centre and foundation of woman: in this case, woman *would* exist – she escapes "male dominance" precisely in so far as she does *not* exist.

35. Karl Marx, *Grundrisse*, Harmondsworth: Penguin 1972, p. 107.

36. Ibid., p. 99.

37. *Hegel's Science of Logic*, p. 583.

38. Ibid.

39. It is because of this original metaphoricity that *ciphering* as such brings about a surplus-enjoyment which cannot be accounted for by the need to get round the censorship which prohibits the direct, "literal" mentioning of some content. One of the supreme cases of the enjoyment procured by the signifier's ciphering is Bertolt Brecht's *Me Ti. Buch der Wendungen*, which transposes the history of socialism into a story about civil war in an ancient Chinese empire (Trotsky becomes "To-Tsi", and so on). The very effect of "estrangement" which serves as the "official" rationale for Brecht's procedure – the need to force the reader to gain distance from his or her own historical constellation and observe it as an exotic, foreign country where things lose their self-evidence – presupposes as the basis of its "efficiency" the enjoyment procured by the act of ciphering as such.

40. *Hegel's Science of Logic*, pp. 82–3.

41. On yet another level, it is the same with the passage of "positing" into "external" reflection: how is it possible for the positing reflection to conceive itself as external with regard to its presuppositions; to assume the existence of some substantial presuppositions and thereby to "forget" that these presuppositions are themselves posited by its activity? How indeed when, at the level of positing reflection enclosed in its circle, there is, strictly speaking, nothing to forget? Or, to put it in another way: how can the reflecting subject suddenly fall victim to the illusion that the substantial content is lost for him, when there was no substantial content to be lost previous to the experience of loss? The answer is, of course, that in order to "forget" (or to "lose") something, one must first forget that there is nothing to forget: this oblivion makes possible the illusion that there *is* something to forget in the first place. Abstract as they may seem, this ruminations apply immediately to the way an ideology functions: the nostalgic lamenting over the forgotten past Values is itself oblivious of the fact that these Values had no existence previous to our lamenting – that we literally invented them through our lamenting over their loss . . .

2

The Wanton Identity

I Impossibility

Hegel's "monism"

The doxa on Hegel against which the whole of our interpretation is directed – a doxa which is today a commonplace on all sides of the philosophical spectrum, from Adorno to "post-structuralism" – reads as follows: it is true that Hegel asserts the right of the Particular – that he, so to speak, opens the door to its wealth and conceives the network of differences as something inherent to the universal Notion, as resulting from the self-articulation of its immanent content; yet it is precisely through this operation that the phenomenal exterior is reduced to the self-mediation of the inner Notion, all differences are "sublated" in advance in so far as they are posited as ideal moments of the Notion's mediated identity with itself . . . . The logic involved here is of course that of the fetishistic disavowal, conveyed by the formula "*je sais bien, mais quand même . . .* ": I know very well that Hegel asserts difference and negativity; nevertheless . . . (by means of the Notion's self-relation, this negativity is ultimately reduced to an abstract moment of the Identity's self-differentiation).

What lies behind this disavowal is the fear of "absolute knowledge" as a monster threatening to suppress all particular, contingent content in the self-mediation of the absolute Idea, and thus to "swallow" our most intimate freedom and unique individuality; a fear which acquires the form of the well-known paradox of the prohibition of the impossible: "absolute knowledge" is impossible, an unattainable Ideal, a philosophical pipe dream – and it is precisely for that reason that we must fight its temptation . . . . In short, "absolute knowledge" is the Real of its critics: the construction of an "impossible", untenable theoretical position which these critics must presuppose in order to define their own position by distancing themselves from it – by asserting, for example, the positivity of the "effective life-process" irreducible to the Notion's logical movement.[1]

The enigma is: why do the critics of Hegel need this adversary of straw to establish their position? What renders it even stranger is the fact that most of Hegel's defenders, with a kind of bad conscience, also tacitly accept the need to distance themselves from the monster of all-swallowing Idea and attempt to "save Hegel" by timidly asserting that "in fact, Hegel does admit a relative autonomy of the Particular and does not simply abolish all differences in the unity of the Idea". They usually take refuge in the notorious formula of "*identity of identity and non-identity*" (which, incidentally, is more Schellingian than Hegelian).

What escapes Hegel's critics as well as such defenders is the crucial fact that Hegel subverts "monism" by, paradoxically, affirming it far more radically than his critics dare to suspect. That is to say, the usual idea of the "dialectical process" runs as follows: there is a split, a dispersion of the original unity, the Particular takes over the Universal; but when the disintegration reaches its utmost, it reverses into its opposite, the Idea succeeds in recollecting-internalizing [*ver-innern*] all the wealth of particular determinations and thus reconciles the opposites . . . at this point, the critics are quick to add that this "sublation" [*Aufhebung*] of the external, contingent determinations never turns out without a certain remainder – that there is always a certain leftover which resists the dialectical sublation–internalization, while being at the same time the condition of its possibility. In other words, what the dialectical movement cannot account for is a certain excess which is simultaneously the condition of its possibility and of its impossibility . . .

What is wrong with this criticism? The key to it is offered by the grammar, in Hegel's use of tense. The final moment of the dialectical process, the "sublation of the difference", does not consist in the act of its sublation, but in the experience of how the difference *was always-already sublated*; of how, in a way, *it never effectively existed*. The dialectical "sublation" is thus always a kind of retroactive "unmaking" [*Ungeschehen-Machen*]; the point is not to overcome the obstacle to Unity but to experience how the obstacle *never was one*; how the appearance of an "obstacle" was due only to our wrong, "finite" perspective.

We could trace this paradoxical logic back to Hegel's particular analyses, to his treatment of crime and punishment in the philosophy of law, for example. The aim of punishment is not to re-establish the balance by recompensing for the crime but to assert how, in a radical ontological sense, the crime did not exist at all – that is, does not possess full effectivity; by means of the punishment, crime is not externally abolished, it is rather posited as something that is already in itself ontologically null. Brought to its extreme, the logic of punishment in Hegel reads: ontologically, crime does not exist, it is nothing but a null and void semblance, *and it is precisely for this reason that it must be punished*.[2]

At this point, we can already locate the first misunderstanding of the Derridean "deconstructive" reading of Hegel: it breaks down an open door. That is to say, Derrida points out the basic paradox of the argument of the "metaphysics of presence" when faced with phenomena which have the status of "supplement" and are exemplified by writing – the recurrence of mutually exclusive arguments on the pattern of the Freudian joke about the borrowed pan (I didn't borrow any pan from you; the pan was already broken when I got it . . .). Writing is totally external to the inner presence of meaning, it simply does not concern its constitution; writing is extremely dangerous in so far as it threatens to obscure the intelligibility of the intention-of-meaning . . . . Yet Hegel, paradoxically and in a way which is unthinkable for Derrida, *openly assumes both these propositions*: that which functions within the traditional metaphysics as a symptom, a slip to be unearthed by the hard labour of deconstructive reading, is with Hegel the very fundamental and explicit thesis – one has to fight crime, for example, precisely because it has no ontological consistency.

The "silent weaving of the Spirit"

The crucial feature of this dialectical "retroactive unmaking" is the interval separating the process of the change of "contents" from the formal closing act – the structural necessity of the *delay* of the latter over the former. In a way, in the dialectical process, "things happen before they effectively happen"; all is already decided, the game is over

* The idea of [illegible] (a) Crime is an unrealizable Ideal

before we are able to take cognizance of it, so that the final "word of reconciliation" is a purely formal act, a simple stating of what has already taken place. Perhaps the subtlest example of this interval is Hegel's treatment of the struggle of the Enlightenment with Superstition in the *Phenomenology of Spirit*, where he speaks of the "silent, ceaseless weaving of the Spirit in the simple inwardness of its substance" which:

> is comparable to a silent expansion or to the *diffusion*, say, of a perfume in the unresisting atmosphere. It is a penetrating infection which does not make itself noticeable beforehand as something opposed to the indifferent element into which it insinuates itself, and therefore cannot be warded off. Only when the infection has become widespread is it that consciousness, which unheedingly yielded to its influence, becomes *aware of it*. . . . when consciousness does become aware of pure insight [of the Enlightenment], the latter is already widespread; the struggle against it betrays the fact that infection has occurred. The struggle is too late, and every remedy adopted only aggravates the disease, for it has laid hold of the marrow of spiritual life, viz. the Notion of consciousness, or the pure essence itself of consciousness. Therefore, too, there is no power in consciousness which could overcome the disease. Because this is present in the essence itself, its manifestations, while still isolated, can be suppressed and the superficial symptoms smothered. This is greatly to its advantage, for it does not now squander its power or show itself unworthy of its real nature, which is the case when it breaks out in symptoms and single eruptions antagonistic to the content of faith and to its connection with the reality of the world outside it. Rather, being now an invisible and imperceptible Spirit, it infiltrates the noble parts through and through and soon has taken complete possession of all the vitals and members of the unconscious idol; then "one fine morning it gives its comrade a shove with the elbow, and bang! crash! the idol lies on the floor" [Diderot, *Rameau's Nephew*]. On "one fine morning" whose noon is bloodless if the infection has penetrated to every organ of spiritual life. Memory alone then still preserves the dead form of the Spirit's previous shape as a vanished history, vanished one knows not how. And the new serpent of wisdom raised high for adoration has this way painlessly cast merely a withered skin.[3]

The dialectical process is thus marked by a double scansion. First, we have the "silent weaving of the Spirit", the unconscious transformation of the entire symbolic network, the entire field of meaning. Then, when the work is already done and when "in itself" all is already decided, it is time for a purely formal act by means of which the previous shape of the Spirit breaks up also "for itself". The crucial point is that *consciousness necessarily comes too late*; it can take cognizance of the fact that the ground is cut from under its feet only when the infectious illness already dominates the field. The strategy of the New, of the spiritual "illness", must therefore be to avoid direct confrontation for as long as possible; a patient "silent weaving", like the underground tunnelling of a mole, waiting for the moment when a light push with the finger will be enough for the mighty edifice to fall to pieces.

Does not this logic spontaneously evoke the well-known cartoon scene where a cat walks calmly over the precipice and drops only when it looks down and becomes aware of having no ground under its feet? The art of subversion is not to fight the cat while it is still walking on firm ground, but to let it continue with head held high and, in the meantime, to undermine the very ground on which it walks, so that when our work is done a simple whistle is enough, a reminder to look down, beneath its feet, and the cat will crumble by itself. Moreover, are we not now in the very midst of the Lacanian notion of "in-between-two-deaths" [*l'entre-deux-morts*]? Apropos of the "shape of consciousness" whose ground is already undermined by the spirit's "silent weaving", although it doesn't yet know it, could we not say that it is already dead without knowing it; that it is still alive only because it doesn't know it is dead?[4] In the passage quoted, Hegel has in mind that by agreeing to take part in the debate, to answer the Enlightenment's arguments, the very reaction to the Enlightenment is already "infected" by it – accepts in advance the logic of its enemy.

Sir Robert Filmer's polemics against John Locke are an exemplary case. Filmer strives to reassert patriarchal authority by means of rational argument proper to the Enlightenment (he refers to Natural Rights, going to great lengths to prove that in the beginning, kings were biological fathers to their subjects, and so on). We encounter a similar paradox with modern neo-conservatives who argue for the need to limit egalitarian-democratic "excesses" using arguments which borrow from the reasoning of their adversary (they point out the beneficent effects of law and order on the individual's freedom and welfare, and so on). In general, we could say that an ideological battle is won when the adversary himself *begins to speak our language*, without being aware of it. What we have here is the lapse of time already mentioned. The break never occurs "now", in the simple present when things are brought to a decision. "In itself", the battle is over before it breaks out: *the very fact that it breaks out is an unequivocal sign that it is really already over*; that the "silent weaving" has already done its job, that the die is already cast. The concluding act of victory thus always has a retroactive character; the final decision has the form of asserting that all is already decided.

It is not without significance that today, the quoted passage from Hegel inevitably evokes psychoanalytic connotations; the "silent weaving of the Spirit" is Hegel's term for the *unconscious working-through*, and we would be quite justified in reading the quoted passage as a refined psychological description of the process of conversion. Let us take the case of an atheist becoming a believer. He is torn by fierce inner struggles, religion obsesses him, he gibes aggressively at believers, looks for historical reasons for the emergence of the "religious illusion", and so on – all this is nothing but proof that the affair is already decided. He *already believes*, although he doesn't yet know it. The inner struggle ends not with the big decision to believe, but with a sense of relief that, without knowing it, he has always-already believed, so that all that remains is for him to renounce his vain resistance and become reconciled to his belief. The refined sense of the psychoanalyst is best attested by his ability to recognize the moment when the "silent weaving" has already done its work, although the patient is still beset by doubts and uncertainty.[5]

"From nothingness through nothingness to nothingness"

A first response to a reproach of Hegel's "monism" would thus be to assert that Hegel is an even more radical "monist" than his critics dare to imagine: in the course of the dialectical process, difference is not "overcome", its very existence is retroactively cancelled. Do we not, however, thus find ourselves occupying the untenable position of defenders of an absurdly "strong" monism: all that effectively exists is the One, differences are only fictitious, with no foundation in reality? The way out of this apparent impasse is shown by the very circular nature of the dialectical process; through it, things *become* what they *always-already were*.

This worn-out commonplace is usually conceived as pointing towards Hegel's supposed ontological evolutionism; development in its entirety is just an explication of what the thing already is "in itself", implicitly – an external realization of its inner potential. The circle of dialectical development is thus closed, nothing really new happens, the seed is "in itself" already the tree, and so on. To dispel the spectre of this ontological evolutionism as a rule imputed to Hegel, one has to reverse the whole perspective by introducing the dimension of radical negativity; the "truth" of any (determined, particular) thing lies in its self-annihilation. The proposition "a thing becomes what it has always-already been" therefore reads "in the course of the dialectical process, a thing reaches its truth by means of sublating its immediate being" – a step towards truth implies by definition a loss of being.

Let us recall the Lacanian distinction between the two deaths and connect it with the Hegelian theory of repetition in history: everybody has to die twice. Napoleon at Elba was already dead (his historical role was over), but he still agitated and tried to recapture power – why? There is only one possible answer: *he wasn't aware that he was dead.* In this precise sense we could say that, with the defeat at Waterloo, Napoleon "became what he already was", dead; he died for the second time. Far from being an exception, a "delay" disturbing the "normal" course of the dialectics of the historical process, Napoleon at Elba is the paradigm of its elementary matrix. The entire span of the dialectical process takes place "between the two deaths", an entity "becomes what it is" by realizing its inherent negativity – in other words, by taking cognizance of its own death. What is "absolute knowledge" but a name for the final moment of this process, when "consciousness" purifies itself of every presupposition of a positive being – the moment paid for by a radical loss, the moment which coincides with pure nothingness?

This "nothingness" reached at the very end of the *Phenomenology of Spirit* is just another name for the fact that "Notion doesn't exist" – or, to use Lacan's terms, that "the big Other doesn't exist", that it is a "dead", purely formal structure without any substantial content. Herein lies the answer to the reproach of "absolute monism". Hegel appears a "monist" only if we impute actual, substantial being to Notion – that is to say, only if we forget the above-described *negative* relationship between knowledge and being. The ill-famed Hegelian formula ascertaining the identity of Reason and Actuality should therefore be read in a way that differs from the usual – it means that neither Reason nor Actuality exists "in itself":

- Actuality is in itself null, without any consistency: it "exists" only in so far as it is grounded in the notional structure – structured through Reason;
- on the other hand, Hegel is anti-Plato *par excellence*: there is nothing more alien to him than a substantialist conception of Notion (claiming that "only Notions effectively exist"). All that "effectively exists" is extra-notional Nature and History; Notion is nothing but their pure logical structure without any substantiality.

In a sense, we could say that "absolute knowledge" implies the recognition of an absolute, insurmountable *impossibility*: the impossibility of accordance between knowledge and being. Here, one should reverse Kant's formula of the transcendental "conditions of possibility"; every positively given object is possible, it emerges only against the background of its impossibility, it can never fully "become itself", realize all its potential, achieve full identity with itself. In so far as we accept the Hegelian definition of truth – the accordance of an object with its Notion – we could say that no object is ever "true", ever fully "becomes what it effectively is". *This discord is a positive condition of the object's ontological consistency* – not because the Notion would be an Ideal never to be achieved by an empirical object, but because Notion itself partakes of the dialectical movement. As soon as an object comes too close to its Notion, this proximity changes, displaces, the Notion itself. Take the three shapes of the "absolute Spirit": art, religion and philosophy. A form of art in total accordance with the Notion of art – in which the Idea appears unmutilated in the medium of the senses – would no longer be art but already religion; with religion, however, the very measure of truth, the Notion to which the object must correspond, changes. In a homologous way, philosophy is nothing but a form of religion which corresponds to its Notion.[6]

The condition of (im)possibility

The picture of the Hegelian system as a closed whole which assigns its proper place to every partial moment is therefore deeply misleading. Every partial moment is, so to speak, "truncated from within", it cannot ever fully become "itself", it cannot ever reach "its own place", it is marked with an inherent impediment, and it is this impediment which "sets in motion" the dialectical development. The "One" of Hegel's "monism" is thus not the One of an Identity encompassing all differences, but rather a paradoxical "One" of radical negativity which forever blocks the fulfilment of any positive identity. The Hegelian "cunning of Reason" is to be conceived precisely against the background of this impossible accordance of the object with its Notion; we do not destroy an object by mangling it from outside but, quite on the contrary, by allowing it freely to evolve its potential and thus to arrive at its Truth:

> Cunning [*List*] is something other than trickery [*Pfiffigkeit*]. *The most open-public activity is the greatest cunning* (the other must be taken in its truth). In other words, with his openness, a man exposes the other in himself, he appears as he is in and for himself, and thereby does away with himself. Cunning is the great art of inducing others to be as they are in and for themselves, and to bring this out to the light of consciousness. Although others are in the right, they do not know how to defend it *by means of speech*. Muteness is bad, mean cunning. Consequently, a true Master is at bottom only he who can provoke *the other to transform himself through his act.*[7]

The "cunning of Reason" simply takes into account the split that is ontologically constitutive of the other: the fact that the other never fully corresponds to its Notion. It does not, therefore, have to be obstructed – it suffices to entice it to reveal its truth, confident that the other will thereby dissolve – transform – itself. Such a procedure has a place in the most intimate interpersonal relationships, as well as in political strategy. When, for example, in a strained interpersonal relationship, somebody complains of the way their partner frustrates them in the realization of their potential, it is wise to withdraw and leave the way open for the supposed victim of oppression. It will soon become clear whether there was any substantial content behind the moaning, or whether the other's entire identity consists in such moaning and groaning – that is, did the other desperately *need* the figure of a "repressive" adversary, in the absence of which their whole identity would disintegrate?

Daniel Sibony recognized the same procedure in what he called "Mitterrand's work as an analyst". Instead of pushing the Communists into a political ghetto, Mitterrand wisely asked them to join the government, putting to test their "capability to govern". The result is known. It became evident that there was no substantial political content behind their "reformist" rhetoric. It should be clear, now, in what sense Lacan, in the early fifties (under the obvious influence of Kojève), equated the position of the psychoanalyst to that of the Hegelian Sage. The psychoanalyst's "inactivity" consists in not intervening actively in the work of the analysand, in refusing to offer him or her any support in the shape of ideals, goals, and so on – the analyst just lets, enables him or her to arrive at his or her repressed content and to articulate it in the medium of speech, whereby this content is tested as to its truth.

One of the great motifs of the Derridean deconstruction is the already-mentioned reversal or complement of the Kantian transcendental formula of the "conditions of possibility". The "infrastructural" condition of possibility of an entity is at the same time the condition of its impossibility, its identity-with-itself is possible only against the background of its self-relationship – of a minimal self-differentiation and self-deferment which opens a gap forever hindering its full identity-with-itself. . . . It should also be clear, now, how the same paradox is inscribed in the very heart of Hegelian dialectics. The key "reversal" of the dialectical process takes place when we recognize in what at first appeared as a "condition of impossibility" – as a hindrance to our full identity, to the realization of our potential – the *condition of the possibility* of our ontological consistency.

Herein lies, strictly speaking, the lesson of the dialectics of "Beautiful Soul" from the *Phenomenology of Spirit*. The "Beautiful Soul" incessantly laments the cruel conditions of the world whose victim it is, which prevent the realization of its good intentions. What it overlooks is the way its own complaints contribute to the preservation of these unfortunate "conditions" – that is, the way the Beautiful Soul is itself an accomplice in the disorder of the world it bemoans. We encounter elements of the Beautiful Soul in a certain type of "dissidence" in decaying "real socialism". Even after the system has begun its terminal disintegration,x such "dissidence" still vehemently maintains that "nothing has really changed" – that behind a new mask, there is still "the same old Bolshevik-totalitarian kernel", and so on. Such "dissidence" literally *needs* a "Bolshevik", a totalitarian adversary. Its compulsive "unmasking" actually *provokes* the adversary into displaying its "totalitarian" character. It lives entirely for the moment, in expectation of the moment when "the mask will fall off" and it will become evident that the adversary is the same old totalitarian Party.

x the greatest vocal resistance occurs at the very moment of its target (object)'s unraveling

ISSUED BY Amtrak®

SUMMARY OF CONDITIONS OF CONTRACT

Not valid for carriage or refund twelve months after date of issue, unless otherwise noted. Reservations must be secured when required; failure to cancel unneeded reservations prior to train departure may result in a substantial service charge. This ticket is not transferable and Amtrak shall not be liable to the purchaser in the event of its loss, destruction or theft, or if it is honored for transportation or refund when presented by any other person.

Carriage hereunder is subject to the Conditions of Contract and the rules and regulations of Amtrak, including those limiting liability for loss of or damage to checked baggage and such Conditions of Contract and rules and regulations are available for inspection by the passenger at any Amtrak ticket office. Amtrak shall not be liable for loss, damage, injury or delay to baggage not placed in checked baggage service, or, in excess of prescribed limits, for loss of or damage to undeclared valuable property contained in checked baggage.

Transportation of automobiles and their contents in Auto Train service is also subject to special rules and regulations available for inspection at any Amtrak office where Auto Train tickets are sold.

Times shown in timetables or elsewhere, and times quoted, are not guaranteed and form no part of this contract. Time schedules and equipment are subject to change without notice. Amtrak expressly reserves the right, without notice, to substitute alternate means of trasportation, and to alter or omit stopping places shown on ticket or timetables. Amtrak assumes no responsibility for inconvenience, expense or other loss, damage or injury resulting from error in schedules, delayed trains, failure to make connections, shortage of equipment or other operating deficiencies.

REV. 9-95

The real "object of desire" of such a "dissident" is not to defeat the adversary, even less to re-establish a democratic order in which the adversary would be forced to accept the role of a rival for power on an equal footing with others, but *one's own defeat*, in accordance with the logic "I have to lose, I must receive a hard blow, since this is the only way to demonstrate that I was right in my accusations against the enemy."

This paradoxical reasoning clearly illustrates the inherently antagonistic character of desire. My "official" desire is for the Communist Party to change into a democratic partner and rival, but in fact I fear such a change more than the plague itself, since I know very well that it would make me lose my footing and force me radically to modify my whole strategy – my real desire is thus for the Party *not* to change; to remain totalitarian. The enemy-figure, the Party supposed to impede my fulfilment, is in truth the very precondition of my position of Beautiful Soul; without it, I would lose the big Culprit, the point by reference to which my subjective position acquires its consistency. It is against this background that we must conceive Hegel's proposition from his *Science of Logic*: "By way of reconciliation, the negative force recognizes in what it fights against its own essence." In the monster of the "Party", the negative force of "dissidence" must recognize an entity on which hangs its own ontological consistency, an entity that confers meaning upon its activity – in other words, its essence.

This paradoxical logic could be further exemplified via a notion which is a kind of analytical-philosophy pendant to the Hegelian "cunning of Reason", that of the "states that are essentially by-products" elaborated by Jon Elster.[8] When, as a result of the subject's activity, a certain non-intended state of things emerges (when, for example, in a "totalitarian" state in disintegration, an attempt at intimidation backfires and strengthens the forces of democratic opposition, like the murder of Chamorro during the last months of the Somoza dictatorship in Nicaragua), the subject has no right to say: "I didn't intend *this*!" and thus elude his responsibility. In so far as "actuality is rational", it is precisely the external, social realization of our aims and intentions that testifies to their true meaning – when we realize our intention, we are confronted with its "truth".

This is also the way to conceive the famous Lacanian proposition that the speaker receives from the other (his addressee) his own message in its inverted – its true – form. The subject whose activity misfires, who achieves the opposite of what he intended, must gather

Hitchcock's Rope (Jimmy Stewart)

enough strength to acknowledge in this unlooked-for result the truth of his intention. That is to say, truth is always the truth of the symbolic "big Other"; it does not occur in the intimacy of my inner self-experience, it results from the way my activity is inscribed in the "public" field of intersubjective relations. To quote the famous final phrase of Lacan's *Seminar on "The Purloined Letter"*, "a letter always arrives at its destination". Although the Beautiful Soul is not prepared to recognize itself as the addressee of the letter returned by (social) reality, although it refuses to decipher in the disorder of the world the truth of its own subjective position, the letter nevertheless reaches its destination: the disorder of the world is a message testifying to the truth of the subject's position – the more this message is ignored, the more it insists and pursues its "silent weaving".

II Reflection

The logic of re-mark

The lesson to be drawn from what we have elaborated so far is that Hegel is to be read carefully and literally. When, for example, he says that the hardest nut of the speculative approach is to recognize the identity of the contraries *as contraries*, to uncover the positivity *in the negative itself*, this does *not* mean that the contraries are to be somehow united, harmonized (against which we could always retort that this operation never works out without some remainder resisting synthesis), or that the negative force is to be somehow "inverted" into positivity, "encompassed" by it (against which we could again always retort that there is an excess of negativity resisting absorption into the positivity of the dialectically mediated identity). As we have seen apropos of the "cunning of Reason", the crucial gesture of the dialectical approach is to exhibit the "positive" (enabling, "productive") dimension that pertains to the Negative as such; to grasp how what appeared at first a purely negative (impending) agency functions as a positive "condition of possibility" of the entity it impedes.

The inappropriateness of the current doxa on Hegel emerges most clearly at this point – apropos of the Negative's inversion into positivity. The hardest nut for the non-dialectical approach is to reconcile it with the Hegelian affirmation of the "infinite force of the Negative". That is to say, it is not sufficient to conceive Hegel as the "thinker of negativity", as the philosopher who displayed the bacchanalian dance of Negativity which sweeps away every positive-substantial identity. What escapes such an approach is simply *identity itself*, the way identity is constituted through the reflexive self-relationship of the Negative. We shall endeavour to shed light on this hardest nut by a symptomatic impasse of the Derridean reading of Hegel.

It would appear that the Derridean treatment of Hegel itself *repeats* the above-mentioned paradoxical logic of the "supplement" elaborated by Derrida apropos of his model analysis of the role of writing in the Platonic text. First, writing is simply excluded as a secondary externality which does not affect the inner presence of the Idea; then, second, he is forced to acknowledge their uncanny proximity, as if the inner essence is always-already affected, constituted even, by the process of writing – which is why we have to repeat the exclusion of writing at another level, within Idea itself. Derrida and the Derridean interpreters (Nancy, Lacoue-Labarthe, Gasche) likewise first oppose Hegel to Derrida by presenting him as a kind of effective antipode of Derrida.

Hegelian dialectics is the culmination of the metaphysics of presence, the logical machine of Notion which, by means of its self-mediation, "sublates" and encompasses all heterogeneity, a closed circle of teleological movement within which every diversity is in advance posited as its own ideal moment – in contrast to Derrida, who affirms the irreducible dissemination of the process of *differance*, the impossibility of ever enclosing this process within the circle of self-mediated identity . . . Second, however, they acknowledge that it is almost impossible to distinguish the self-differentiation process of the Notion from the movement of *differance*, that the line separating them is almost imperceptible, that their proximity is almost absolute. For this reason, their delimitation must be repeated – and, as we have already pointed out, the form of this repetition uncannily resembles that of the fetishistic disavowal, the formula "*je sais bien, mais quand même . . .* ". Its first part articulates the *knowledge* which subverts the point of departure (Hegel as the philosopher of metaphysical identity, and so on); whereas the second part does not refute the first, it simply returns to the point of departure and clings to it as to an article of *faith* – "I know very well that with Hegel, any identity is just a passing moment in the process of difference, yet for all that (I still believe that) the speculative identity ultimately sublates all differences."

We encounter perhaps the clearest example of this discord in Rodolphe Gasche's *The Tain of the Mirror*,[9] in which the relationship of Derridean deconstruction to the philosophy of reflection is elaborated with immense theoretical erudition and acuteness. The first surprise, however, is the way Gasche presents as specifically "Derridean" a whole series of propositions which sound as if they were taken from Hegel's *Logic* – for example, on pages 201–2: ". . . any entity is what it is only by being divided by the Other to which it refers in order to constitute itself" – an almost literal quote from the beginning of Hegel's "logic of essence"! In order to maintain the distance between Hegel and Derrida, Gasche is thus forced to impute to Hegel a nonsensically simplified version of "absolute idealism", summarizing the worn-out textbook platitudes on "the dialectical One encompassing both the One and the manifold"(p. 277) and suchlike. Matters reach a peak when Gasche *refutes Hegel by means of Hegel himself* – presents as a limit supposed to escape Hegel the elementary propositions of Hegelian logic itself, as, for example, in the following characteristic passage:

> The possibility of dialectically comprehending the opposition between what is doubled and its double as a relation of exteriorization and reappropriation of the double as the negative of what is doubled is logically dependent on the originary duplication according to which no *on* can refer in its appearing to itself except by doubling itself in an Other. (p. 228)

In short, first one imputes to Hegel an absurdly oversimplified notion of dialectical reflection ("reappropriation of the double as the negative of what is doubled"); subsequently one states as a condition of such a reappropriation, supposed to escape the dialectics, the elementary dialectical insight that an entity can refer to itself only by doubling itself in an Other!

This inherent ambiguity of the "deconstructive" reading of Hegel emerges most violently apropos of the crucial notion of "sublation" [*Aufhebung*]. In the first stage, Hegel and Derrida are of course clearly opposed. *Aufhebung* names the dialectical overcoming of differences, the very way Notion encompasses heterogeneity, diversity, by transforming it into an ideal-sublated moment of its own identity – differences are recognized *qua* "sublated", *qua* moments of an articulated totality, whereas Derrida's entire emphasis is on an "infrastructural" remainder which *resists sublation*, which persists in its heterogeneity and is precisely as such – as the limit of sublation, as a rock on which sublation necessarily founders – its positive condition. In a second stage, however, this opposition between *Aufhebung* and its leftover becomes blurred. When, for example, in *Dissémination*, Derrida deals with the Mallarméan problematic of "re-mark" [*ré-marque*], he concedes that *Aufhebung* as the elementary matrix of Hegelian speculative reflection is almost indistinguishable from the graphics of re-mark, so that the gesture of differentiation has to be repeated in a far more refined and ambiguous way. This Derridean reading/rewriting of the Mallarméan re-mark deserves closer examination since, as we shall see, it is here that Derrida comes closest to the Lacanian logic of the signifier.

How do we get from the mark [*marque*] to the re-mark? Why must every mark (every signifying trace) be re-marked? Derrida's point of departure is the differential character of the texture of marks. A mark is nothing but a trace, a sheaf of features that differentiate it from other marks, in which this differentiality must be brought to its self-reference – in which every series of marks as semic (bearers of meaning) "must contain *an additional* tropological movement by which the seme *mark* refers to what demarcates the marks, to the blanks between the marks that relate the different marks to each other".[10] In short, in any series of marks there is always at least one which functions as "empty", "asemic" – that is to say, which re-marks the differential space of the inscription of marks. It is only through the gesture of re-marking that a mark becomes mark, since it is only the re-mark which opens and sustains the place of its inscription . . .

Are we not thus in the midst of the "logic of the signifier" as elaborated by Jacques-Alain Miller in his two short "canonic" writings, "Suture" and "Matrix",[11] in the second of which he even uses the same terms as Derrida (the mark and the empty place of its inscription, sustained by an additional empty mark, and so on)? Is not the elementary proposition of the "logic of the signifier" (dismissed by Derrida in a short note – *remark* – in *On Grammatology*) that every series of signifiers must contain a paradoxical surplus-element which holds the place, within this series, of the very absence of the signifier – to resort to the formula which has been part of the jargon for a long time, a signifier of the lack of the signifier? That is to say, in so far as the order of the signifier is differential, the very difference between the signifier and its absence must be inscribed within it; and is not this "valence that is not just one among others"[12] the Lacanian S1, the Master-Signifier, the "asemic" signifier-without-signified, always supplementing the chain of "knowledge" (S2) and thus enabling it? Moreover, is not the empty place represented by the re-mark the Lacanian "*sujet barré*", the subject of the signifier, so that this most elementary matrix already makes possible the inference of the Lacanian definition of the signifier as that which "represents the subject for all other signifiers"? Does not the re-mark represent the empty space of inscription for all other marks?

To render this logic of re-mark "palpable", let us just recall a certain procedure found in different domains of art, from painting (the relation between figure and its ground) to music (the relation of motif and accompaniment) and cinema: the paradoxical inversion by means of which what at first appears as motif (figure) retroactively, after being re-marked by a new motif (figure), changes into accompaniment (ground) – and the complementary inversion whereby what at first appears as "mere accompaniment" changes retroactively into the principal motif. Let us begin with Escher's graphic paradoxes. Their basic procedure is that of the dialectical interplay of figure and ground, of gradual transformation of ground into figure, of retroactive re-marking of ground as figure, and vice versa. The paradoxical result of such an interplay – the inconsistency of a series of staircases where, by going all the way down, we find ourselves at the top again, for example – attests the presence of *subject*: the subject "is" this very inconsistency of the structure – in our case, the void, the invisible and "impossible" gap between the lowest and the highest step bridged by optical illusion. And is not Escher's best-known visual paradox, that of two hands holding a pencil and drawing each other, a perfect case of two marks simultaneously re-marking each other?

However, to detect the logic of re-mark, one does not need to look on the fringes of art, where art approaches technical trickery (paradoxes, anamorphoses, and so on). It is enough to view "mainstream" works in another light. Mozart, for example: we all know the cliché about Mozart's music being "heavenly", "divine" – this characterization nevertheless contains a grain of truth. It points towards a typical Mozartian procedure in which the initial melody is joined by another melodic line which, so to speak, descends "from above" and changes the status of the first melody retroactively into that of an "accompaniment" (the best-known instance is the third movement of Serenade No. 10 in B Major, KV 361). We could say that this second, "heavenly" motif re-marks, reframes anew, the initial motif. Perhaps we could also risk the elementary hypothesis that precisely such a re-marking of motifs, their passage into accompaniment, is lost with Beethoven – it appears in his work only by way of exception (in the third movement of the Ninth Symphony, for example).[13]

In the domain of cinema, a homologous inversion is often practised by Alfred Hitchcock – in *The Birds*, for example, the famous panoramic shot from great height of a small town in which a fire has just burst out. Suddenly, a lone bird enters the frame from behind the camera; soon it is joined by a couple, followed by the entire flock. The same shot is thus re-marked. What seemed at first to be an establishing shot of the entire scene, taken from a "neutral", objective point of view, is *subjectivized* and proved to be the threatening view of the birds themselves of their victims. A similar, albeit symmetrically inverted, procedure is used by Francis Ford Coppola in the opening titles of his *Conversation*. The camera shows various scenes from a park full of walkers during a lunch-time break, with a soundtrack of strangely distorted voices. We, the spectators, automatically take this to be a neutral, purely illustrative background for the titles, whose sole function is to create the right "feeling". However, it soon becomes evident that the scene shown during the titles is the key scene of the entire film (a detective agency in the middle of bugging an adulterous couple). The crucial point not to be missed here is that reference to the imaginary level of *Gestalt* does not suffice to explain this dialectical interplay of "figure" and "background". Inversions of this kind are possible only within the universe of the signifier – that is to say, within a universe in which at least one element represents the place of inscription of and for all other elements. Without the inscription, within the series of elements, of an element which re-marks their very place of inscription, the distance between "figure" and its "ground" cannot be established.

This dialectics of "figure" and "ground" makes it possible to discern the homology between re-mark and *Aufhebung* pointed out by Derrida himself. An element is "sublated" – suppressed and at the same time preserved – when it is re-marked by a new frame, included in a new symbolic network, "elevated" into its element. In the above-mentioned shot from *The Birds*, for example, the "objective" view from above the town is suppressed-and-preserved by being re-marked as the "subjective" view of the birds themselves. "The thing remains exactly the same as before, yet all of a sudden, its meaning changes totally"; it remains the same *qua* mark, yet it is re-marked in a different way. In this sense, the dialectical inversion always follows the logic of re-mark: the thing itself in its immediacy does not change; all that changes is the modality of its inscription in the symbolic network. In this sense, it also becomes clear why the re-mark coincides with the Lacanian S1, the Master-Signifier, the "quilting point" [*point de capiton*]. The effect of "quilting" takes place when, with a sudden reversal of perspective, what was a moment ago still perceived as defeat appears as victory.

Let us take the case of Saint Paul, whose rereading of the death of Christ gave Christianity its definitive contours. He did not add any new content to the already-existing dogmas – all he did was to re-mark as the greatest triumph, as the fulfilment of Christ's supreme mission (reconciliation of God with mankind), what was before experienced as traumatic loss (the defeat of Christ's mundane mission, his infamous death on the cross).[14] Here we encounter again the fundamental Hegelian motif: "reconciliation" does not convey any kind of miraculous healing of the wound of scission, it consists solely in a reversal of perspective by means of which we perceive how the scission is in itself already reconciliation – how, for example, Christ's defeat and infamous death are already in themselves reconciliation. To accomplish "reconciliation" we do not have to "overcome" the scission, we just have to *re-mark* it.[15]

Furthermore, does this logic of re-mark not point towards the *self-reflective* character of what Derrida calls "textuality" – towards the way every texture of marks necessarily "reflects" into itself, within itself, its own space of inscription, its own conditions of possibility – in the shape of its opposite, to be sure? The empty space of inscription (the lack) reflects itself in the shape of a positive mark, of "one among others". Gasche proposes the following concise formulation: "In affecting itself by the re-mark, designating its own space of engenderment, the mark inscribes itself within itself, *reflects itself within itself* under the form of what it is not."[16] Is the logic of re-mark therefore not the elementary matrix of the Hegelian self-reflective movement of the Notion? In *On Grammatology*, Derrida articulates how Rousseau "inscribes textuality within the text", how he "tells us in the text what is text". The themes upon which the Derridean reading of Rousseau is centred ("supplementarity", for example) are not simply themes among others in the chain; they are themes which describe (reflect within the text) the textual chain itself, the very way the text "operates". If, thence, as Gasche points out, referring to Derrida, there is a near-perfect coincidence between the logic of re-mark and the reflexive movement of *Aufhebung*, how does one distinguish them?

Gasche's basic strategy consists in drawing a distinction between the self-reflective layer of the text (elements, motifs, by means of which textuality is reflected, represented, within the text) and its "infrastructural" background, the textual operations that render possible and, by the same gesture, hinder such reflectivity – which open its space, but simultaneously prevent it from fully succeeding and thus coinciding with itself in accomplished self-mirroring. He quotes the following passage from *Grammatology*: "If a text always gives itself a certain representation of its own roots, those roots live only by that representation, by never touching the soil, so to speak", and comments upon it: "The circumscribed discourse in which a text presents itself is a representation that is constantly overrun by the entire system of the text's own resources and laws."[17]

Here, we should indulge in a short "deconstructive" reading of Gasche himself. His commentary misses – or rather misplaces – the emphasis of Derrida's proposition. That is to say, Gasche puts the emphasis on the way self-reflection is "embedded" in infrastructural mechanisms which exceed it, whereas the whole point of Derrida's quoted proposition is its exact opposite. These infrastructural mechanisms "live only by that representation" – that is, the very textuality of the text is sustained by this self-reflection. There is no primordial textual "infrastructure" that could as a result reflect itself in a distorted, partial way within the text – "textuality" is nothing but a name for this very process of textual self-reflection: in other words, of this process of re-marking. Let us, however, turn to Gasche's principal argument against identifying the "infrastructure of re-mark" with the Hegelian movement of reflection:

> This theme [that describes the chain itself] does not reflect the whole chain, if reflection means what it has always meant, a mirroring representation through which a self reappropriates itself. Instead of reflecting the chain of the text into itself, "supplementarity" *re-marks* that chain in the same way as it is itself re-marked, that is, put back into the position of a mark within the textual chain. . . . The illusion of a reflexive totalization by a theme or a concept is grounded in the representational effacement of their position as

> marks within the chain that they tend to govern. Because of the re-mark, self-representation and self-reflection never quite take place. A theme or concept can only designate the text *en abyme*; that is, its representation is the representation of a representation.[18]

The first phrase is already revealing: one can discern re-mark from reflection only by presupposing that "reflection means what it has always meant" – this statement is doubly questionable, formally as well as on the level of content. On the level of content, it is – to resort to naive terms which are quite appropriate here – *simply wrong*. It imputes to Hegel a strictly pre-Hegelian notion of reflection ("a mirroring representation through which a self reappropriates itself") – a notion which misses what Hegel endeavoured to circumscribe by "absolute reflection". If this were the Hegelian notion of reflection, then we certainly could not speak of a "similarity" between the movement of reflection and re-mark. Formally, such a statement cannot but sound somewhat odd, coming from the mouth of a "deconstructivist". Is not the entire effort of "deconstruction" directed towards displaying how words *never* simply "mean what they have always meant" – how they can never reach the full identity of their "proper meaning"? Here, however, all of a sudden, we are obliged to appeal to what reflection "has always meant" . . . . What if Hegel himself had already "deconstructed" the notion of reflection, making it function in a way unheard of within the pre-Hegelian (and, perhaps, also post-Hegelian) tradition? What if, precisely with Hegel, "reflection" *no longer* "means what it has always meant"?

The abyss re-marked

To decide on this crucial point, we have to look closely at Gasche's line of argument. Contrary to the movement of reflection – where, by means of reflexive totalization, its agent "dominates" the entire chain and "reappropriates" the reflected contents – in the Derridean logic of re-mark the element through which textuality reflects itself within the text – the element which re-marks the place of the chain as such – never "dominates" the chain, since it occupies itself the position of one of its elements and is thus remarked anew by other elements.[19] For this reason, any element can reflect textuality only *en abyme*, through endless deferment – there is always a certain excess of re-mark which eludes dialectical totalization:

> . . . one trope too many is thus added to the series, and, in the form of a proxy . . . , it represents what does not really belong to the series of semes, the nonmeaning against which the full marks stand out. If that trope is subtracted from the series to be totalized by the concept [of the mark], however, this totalization leaves at least one mark unaccounted for. Thus re-marked by the space of inscription that demarcates all marks, no concept or theme of the mark could hope to coincide with what it aims to embrace. The re-mark is an essential limit to all coinciding reflection or mirroring, a doubling of the mark that makes all self-reflective adequation impossible. For structural reasons, there is always more than totality; the extra valence added by the delegate of the asemic space of diacritical differentiation of the totality of semes always – infinitely – remains to be accounted for.[20]

The argument is clear. The (conceptual) totalization of a chain of marks is always re-marked by an additional mark which, within the series of semic marks, represents (holds the place of) their ground, their field of inscription – that is, their very differentiality, the difference between marks as such. Totality takes place only as re-marked; as soon as it occurs, a surplus-mark is always added. In other words, totalization never totalizes all; because of a structural necessity, it is accomplished by means of an excess which itself remains non-totalized, non-accounted-for. What is not possible is a totalization which, through a self-reflective equation to itself, would comprise itself, its own re-mark – which would re-mark itself and thus achieve transparent self-coincidence. Yet Hegelian reflective reappropriation is precisely such an impossible totalization in which the field of marks re-marks (reflects) its own conditions without remainder; in which the frame of the text is inscribed into, accounted for, by the text itself.

Does this argument hold? Is it effectively an argument against Hegel? Instead of providing a formal answer, I will risk an "empirical refutation", however naive it may appear, by referring to a particular line of thought from Hegel which suits perfectly Gasche's description of the way re-mark functions as a surplus by means of which totalization takes place: Hegel's deduction of monarchy from his philosophy of right.

This deduction is, as a rule, looked down upon. One sees in it evidence of Hegel's concession to pre-bourgeois historical circumstances, if not outright proof of his conformism. There is surprise at the absurdity and inconsistency of Hegel, the philosopher of absolute Reason, advocating that the decision on who will be the head of state should depend upon the non-rational, biological fact of descent. It is pointed out how the whole of Hegel's argumentation clings to a wordplay on "immediacy". To be effective, the unity of the State must be again embodied in an individual in whose existence alone Will exists for itself – achieves immediate existence – and this demand for natural immediacy is best met precisely by lineage . . . . This criticism, however, misfires totally: not because it is simply wrong – the point is rather that, unknowingly, it confirms Hegel's basic idea. The constitutional monarchy is a rationally articulated organic Whole at the head of which there is an "irrational" element, the person of the King. What is crucial here is precisely the fact accentuated by Hegel's critics: the abyss separating the State as an organic rational totality from the "irrational" *factum brutum* of the person who embodies supreme power – that is to say, by means of which the State assumes the form of subjectivity. Against the reproach that the fate of the State is thus left to the natural contingency of the sovereign's psychic constitution (his wisdom, honesty, courage, and so on), Hegel retorts:

> . . . all this rests on a presupposition which is nugatory, namely that everything depends on the monarch's particular character. In a completely organized state, it is only a question of the culminatory point of formal decision . . . . It is wrong therefore to demand objective qualities in a monarch; he has only to say "yes" and dot the "i" . . . whatever else the monarch may have in addition to this power of final decision is part and parcel of his private character and should be of no consequence. . . . In a well-organized monarchy, the objective aspect belongs to law alone, and the monarch's part is merely to set to the law the subjective "I will".[21]

The act of the monarch is thus of a purely formal nature: its framework is determined by the Constitution, the concrete content of his decisions is proposed to him by his counsellors, so that "he has often no more to do than sign his name. But this name is important. It is the last word beyond which it is impossible to go."[22]

Hereby, all is actually said. The monarch functions as a "pure" signifier, a signifier-without-signified; his entire actuality (and authority) consists in his Name, and it is precisely for this reason that his physical reality is wholly arbitrary and could be left to the biological contingency of lineage. The monarch thus embodies the function of the Master-Signifier at its purest; it is the One of the Exception, the "irrational" protuberance of the social edifice which transforms the amorphous mass of "people" into a concrete totality of mores. By means of his ex-sistence of a pure signifier, he constitutes the Whole of the social fabric in its "organic articulation" [*organische Gliederung*] – the "irrational" surplus as a condition of the rational totality, the excess of the "pure" signifier without signified as a condition of the organic Whole of signifier/signified: "Taken without its monarch and the articulation of the whole which is the indispensable and direct concomitant of monarchy, the people is a formless mass and no longer a state."[23]

In other words, the monarch is not just a "symbol" of community, he is something decidedly more. Through him, in him, the community itself reaches its "being-for-itself" and thus realizes itself – it is a paradoxical "symbol" by means of which the symbolized content actualizes itself. The monarch can accomplish this task only in so far as his authority is of a purely "performative" nature and not founded in his effective capacities. It is only his counsellors, the State bureaucracy in general, which are supposed to be chosen according to their respective capabilities and their fitness to do the required job. One thus maintains the *gap* between State employees who must obtain their post by hard effort, by proving themselves worthy of it, and the monarch himself as the point of pure authority of the signifier:

> the multitude of individuals, the mass of people, is confronted with a Unique individual, the monarch – they are the multitude, movement, fluidity; – he is the immediacy, *naturalness* – it is only he who is *natural*, that is to say, with him, *nature took refuge*; he is *its last remainder, as a positive remainder* – the family of the prince is the only positive family – all other families must be left behind – other individuals *have value only in so far as they are dispossessed*, in so far as they have made themselves.[24]

This coincidence of pure Culture (the empty signifier) with the left-over of Nature in the person of the king entails the paradox of the king's relationship towards law: strictly speaking, the king cannot break the law since his word immediately *makes* law; it is only against this background that Kant's unconditional prohibition of the violent overthrow of the king obtains its rationale. In this sense, monarch functions as a personification of Wittgenstein's "sceptical paradox":

we cannot say that his act violates the Rule, since it (re)defines it. All other subjects are marked by the gap forever separating their "pathological" reality, what they effectively are and do, from the ideal order of what they ought to be – they never fully correspond to their Notion and, consequently, can be judged and measured by their (in)adequacy to it; whereas the monarch immediately *is* the actuality of his own Notion. To resort to Kantian terms: the king is a Thing which acquired phenomenal existence, a point of short circuit between the noumenal order of freedom (moral law) and the level of phenomenal experience – more precisely: although he is not it, we, the subjects, are obliged to act *as if* he is the Thing embodied.

The paradox of the Hegelian monarch is thus that, in a sense, he is the point of madness of the social fabric; his social position is determined immediately by his lineage, by biology; he is the only one among individuals who already by his "nature" is what he (socially) is – all others must "invent" themselves, elaborate the content of their being by their activity. As always, Saint-Just was right when, in his accusation against the king, he demanded his execution not because of any of his specific deeds but simply *because he was king*. From a radically republican point of view, the supreme crime consists in the very fact of *being* the king, not in what one *does* as a king.

Here Hegel is far more ambiguous than it may seem. His conclusion is roughly as follows: in so far as a Master is indispensable in politics, we should not condescend to the common-sense reasoning which tells us that "the Master should be at least as wise, brave and good as possible . . . ". On the contrary, we should maintain the greatest possible gap between the Master's symbolic legitimation and the level of "effective" qualifications; localize the function of the Master to a place excluded from the Whole, reduce him to an agency of purely formal decision whereby it does not matter if he is effectively an idiot . . . [25] At the very point where Hegel seems to praise monarchy, he carries out a kind of *separation* between S1 and *a*, between pure signifier and object. If the king's charismatic power of fascination depends on a *concomitance* of S1 and *a* – on the illusion that the Master-Signifier covers, deep within itself, the precious object – Hegel separates them and shows us, on the one hand, S1 in its imbecilic tautology of an empty name; and on the other, the object (the body of the monarch) as a pure excrement, a remainder appended to the Name.[26]

From failed reflection to reflected failure

The crucial feature is thus that the Hegelian monarch *falls out* from the dialectical mediation of Nature and Spirit. He presents a point of the *immediate* passage of one into the other, a paradoxical point at which the pure Name, the pure agency of the signifier, *immediately* clings to the "last residue" of positive naturalness – to what is NOT *aufgehoben*, sublated through the work of mediation . . . . Have we not here, in this position of the monarch, a clear case of an element which, in its relation to the semic totality (of the State), functions precisely as a "re-mark" in the Derridean sense of the term? Of an element which is "more than totality", which "sticks out" from the rational totality of the State, in so far as it is the last residue of Nature – of non-Reason – but which precisely as such "reflects" the very space of articulation of the rational totality? Of an element which literally "represents what does not belong to the series of semes"; Nature in its immediacy? The Monarch is a strange body within the fabric of the State; he remains "unaccounted for" by rational mediation. However, precisely as such, he is the element through which rational totality constitutes itself. Herein lies the "secret" of the dialectical mediation of social elements by the State's rational totality. This mediation can be brought about only by way of an "irrational" residue of non-mediated Nature – that is, the stupid biological fact of the monarch's body. In other words, what the Derridean "deconstruction" brings out after a great struggle and declares to be the inherent limit of the dialectical mediation – the point at which the movement of *Aufhebung* necessarily fails – Hegel posits directly as the crucial moment of this movement. "Everything can be mediated", sublated in its immediacy and posited as an ideal moment of rational totality – on condition that this very power of absolute mediation is embodied anew in the form of its opposite; of an inert, non-rational residue of natural immediacy. We can now perhaps see why the conception of the monarch is "of all conceptions the hardest for ratiocination",[27] inclusive of the deconstructive one.[28]

For that reason, Gasche's proposition "Thus re-marked by the space of inscription that demarcates all marks, no concept or theme of the mark could hope to coincide with what it aims to embrace" is to be given its full weight and taken more literally than it was probably meant. By its mere presence, the re-mark (which represents the place of inscription of other marks – themes) hinders, prevents the other marks from coinciding with themselves, from achieving their full identity. The very identity-with-itself of a re-mark embodies negativity, auto-fissure, inherent to all marks, in so far as this identity consists in the impossible coincidence of an element with the empty place of its inscription (which is the Hegelian–Wittgensteinian definition of identity). By his mere presence, the monarch serves as a reminder of the ultimate instability of the social fabric; of the fact that what we call "society" is the congelation of an original violence which can at any moment erupt again and pulverize the established order. The monarch is therefore simultaneously the point guaranteeing stability and consistency, and the embodiment of a radical negativity – the central element by reference to which the structure obtains stability and meaning; the point of identity in its very heart, coincides with its own opposite.[29]

It should be clear, now, why the basic premiss of the Derridean criticism of Hegel – that *Aufhebung* itself cannot be *aufgehoben*, that re-mark itself is in its turn always-already re-marked by the series within which it is inscribed – misfires completely. According to Derrida, *Aufhebung* would mean a "successful" inscription/re-mark of the space into the series of marks – that is, of textuality into the text. Against this "illusion" he then points out how re-mark could never entirely reflect the chain of marks, how it could never fully coincide with itself in a perfect self-mirroring – how the text is always reflected-into-itself in a distorted, displaced, "biased" – in short, *re-marked* perspective. Herewith, Derrida misplaces as a *limit* of reflection what is in Hegel the very fundamental feature of "absolute" reflection. Reflection, to be sure, ultimately always fails – any positive mark included in the series could never "successfully" represent/reflect the empty space of the inscription of marks. It is, however, *this very failure as such which "constitutes" the space of inscription.* The "place" of the inscription of marks is *nothing* but the void opened by the failure of the re-mark. In other words, there is no infrastructural space of the inscription of marks without the re-mark. Re-mark does not "represent"/reflect some previously constituted infrastructural network – *the very act of reflection as failed constitutes retroactively that which eludes it*.

To clear up this crucial problem, let us return again to Gasche. According to him, the "limits of speculative *Aufhebung*" consist in the fact that it

> is incapable of accounting for the re-mark *as such*, not only because this infrastructure cannot be phenomenologized and experienced, but also

> because at least one representation of it – that is, at least one figure in which it disappears – is left unaccounted for. This last figure is ultimately the figure of *Aufhebung* itself.[30]

What should arouse our suspicion is the use of the seemingly innocent figure "not only . . . but also . . . "; the enumeration of *two* reasons why *Aufhebung* necessarily fails: on the one hand, the unattainable, ever-elusive excess of the "infrastructure" which can never be fully mirrored within the text; on the other, the unaccountable excess of the very figure of *Aufhebung* which can never totalize *itself.* The paradox is that the relation between these two "excesses" supposed to escape the movement of reflection is *in itself reflective.* First, we have the excess of what escapes the reflective movement of *Aufhebung*, then we have the excess of this very movement of *Aufhebung* – and we pass from Gasche (and Derrida) to Hegel the moment we realize that this "not only . . . but also . . . " is *superfluous*; that the two excesses are nothing but two aspects of the same gesture; that instead of "not only . . . but also . . . " there should be "*videlicet*" – that the unattainable excess of the "infrastructure" constitutes itself by means of the *Aufhebung* as "unaccountable". The Hegelian "absolute reflection" is nothing but the name for such a "reflective" relationship between these two excesses. It is, so to speak, a redoubled reflection, the reflective re-marking of the very surplus that escapes reflection.[31]

The contours of a possible Hegelian criticism of Derrida are thus beginning to take shape. What eludes Derrida is the "negative" kernel of identity itself – the fact that identity as such is a "reflective determination", an inverted presentation of its opposite. Let us take the following proposition from Gasche:

> To the extent that [the] asemic space is represented by a proxy within, and in addition to, the series, it becomes metaphorically or metonymically transformed into a mark, that is, into precisely what it is supposed to make possible.[32]

The paradox of re-mark is therefore that its identity stands proxy for its own opposite (pure difference, the space between marks), that the One of the re-mark stands proxy for the blank of its own place of inscription, and so on. All that needs to be added is that this paradox, far from characterizing the additional identity of the re-mark, supplement to the identity of "ordinary" marks, *defines identity as such.*

The "identity" of an object consists in the feature which re-marks the asemic space of its inscription (the Lacanian "signifier without signified"). In other words, *every* identity-with-itself is nothing but the "semic substitute[s] for the spaced-out semiopening that makes [it] possible"[33] – that is, the inverted representative of the space of its own condition of (im)possibility. Consequently, when Gasche speaks about "one trope too many" added to the series of semic marks, what should be pointed out is that *this "one too many" is precisely the One as such*; there is no One to which, subsequently, "one too many" would be added – the One is "originally" one-too-many, the signifier-One whose signified is Void.[34]

In a paradoxical way, Derrida remains prisoner of the – ultimately "commonsensical" – conception which aims at freeing heterogeneity from the constraints of identity; of a conception which is obliged to presuppose a constituted field of identity (the "metaphysics of presence") in order to be able to set to the unending work of its subversion. The Hegelian answer to this would be: we "deconstruct" identity by retroactively ascertaining how identity itself is a "reflective determination", a form of appearance of its opposite – identity as such is the highest affirmation of difference; it is the very way differentiality, the space of differences "as such", inscribes-reflects itself within the field of differences (of the series of different determinations).

This is a hard nut to crack even for those followers of Hegel who remain fascinated by the "power of the Negative", by the wild dance of negativity which "liquefies" all positive, solid determinations. For them, the "ultimate secret" of dialectical speculation is still unapproachable. The "standpoint of Understanding" – what Hegel calls "abstract ratiocination" – is bewitched by the eternal "flow of things" whereby every definite, solid form is doomed to death, whereby every fixed identity is just a passing moment of the all-embracing whirlpool of generation and corruption. What eludes this approach is not the "mediation" of all solid, fixed forms by the negative power of "liquefaction" but the *immediate* passage of this "liquefaction" into a point of inert, fixed identity-with-itself, the way the State as the agency of rational "mediation" of society acquires full actuality, realizes itself, only in the inert, "irrational" immediacy of the monarch's body, for example. For the "standpoint of Understanding", this could only mean that the person of the monarch "symbolizes", "represents" the totality of the State – what it cannot grasp is that the monarch, in his very corporality, "is" the State in a way which is far from "metaphoric". It cannot grasp how what the monarch "symbolizes" – "represents" – has no consistency outside this "representation".

The tain of the mirror

Actually, the basic misunderstanding of Gasche's book is best exemplified by its very title: *the tain of the mirror*, the part where the reflecting surface is scraped, so that we see the dark rear. Within Gasche's line of argument, this tain of the mirror serves, of course, as a metaphor for the limit of (philosophical) reflection–mirroring. Reflection – the mirroring of the subject in the object, the reappropriation of the object by means of the subject recognizing in it itself, its own product – encounters its limit in the "tain of the mirror"; in the points where, instead of returning to the viewer his own image, the mirror confronts him with a meaningless dark spot. These dark spots are, of course, simultaneously the condition of the possibility and the impossibility of mirroring. Precisely by limiting reflection, they create the minimal distance between what is being mirrored and its mirror-image, the distance which makes the very process of mirroring possible.

Here, Gasche pays the price for the fact that – in a book which is ultimately dedicated to a criticism of the dialectical notion of reflection – he fails to elaborate the elementary structure of the Hegelian notion of reflection (positing, external, determining reflection). That is to say, the examination of this structure would immediately confront us with the way Hegelian "absolute" reflection is in itself always-already *redoubled*, "mediated" by its own impossibility. Hegel knows perfectly well that reflection always fails, that the subject always encounters in a mirror some dark spot, a point which does not return him his mirror-picture – in which he cannot "recognize himself". It is, however, precisely at this point of "absolute strangeness" that the subject (the subject of the signifier, $\$$, not the imaginary *ego*, caught in the miror-relationship $m - i(a)$) is inscribed into the picture. The spot of the mirror-picture is thus strictly constitutive of the subject; the subject *qua* subject of the look "is" only in so far as the mirror-picture he is looking at is inherently "incomplete" – in so far, that is, as it contains a "pathological" stain – the subject is correlative to this stain.

Therein ultimately consists the point of Lacan's constant reference to anamorphosis: Holbein's *Ambassadors* exemplifies literally the Hegelian speculative proposition on phrenology "spirit (= subject) is a bone (= skull)": the blind spot of the picture. In the reversal proper to the process of reflection, the subject experiences itself as correlative to the point in his Other in which he comes across an absolutely strange power, a power with which no mirror-exchange is possible. In the Hegelian reading of the Terror of the French Revolution, for example, the subject must recognize, in the arbitrary power which can at any time cut off his head, a materialization of his own essence. The guillotine, this image of uncontrollable Otherness with which no identification seems possible, is nothing but the "objective correlate" of the abstract negativity that defines the subject. The passage of "external" into "absolute" reflection consists precisely in this *redoubling* of reflection. Reflection as symmetrical mirroring of the subject in objectivity fails, there is always some residue which resists integration, and it is in this residue escaping the reflective grasp that the proper dimension of the subject is "reflected". In other words, *the subject is the tain of the mirror.*[35]

In Kafka's apologue about the Door of the Law (from his *Trial*) the man from the country occupies, until the final dénouement, the position of "external reflection". He is confronted with the transcendent image of the Palace of Law where, behind every door, there is another door hiding an unapproachable Secret, and whose representative (the doorkeeper) treats him with utter indifference and contempt. The crucial reversal takes place when the doorkeeper explains to the dying man that the Door was meant only for him from the very beginning – in other words, the Law that the man from the country viewed with awed respect, assuming automatically that it did not even notice his presence, had regarded him from the very beginning; precisely as excluded, he was always-already *taken into account*. "Absolute reflection" is simply the name for this experience of how the subject, by means of his very failure to grasp the secret of the Other, is already inscribed in the Other's "accountancy", *reflected* into the Other: the experience of how his "external" reflection of the Other is already a "reflective determination" of the Other itself.

Hegel's often quoted and even more often misunderstood proposition from the Introduction to *Phenomenology of Spirit* that it would be vain for the subject to try to grasp the Absolute if the Absolute were not and did not want to be in- and for-itself already with us, has to be comprehended against this background. By restating it as "the Absolute is always with us", even Heidegger misses its crucial point. What is at stake here is not the notion that the Absolute is (always) with us, still less the notion that, by means of a final synthesis – reconciliation – it will be with us, but the experience of how it *always-already was* with us. Our experience of the "loss", of the fissure between us (the subject) and the Absolute, is the very way the Absolute is already with us. In this sense, the final assertion of the doorkeeper that from the very beginning the Door was meant only for the man from the country is Kafka's version of the Hegelian proposition that the Absolute was always-already with us. The very appearance of the inaccessible transcendence, of the Secret hidden beyond the endless series of Doors, is an appearance "for the consciousness" – it is the way the Law addresses the subject. This is how we should grasp the passage of "external" into "determining" (absolute) reflection. The notion of the inaccessible, transcendent Absolute makes sense only in so far as the subject's gaze is already here – in its very notion, the inaccessible Other implies a relation to its own other (the subject). The subject does not "internalize", "mediate", the Being-in-itself of the Absolute; it simply takes cognizance of the fact that this In-itself is in-itself *for* the subject.

Notes

1. Such a paradoxical status of the Real *qua* construction could be exemplified by the mathematical notion of the "non-constructive proof", elaborated by Michael Dummett apropos of intuitionism (see his *Truth and Other Enigmas*, Cambridge, MA: Harvard University Press 1978). Dummett has in mind a procedure whereby we can prove (construct) the existence of a certain mathematical entity (of a certain number, for example), although we are not able to exhibit this entity (number) in its positive determination – statements of the type "it is hereby proven that a cardinal number must exist which is a multiple of. . . " which are fully valid notwithstanding the fact that we will never be able to state precisely what this number is.

The status of the Freudian–Lacanian Real (the traumatism of the primal parricide, for example) is exactly the same. We can deduce the fact of the parricide by means of a "non-constructive proof"; we can prove that the parricide must be presupposed for (subsequent) history to retain its consistency, although we will never be able to exhibit its empirical reality; and, incidentally, in his "A Child Is Being Beaten", Freud describes in the same way the status of the middle term in the fantasy chain which runs from "father beats a child" to "a child is being beaten"; the scene "father is beating me" is wholly inaccessible to the consciousness, but we must construct it to be able to account for the passage from the first to the third form.

2. See Slavoj Žižek, *Le plus sublime des hystériques – Hegel passe*, Paris: Point-hors-ligne 1988, pp. 100–3.

3. G.W.F. Hegel, *Phenomenology of Spirit*, Oxford: Oxford University Press 1977, pp. 331–2.

4. For a more detailed elaboration of the notion of "in-between-two-deaths", see Slavoj Žižek, *The Sublime Object of Ideology*, London: Verso 1989, pp. 131–6.

6. This paradoxical logic of a moment when, before the formal act of decision, things are already decided, enables us perhaps to throw new light upon a typical Wagnerian scene to which Claude Lévi-Strauss has already drawn attention: the scene of the hero's inner peace, of his conciliation, harmony with the world, surrender to the flow of the world, just before the crucial ordeal. There are three versions of this scene in Wagner's operas: the idyll of the "murmur of the forest" before the struggle with the dragon in Act II of *Siegfried*; the sextet preceding the final singing contest in the *Meistersinger von Nürnberg*; and the "enchantment of Good Friday" before Parsifal's healing of Amfortas's wound in *Parsifal*. In all these cases, is not the inner peace before the crucial ordeal expressive of the presentiment that the decision has already been made, that the "silent weaving of the Spirit" has already done its work, and that what awaits us is a purely formal act proclaiming the outcome? The dimension of this scene of conciliation is especially delicate in *Meistersinger*, where it immediately follows the forceful burst of passion between Hans Sachs and the future bride of Walter von Stolzing. Suddenly and violently the truth emerges that the real libidinous tension radiates between the young girl and the fatherly figure of Hans, not between her and Walter, who is predestined to win the contest and marry her. The significance of the "sextet of conciliation" is thus overdetermined; beside Walter's calming influence in the face of the coming ordeal, it enacts the cathartic acknowledgement and, by means of the same gesture, renunciation of the "impossible" incestuous link between the girl and Hans.

It would be extremely interesting to compare this Wagnerian repose of the hero before the ordeal with those moments in Raymond Chandler's novels when, exhausted by his activity, Philip Marlowe disconnects from the frenetic run of things, lies down and takes a rest. Far from bringing about any kind of inner conciliation, these moments when Marlowe yields to the "flow of the world" mark the intrusion of "things" in their filth and corruption. When his vigilance slackens, Marlowe finds himself face to face with the nausea of existence. Through the luminescence of advertisements, through the stench of alcohol and garbage, through the intrusive noise of a big city, all the rot and decay from which he has tried to escape by means of activity return to strike him in the face. There is nothing calming or reassuring in these moments; the passive thought, confronted with the positivity of existence, is, on the contrary, pervaded by paranoia. Marlowe "thinks", yet his thought is not a free-floating, calming reflection, but rather a sneaking crawling under the watchful eye of a cruel superego: "I thought, and thought in my mind moved with a kind of sluggish stealthiness, as if it was being watched by bitter and sadistic eyes" (*Farewell, My Lovely*). This would be, then, Marlowe's *cogito*: I think, therefore an obscene, sadistic superego is watching me.

6. The logic at work here is therefore the very opposite of the surplus of the Ideal over its actual realization; of the "idealist" insistence that empirical reality can never fully correspond to its Notion. What we have here is, quite on the contrary, an (actual)

element which, although it is not a member of the genus X, is "more X than X itself". This dialectic is often referred to in everyday expressions, as when we say of a resolute woman that she is "more man than men themselves", or of a religious convert that he is "more Catholic than the pope", or of the legal plundering via stock exchange transactions that it "outcrimes crime itself". The above-mentioned relation of Art and Religion is to be grasped according to this logic: Religion is "more Art than Art itself" – it realizes the Notion of Art and hereby subverts it, transforms it into something else. The "surplus" is therefore on the side of the "example", not on the side of the ideal Notion; Religion is an "example" of Art which is "more Art than Art itself" and thus accomplishes the passage into a new Notion. (See Chapter 3 below.)

7. G.W.F. Hegel, *Jenaer Realphilosophie, Werke* 5–6, Hamburg: Meiner Verlag 1967, p. 199.

8. Jon Elster, *Sour Grapes*, Cambridge: Cambridge University Press 1983.

9. Rodolphe Gasche, *The Tain of the Mirror*, Cambridge, (MA): Harvard University Press 1987.

10. Ibid., p. 219.

11. Jacques-Alain Miller, "Suture", *Cahiers pour l'Analyse* 1, Paris 1967; and "Matrice" (Matrix), *Ornicar?* 4, Paris 1975.

12. Gasche, p. 221.

13. An interesting variation of this procedure is offered by the opening of Wagner's *Rheingold*. The "motif" consists of the rhythmic repetition of a single note, while the "accompaniment" contains a rich melodic texture. Such a reversal of the "normal" proportion creates an extreme tension discharged with the instantaneous passage into the singing of the "Rhine maidens" whereby the hitherto "accompaniment" takes on the status of the main melody.

14. As to the notion of "quilting point", Slavoj Žižek, *The Sublime Object of Ideology*, London: Verso 1989, Chapter 3.

15. Žižek, *Le plus sublime des hystériques*, Chapters 2 and 6.

16. Gasche, p. 222 (emphasis added).

17. Ibid., pp. 290–91.

18. Ibid., p. 291.

19. Note here the way Gasche, by a kind of structural necessity, entangles himself in a "contradiction". In the quoted passage, the "illusion of a reflexive totalization" equates to the *effacement* of the fact that re-mark itself is inscribed anew within the series of marks it is supposed to dominate, whereas sixty pages earlier (on p. 221) he qualifies the "metaphysical illusion of the self-present referent" by a reduction of re-mark to a mere semic function. We fall prey to metaphysical illusion as soon as we level re-mark with other marks; as soon as we efface its *exceptional* character, the fact that it is not just another bearer of a semic function but represents the empty space of their inscription.

20. Gasche, p. 221.

21. G.W.F. Hegel, *Philosophy of Right*, Oxford: Oxford University Press 1967, pp. 288–9.

22. Ibid., p. 288.

23. Ibid., p. 183.

24. G.W.F. Hegel, *Naissance de la philosophie hégélienne d'état*, Jacques Taminiaux, ed. Paris: Payot 1984, p. 268.

25. One of the reasons for the public success of Ronald Reagan's presidency was that

what a lot of his critics mocked as his weaknesses – the obvious limits to what he was able to understand, and so on – were effectively positive conditions of his reign. Reagan was perceived precisely as somebody who reigned in a king-like fashion: making empty gestures, putting the dots on (other's) i's, not really grasping what was going on . . . . So much for the idea that the logic of the Hegelian monarch is an eccentric witticism of no importance for today's world.

26. What is therefore crucial about the Hegelian monarch is that he cannot be reduced to a pure agency of nonsensical Master-Signifier: his status is simultaneously that of the Real. We should not be surprised, then, to find Hegel himself assigning the monarch a place in the series of the "answers of the Real". In para. 279 of the *Philosophy of Right*, he deals with the difference between ancient aristocracy or democracy and modern monarchy: in aristocracy or democracy, the "moment of the final, self-determining decision of the will" is not yet explicitly posited as an "organic moment immanent to the State"; the pure performative point of decision, the "So be it!" which transforms an opinion into a state's decision, has not yet acquired the form of subjectivity; the power of a pure unambiguous decision is therefore delegated to:

> a *fatum*, determining affairs from without. As a moment of the Idea, this decision had to come into existence, though rooted in something outside the circle of human freedom with which the state is concerned. Herein lies the origin of the need for deriving the last word on great events and important affairs of state from oracles, a "divine sign" (in the case of Socrates), the entrails of animals, the feeding and flight of birds, etc. It was when men had not yet plumbed the depths of self-consciousness or risen out of their undifferentiated unity of substance to their independence that they lacked strength to look within their own being for the final word. (G.W.F. Hegel, *Philosophy of Right*, pp. 183–4)

Oracles, entrails . . . so many names for an answer supposedly written in the Real itself – the status of the oracles is by definition that of a *writing* to be interpreted, to be integrated into our symbolic universe. The subjectivity of the monarch occupies this very place of the "answers of the Real": instead of looking for the "final word" (the Master-Signifier) in a writing contained within the Real itself (entrails, feeding of birds . . .) it is the person of the monarch who assumes the act of transforming the opinion of his ministers into a state's decision.

27. Hegel, *Philosophy of Right*, p. 182.

28. The paradox of Lacan is that, although in his explicit statements he also subscribes to what later became the "deconstructivist" argumentation against Hegel (the-"there-is-always-a-remainder-that-resists-*Aufhebung*"-story), his actual theoretical work goes against it and is Hegelian precisely where he himself does not know it. The effect of it is that Lacan often "refutes" Hegel by means of an argument which is itself deeply Hegelian, as, for example, in this passage from *Écrits*:

> Certainly there is in all this what is called a bone. Though it is precisely what is suggested here, namely, that it is structural of the subject, it constitutes in it essentially that margin that all thought has avoided, skipped over, circumvented, or blocked whenever it seems to succeed in being sustained by a circle, whether that circle be dialectical or mathematical. (Jacques Lacan, *Écrits: A Selection*, London: Tavistock 1977, p. 318)

How can one not recognize in this "bone" which is structural of the subject precisely in so far as it resists symbolization (dialectical mediation) an allusion to the Hegelian thesis "the Spirit is a bone"?

29. It is for this reason that, in Hegel's *Logic*, identity appears as the first "determination-of-reflection" [*Reflexionsbestimmung*]. Identity of an object with itself is the point at which, within the series of its predicates–determinations, this object encounters "itself", the empty place of its inscription; in the shape of "identity", this empty place is "reflected" into the object itself. The structure of identity-with-itself is therefore precisely that of the re-mark: identity "represents" the place of inscription of all predicates and thus re-marks them. Let us take the case of the tautology "law is law": its emptiness holds open the space in which all other positive predicates–determinations of the law could inscribe themselves.

30. Gasche, p. 223.

31. In psychoanalytic theory, this paradox assumes the shape of the relationship between the Unconscious *qua* repressed and its "returns" in symptoms. Against the usual conception according to which symptoms "reflect" in a fragmentary, distorted way the previously given unconscious "infrastructure", we should follow Lacan and assert that *repression and the return of the repressed are two sides of the same process*. The "repressed" content constitutes itself retroactively, by means of its failed/distorted return in symptoms, in these "unaccounted for" excesses: there is no Unconscious outside its "returns".

32. Gasche, p. 222.

33. Ibid.

34. This was perfectly clear to Hegel – one has only to examine the way he articulates the passage of being-for-another into being-for-itself apropos of the German idiom "*Was für ein Ding ist das?*" (What for a/one thing is this?). See Chapter I above.

35. At this point, the difference between the Derridean and Lacanian notions of the subject emerges forcefully. With Derrida, as with Lacan, the identity of the subject – the process leading to it (identification, interpellation, "recognizing oneself as subject") – is always truncated, failed, the subject's condition of possibility is simultaneously the condition of its impossibility: to constitute itself, the subject must deliver itself to the play of auto-affection, self-deferral: that is, the very gesture that constitutes it damages it irreparably.

With Lacan, however, it is not enough to say that the subject's identity is always, constitutively, truncated, dispersed because of the intrusion of an irreducible outside. The point is rather that the "subject" is nothing but the name for this "mutilation", for this impossibility of the "substance" to realize itself fully, to achieve its full identity-with-itself. And in Lacanian theory, this irreducible outside, this foreign body, this intruder that prevents the full constitution of the subject and to which subject is strictly correlative, has a precise name: object [*objet petit a*]. In its very ontological (non)status, the subject is the negative of the strange body which prevents substance from achieving identity with itself. It is of course no accident that this difference between Derrida and Lacan can be articulated by means of a Hegelian figure of reflective inversion: the inversion of "mutilated subject" into "subject *qua* mutilation". As to this crucial difference between "deconstructive" and Lacanian notions of the subject, see Joan Copjec, "The Orthopsychic Subject", *October* 49, Cambridge: MIT 1989.

PART II

Dialectics and its Discontents

3

Hegelian Llanguage

I With an Eye to Our Gaze

How to do a totality with failures

Today's "post-modern" thought seems to be dominated by the alternative of dialectical totalization and dissemination: is it possible to "mediate" the heterogeneous elements that we encounter in our experience, to posit them as ideal moments of a rational totality, or are we condemned to an interplay of fragments that can never be totalized? The way one raises this question is of course far from neutral, since it clearly gives predominance to the second term of the alternative: following the post-modern pop-ideological topic on "the end of big stories", it silently assumes that every attempt at rational totalization is in advance doomed to failure, that there is always some leftover that eludes the totalizing seizure, and so on.

The problem with this alternative, however, is not in the advance choice it implies but in the fact that it falsifies the choice by crucially misrepresenting the authentic Hegelian notion of a rational totality. Hegel knows very well that every attempt at rational totalization ultimately fails, this failure is the very impetus of the "dialectical progress"; his "wager" is located on another level – it concerns, so to speak, the "squared totalization": the possibility of "making a system" out of the very series of *failed* totalizations, to enchain them in a rational way, to discern the strange "logic" that regulates the process by means of which the breakdown of a totalization itself begets another totalization. What is *Phenomenology of Spirit* ultimately if not the presentation of a series of aborted attempts by the subject to define the Absolute and thus arrive at the longed-for synchronism of subject and object? This is why its final outcome ("absolute knowledge") does not bring about a finally found harmony but rather entails a kind of reflective inversion: it confronts the subject with the fact that *the true Absolute is nothing but the logical disposition of its previous failed attempts to conceive the Absolute* – that is, with the vertiginous experience that Truth itself coincides with the path towards Truth.

Similar misunderstandings are usually aroused by the Marxist notion of the *class struggle*. True, class struggle is the "totalizing" moment of society, its structuring principle; this, however, does *not* mean that it is a kind of ultimate guarantee authorizing us to grasp society as a rational totality ("the ultimate meaning of every social phenomenon is determined by its position within the class struggle"): the ultimate paradox of the notion of "class struggle" is that society is "held together" by the very antagonism, split, that forever prevents its closure in a harmonious, transparent, rational Whole – by the very impediment that undermines every rational totalization. Although "class struggle" is nowhere directly given as a positive entity, it none the less functions, *in its very absence*, as the point of reference enabling us to locate every social phenomenon not by relating it to class struggle as its ultimate meaning ("transcendental signified") but by conceiving it as an(other) attempt to conceal and "patch up" the rift of the class struggle, to efface its traces – what we have here is the typical structural–dialectical paradox of *an effect which exists only in order to efface the causes of its existence*; of an effect which in a way "resists" its own cause.

In other words, class struggle is *real* in the strict Lacanian sense: a "hitch", an impediment which gives rise to ever-new symbolizations by means of which one endeavours to integrate and domesticate it (the translation of the class struggle into the organic articulation of the "members" of the "social body", for example), but which simultaneously condemns these endeavours to ultimate failure. Class struggle is therefore, if one refers to the Hegelian opposition of Substance and Subject, *the Subject* (not the Substance) of history; Substance is the Universal *qua* positive space of mediation of its particular content, the receptacle containing all its particular wealth, whereas the subject is the Universal in so far as it entertains a *negative* relationship towards its particular content: the unfathomable limit that forever *eludes* its particular effects. In short, the Marxist version of the Hegelian motto that the Absolute is to be conceived not only as Substance but also as

Subject is that history is to be conceived not only as the progression of the "economic basis" (the dialectic of productive forces and the relationship of production) but also as class struggle.

This kernel of the Real encircled by failed attempts to symbolize–totalize it is radically *non-historical*: history itself is nothing but a succession of failed attempts to grasp, conceive, specify this strange kernel. This is why, far from rejecting the reproach that psychoanalysis is non-historical, one has to acknowledge it fully and thus simply transform it from a reproach into a positive theoretical proposition. Therein consists the difference between hysteria and psychosis: *hysteria/history* is more than a trivial word game – hysteria is the subject's way of resisting the prevailing, historically specified form of interpellation or symbolic indentification.

Hysteria means failed interpellation, it means that the subject in the name of that which is "in him more than himself" – the object in himself – refuses the mandate which is conferred on him in the symbolic universe; as such, it falls conditional with the dominant form of symbolic identification – that is, it is its reverse; while psychosis, the maintenance of an external distance from the symbolic order, is "unhistorical" – that is, on the level of psychosis it is not difficult for us to pose equality between psychotic outbursts reported in classical sources, and contemporary clinical cases. The act *qua* "psychotic" in this sense is ahistorical. However, an ahistoric kernel of the Real is present also in history/hysteria: the ultimate mistake of *historicism* in which all historical content is "relativized", made dependent on "historical circumstances", – that is to say, of historicism as opposed to *historicity* – is that it evades the encounter with the Real.

Let us take the usual attitude of the university discourse towards the great "Masters of Thought" of our century – towards Heidegger, towards Lacan: its first compulsion is to carry out an arrangement of their theoretical edifices into "phases": Heidegger I (*Being and Time*) in contrast to Heidegger II ("thought of Being"); phenomenologically Hegelian Lacan of the 1950s, then structuralist Lacan, then the Lacan of the "logic of the Real". In such an arrangement there is of course some pacifying effect, the thought is rendered transparent, properly classified . . . but we have nevertheless lost something with such a disposition into "phases": we have actually lost what is crucial, the encounter with the Real. We have lost (with Heidegger) the fact that Heidegger's various phases are only so many attempts to grasp, to indicate, to "encircle", the same kernel, the "Thing of thought" which he constantly tackles, dodges and returns to.[2] The paradox is thus that historicity differs from historicism by the way it presupposes some traumatic kernel which endures as "the same", non-historical; and so various historical epochs are conceived as failed attempts to capture this kernel.

The trouble with the alleged "Eurocentricity" of psychoanalysis is homologous. Today it is a commonplace to draw attention to the way Freud's myth in *Totem and Taboo* is based on the Eurocentric anthropology of his time: the anthropologies on which Freud relied were "unhistorical" projections of the modern patriarchal family and society into primeval times – it was only on this basis that Freud could construct the myth of the "primeval father". A breakthrough was only later achieved with Malinowski, Mead, and others who demonstrated how sexual life in primitive societies was organized in a completely different way, how we cannot therefore talk about an "Oedipus complex", how inhibition and anxiety were not associated with sexuality. Things thus appear clear, we know where we are, where the "primitives" are; we have not reduced the Other, we have preserved its diversity . . . nevertheless such historicizing is false: in the simple distinction between our own and past societies we avoid calling into question our own position, the place from which we ourselves speak.

The fascinating "diversity" of the Other functions as a fetish by means of which we are able to preserve the unproblematic *identity* of our subjective position: although we pretend to "historically relativize" our position, we actually conceal its split; we deceive ourselves as to how this position is already "decentred from within". What Freud called the "Oedipus complex" is such an "unhistorical" traumatic kernel (the trauma of prohibition on which the social order is based) and the miscellaneous historical regulations of sexuality and society are none other than so many ways (in the final analysis always unsuccessful) of mastering this traumatic kernel. To "understand the Other" means to pacify it, to prevent the meeting with the Other from becoming a meeting with the Real that undermines our own position. We come across the Real as that which "always returns to its place" when we identify with the Real in the Other – that is to say: when we recognize in the deadlock, hindrance, because of which the Other failed, our own hindrance, that which is "in us more than ourselves".[3]

Much more subversive than "entering the spirit of the past" is thus in contrast the procedure by which we consciously treat it "anti-historically", "reduce the past to the present". Brecht made use of this procedure in *The Affairs of Mr Julius Caesar*, where Caesar's rise to power is presented in twentieth-century capitalist terms: Caesar is concerned with stock market movements and speculation with capital, he organizes Fascist-style "spontaneous" demonstrations of the *Lumpenproletariat*, and so on. Such a procedure could be brought to self-reference when the contemporary image of the past is projected into the past. So, today, pre-Socratic times are known only in fragments which have survived a turbulent history; we thus inadvertently forget that Heraclitus and Parmenides did not write "fragments" but long, verbose philosophical poems. So it would really be some kind of subversive philosophical humour if we were to represent Heraclitus, let us say, as saying: "I can't write any good fragments today!" (or, on another level, the unknown sculptor of Milos saying: "I can't break the arm off my Venus today!"). Relying on a similar "reductionist", "unhistorical" procedure, Adorno's and Horkheimer's *Dialectic of Enlightenment*[4] reads *The Odyssey* retroactively, from the experience of contemporary technical-instrumental reason: of course, such a procedure is "unhistorical"; however, precisely through the feeling of the absurd which it awakens in us, it opens actual historical distance to us (just as with Hegel's claim "the Spirit is a bone", where the real effect of the absurd contradiction is the discord that it awakens in the reader).

The speculative (lack of) identity

It is against this background that one has to grasp the fundamental paradox of the *speculative identity* as it was recently restated by Gillian Rose:[5] in the dialectical judgement of identity, the mark of identity between its subject and predicate designates only and precisely the specific modality of their *lack of identity*. Let us recall the case evoked by Rose herself: that of the ultimate identity of religion and State, the Hegelian proposition that "In general religion and the foundation of the State is one and the same thing; they are identical in and for themselves." If we read this thesis in a non-speculative way, as a description of the factual state of things, it can of course easily be "refuted": it applies only to theocracies, and even there not without restraints, and so on. A way to save its legitimacy would be, of course, to read it as a statement that concerns not facts but values; as a statement about the Ought [*Sollen*]: the ideal, perfect state would be a state founded in religion, and existing states can approach this Ideal only to a greater or lesser degree . . .

Yet Hegel's point lies elsewhere; let us take a particular state – the medieval European feudal state, for example. Although directly founded on religion, this state was of course far from ideal; in it, the Christian content was cruelly perverted, it found expression in a distorted way; the ultimate ground for this deficiency is not, however, to be sought in the external social circumstances which prevented the adequate and full realization of the Christian values within state institutions but in the insufficiently articulated notion of Christian religion itself, in the Church's lifeless asceticism, its obsession with the religious Beyond, and its necessary reverse: the depravity of the Church as social institution (according to Hegel, it was only with Protestantism that the Christian religion arrived at its truth). The deficiency is thus redoubled, "reflected-into-itself": the inadequacy of the actual state to the Christian religion *qua* its foundation corresponds to and has its ground in the inadequacy of the Christian religion itself to its own Notion. Therein consists the speculative identity of State and religion: in the overlap of the two lacks, in the co-dependence between the deficiency of the State (its lack of identity with religion) and the inherent deficiency of the determinate form of religion to which this State refers as its foundation – State and religion are thus identical *per negationem*; their identity consists in the correlation of their lack of identity with the inherent lack (deficiency) of the central term that grounds their relationship (religion).

In other words, Hegel fully accepts the underlying premiss of the Kantian–Fichteian logic of *Sollen*, the fact that the identity of State and religion is always realized in an incomplete, distorted way, that the relationship of the universal Idea to its particular actualizations is a negative one; what this logic of *Sollen* – of the infinite approach to the ultimately unattainable Ideal – overlooks, however, is that *the very series of failed attempts to embody religion in the constitution of the State presents the actuality of their speculative identity* – the "concrete content" of this identity is the logic which "regulates" their lack of identity; the conceptual constraint that links the gap separating the State from its religious foundation to the inherent deficiency of this foundation itself.[6]

The supreme case of such a "negative" relationship between the Universal and its particular exemplifications is of course the Oedipal parricide, this paradigm of the crime, this crime *kat' exochen*, this act of which every human being is guilty as a being-of-language, since we are able to speak only under the aegis of the paternal metaphor – of the *dead* (murdered) father who returns as his Name. Lacan's version of the *cogito* is accordingly "I'm guilty, therefore I am" – the very existence of man *qua* being-of-language implies a fundamental guilt, and the so-called "Oedipus complex" is nothing but a way to avoid this guilt. The fact that, as Lacan put it, Oedipus himself had no Oedipus complex means precisely that he went to the extreme, to the utmost limit of human destiny, and fully assumed his guilt. The relationship of particular, "actual" crimes to this Crime *par excellence* is radically ambiguous: by means of assuming responsibility for a particular crime, the subject endeavours to blot out the guilt that stains his very existence.

The notorious "sentiment of guilt" is therefore nothing but a stratagem to deceive the big Other, to divert its attention from the real crime[7] – therein consists the negative relationship between the Universal and the Particular: the particular crime is here in order to conceal the Universality of Crime *kat' exochen*; there is a dialectical tension between the Universal and the Particular, the Particular disavows and subverts the Universal whose exemplification it is. As to the status of the Universal, Lacan is therefore not a nominalist but definitely a *realist* – Universal is "real": not the pacifying medium that unites diverging particularities but the unfathomable limit that prevents the Particular from achieving identity with itself. And it is precisely in the light of this paradox that it becomes manifest how "everything turns on grasping and expressing the True, not only as *Substance*, but equally as *Subject*":[8] *the entire "content" of the Substance consists in the series of failed, distorted ways the Substance (mis)recognizes itself.*

The best remedy against the misapprehension of the Hegelian thesis on Substance as Subject is to rely on the everyday, commonsensical notion of the "subjective", as when we say of some opinion that it represents a "subjective" (distorted, partial) view of the Thing in question: "Substance as Subject" means (also) that non-truth, error, is inherent to Truth itself – to resume Rose's perspicacious formula, that Substance "is untrue as Subject". This is, again, what the speculative identity of Substance and Subject means: their very lack of identity – that is to say, the way their non-identity (the gap separating the Subject from the Substance) is strictly correlative to the inherent non-identity, split, of the Substance itself. What better way to exemplify this speculative (non)identity of Substance and Subject than to refer again to Kafka's parable on the Door of the Law from his *Trial* – to the position of the "man from the country" (Subject) who finds himself impotent and null in front of the impenetrable Palace of Law (Substance)? It is as if the following passage from Hegel's *Phenomenology* was written as a kind of comment *avant la lettre* on Kafka's parable:

> The disparity which exists in consciousness between the "I" and the Substance which is its object is the distinction between them, the *negative* in general. This can be regarded as the *defect* of both, though it is their soul, or that which moves them. . . . Now, although this negative appears at first as a disparity between the "I" and its object, it is just as much the disparity of the Substance with itself. Thus what seems to happen outside of it, to be an activity directed against it, is really its own doing, and Substance shows itself to be essentially Subject.[9]

What the "man from the country", in his bewilderment at the horrifying and magnificent Palace of the Law, fails to notice is that his externality to the Substance, the disparity between him and the Substance, is always-already the "disparity of the Substance with itself": his gaze which perceives the Substance (the Palace of Law) from outside, as the unattainable, transcendent Mystery, is simultaneously the gaze by means of which the Substance *perceives itself, appears to itself*, as an unfathomable Mystery (how can we not recall here Hegel's dictum that the secrets of the Egyptians were secrets for the Egyptians themselves?). In other words, the doorkeeper's final word to the dying man from the country (" . . . this door was intended only for you") is nothing but Kafka's paraphrase of the Hegelian speculative identity of Substance and Subject: the external gaze of the Subject upon the inscrutable Substance is from the very beginning included in the Substance itself as an index of its disparity with itself. This is what escapes the position of "external reflection" (the position which perceives the Substance as an unattainable Thing-in-itself): how its externality to the Substance is a self-alienation of this Substance itself; the way Substance is external to itself.

To explain this paradoxical "short circuit" between externality and internal self-relationship, let us bring to mind a (falsely) "concrete" case, that of the "atomized" bourgeois subject who experiences himself as an abstract, isolated individual and views Society as a foreign, impenetrable Entity that rules his life like an all-powerful

Destiny: what he overlooks is that his externality to Society is *a product of this very Society* – an index of how Society is in itself splintered, reduced to a network of abstract individuals "held together" by an external, mechanical coercion, not yet Society consistent with its notion: a living community of individuals to whom their social bond does not appear as a foreign coercion but as part of their innermost "nature", opening up the field of the actualization of their most intimate potentials. In short, the *surplus* of Society over the individual (Society as unattainable, mysterious Thing-in-itself) is nothing but the inverted form of appearance of its *lack*, of the fact that Society itself does not yet correspond to its notion, but remains an external "mechanical" network linking individuals. The "transcendent" character of the Substance, its surplus eluding the Subject's grasp, results from a kind of illusion of perspective: from the Subject's forgetting to include his own gaze in the picture.

Let us recall the enigmatic Sarah from John Fowles's *The French Lieutenant's Woman*, this social outcast stigmatized by her sinful past, who fully enjoys her suffering. It is not sufficient to say that her enigma fascinates the novel's male hero; what one has to do is to accomplish a decisive step further and ascertain that her enigma *is staged in order to fascinate the hero's gaze*. A similar strategy must be adopted apropos of Kafka's enigmatic and horrifying agency of Power (the Court, the Castle): its entire spectacle is staged in order to fascinate the gaze of those who endeavour in vain to penetrate its mystery – the horrifying and imposing edifice of Power, totally indifferent towards the miserable individual, *feigns this indifference in order to attract his gaze*. In so far as Sarah is a hysteric who builds up her fantasy of the "French lieutenant" so that her desire is sustained as unsatisfied, she stages her hysterical theatre to attract the gaze of the bystanders: taking a lone walk in a state of oblivious trance on the Cob in stormy weather – and reckoning upon the fact that her lone trance will be noticed.

Now we can perhaps understand why, for Lacan, Hegel is "the most sublime of all hysterics": the elementary dialectical inversion consists precisely in such a reversal of transcendence into immanence that characterizes hysterical theatre – the mystery of an enigmatic apparition is to be sought not *beyond* its appearance but in the very *appearance of mystery*. This paradox is best expressed in the French phrase "*il me regarde en me donnant à voir le tableau*" (he looks at me by offering the picture to my view). The ambiguity of the French verb *regarder* (concern; look at) is crucial here: it is precisely by offering to my view the picture of the horrifying and unattainable Mystery (of the Court, of the Castle, of the Woman, and so on) which does not trouble about me – where, to refer again to a French expression, "*je n'y suis pour rien*" (I'm nothing in it) – that the Thing, the Substance, concerns me, takes my gaze into account: the entire spectacle of Mystery is staged for this "nothing" of the Subject's gaze.

There is a well-known true story about an anthropological expedition trying to contact a wild tribe in the New Zealand jungle who allegedly danced a terrible war dance in grotesque masks; when they reached this tribe, they begged them to dance it for them, and the dance did in fact match the description; so the explorers obtained the desired material about the strange, terrible customs of the aborigines. However, shortly afterwards, it was shown that this wild dance did not itself exist at all: the aborigines had only tried to meet the wishes of the explorers, in their discussions with them they had discovered what they wanted and had reproduced it for them . . . . This is what Lacan means when he says that the subject's desire is the desire of the Other: the explorers received back from the aborigines their own desire; the perverse strangeness which seemed to them uncannily terrible was staged for their benefit. The same paradox is nicely satirized in *Top Secret* (Zucker, Abrahams and Abrahams, 1978), a comedy about Western tourists in (now the former) GDR: at the railway station at the border, they see a terrible sight through the window: brutal police, dogs, beaten children. However, when the inspection is over, the entire Customs post shifts, the beaten children get up and brush the dust from themselves – in short, the whole display of "Communist brutality" was laid on *for Western eyes*.

The Kafkaesque illusion of an all-powerful Thing paying no attention to us, indifferent to our gaze, is the inverse–symmetrical counterpoint to the illusion that defines the ideological interpellation – namely, the illusion that the Other always-already looks at us, addresses us. When we *recognize* ourselves as interpellated, as the addressees of an ideological call, we *misrecognize* the radical contingency of finding ourselves at the place of interpellation; we fail to notice how our "spontaneous" perception that the Other (God, Nation, and so on) has chosen *us* as its addressee results from the retroactive inversion of contingency into necessity: we do not recognize ourselves in the ideological call because we were chosen; on the contrary, we perceive ourselves as chosen, as the addressee of a call, because we recognized ourselves in it – *the contingent act of recognition engenders retroactively its own necessity* (the same illusion as that of the reader of a horoscope who "recognizes" himself as its addressee by taking contingent coincidences of the obscure predictions with his actual life as proof that the horoscope "speaks about *him*"). The Kafkaesque illusion, on the other hand, is far more cunning: while we perceive ourselves as external bystanders stealing a furtive glance into some majestic Mystery indifferent to us, we are blinded to the fact that the entire spectacle of Mystery is staged *with an eye to our gaze*; to attract and fascinate our gaze – here, the Other deceives us in so far as it induces us to believe that we were *not* chosen; here, it is the true addressee himself who mistakes his position for that of an accidental bystander.[10]

What the two illusions have in common is that in both cases, the subject fails to notice how he himself *posits* the Other: by means of the very act of recognizing myself as the addressee of the ideological call, I (presup)posit the Other as the agency which confers meaning upon the contingency of the Real; by means of the very act of perceiving myself as the impotent, negligible, insignificant witness of the spectacle of the Other, I constitute its mysterious, transcendent character. The psychoanalytic intersubjective relationship exhibits this aspect, passed over in silence by the Althusserian theory of interpellation, in its pure, so to speak distilled form: in the act of transference, the analysand (presup)posits the Other (the analyst) as "the subject supposed to know" – as a guarantee that his contingent "free associations" will ultimately receive meaning; and the function of the analyst's "passivity" and "neutrality" is precisely to frustrate the analysand's demand for an interpellation, namely his expectation that the analyst will offer him a point of symbolic identification – in this way, the analyst forces the analysand to confront *his own act of presupposing the Other.*

Llanguage and its limit

This negative relationship between the Universal and the Particular also offers a clue to the Hegelian distinction between boundary and limit: *boundary* is the external limitation of an object, its qualitative confines which confer upon it its identity (an object is "itself" only within these confines, in so far as it fulfils a set of qualitative conditions); whereas *limit* results from a "reflection-into-itself" of the boundary: it emerges when the determinatedness which defines the identity of an object is reflected into this object itself and assumes the shape of its own unattainable limit, of what the object can never fully become, of what it can only approach into (bad) infinity – in other words, limit is what the object *ought to* (although it never actually *can*) become. In the course of the dialectical progression, every boundary proves itself a limit: apropos of every identity, we are sooner or later bound to experience how its condition of possibility (the boundary that delimits its conditions) is simultaneously its condition of impossibility.

National identification is an exemplary case of how an external border is reflected into an internal limit. Of course, the first step towards the identity of the nation is defined through differences from other nations, via an external border: if I identify myself as an Englishman, I distinguish myself from the French, Germans, Scots, Irish, and so on. However, in the next stage, the question is raised of who among the English are "the real English", the paradigm of Englishness; who are the Englishmen who correspond in full to the notion of English? Are they the remaining landed gentry? Factory workers? Bankers? Actually, in the political imagery of Thatcher's government, a revolution has taken place, with a shift in the centre of gravity of "the real Englishness": it is no longer the landed gentry who preserve the old traditions, but self-made men from the lower strata who have "made themselves" English. However, the final answer is of course that *nobody* is fully English, that every empirical Englishman contains something "non-English" – Englishness thus becomes an "internal limit", an unattainable point which prevents empirical Englishmen from achieving full identity-with-themselves.

On another level, the same dyad can serve as a conceptual tool to define the break between traditional and modern art. The traditional work of art presents a well-rounded organic Whole upon which harmony is bestowed by means of the boundary separating it from its Outside; whereas modernism, so to speak, internalizes this external boundary which thereby starts to function as limit, as the internal impediment to its identity: the work of art can no longer attain its organic roundness, "fully become itself"; it bears an indelible mark of failure and the Ought [*Sollen*] – and thereby its inherent *ethical* character. Already with Mallarmé, his entire writing is nothing but a series of failed attempts to produce "*the* Book"; this constitutive failure is what justifies the definition of modern art as "experimental".

Contrary to the prevailing doxa which conceives the advent of modern art as a break out of the Oedipal confines of the paternal metaphor, one has to recognize its fundamental feature in the emergence of the ethical agency of an irreparable symbolic debt which undermines the "regression" to the pre-Oedipal fetishism that pertains to the status of the traditional work of art.

The Lacanian notion of *llanguage* [*lalangue*][11] concerns the field of language in so far as it is "barred" by just such an inherent limit which prevents it from constituting itself as a consistent Whole. That is to say: "llanguage" is language in so far as its external boundary that guarantees its identity-with-itself is reflected-into-it and assumes the shape of an inherent impediment that transforms its field into an inconsistent, "non-all" totality. Lacan's crucial point is, of course, that the logical sequence of it has to be *reversed*: llanguage is logically "primordial", and the way to make out of its inconsistent, non-universal field a closed and coherent totality is to "evict", to exclude its inherent limit into an external boundary. To evoke the well-known ironic phrase, one has to speak of "all things possible and some others besides": of what has to be excluded so that the field of "all things possible" can constitute itself. In other words, every Whole is founded on a constitutive Exception: what we can never obtain is a complete set of signifiers without exception, since the very gesture of completion entails exclusion.

Therein consists the fundamental paradox of the "logic of the signifier": from a non-all, non-universal collection, we constitute a Totality not by adding something to it but on the contrary by *subtracting* something from it, namely the excessive "besides" the exclusion of which opens up the totality of "all things possible". A totality without exception serving as its boundary remains an inconsistent, flawed set which "doesn't hold together", a "non-all" [*pas-tout*] set. Take Truth, for example: it can be said to be "all" only in so far as it is conceived as *adequatio* to an external object-boundary ("reality", "pure thought", and so on) – to purport that Truth is "non-all" equals saying that it does not consist in an external relationship of the proposition to some external measure but that it dwells within language itself; that it is an immanent effect of the signifier.

If, therefore, there is no (external) boundary to llanguage, this very absence of boundary is a token of the circular movement that characterizes the field of llanguage: since the signifier lacks an external support, it ultimately relates only to itself. Therein consists the difference between the "arbitrariness" (of the sign) and the "differentiality" (of the signifier): we have to do with "arbitrariness" in so far as we can trace an external boundary with reference to which signs are "arbitrary" ("reality", "pure thought", "immediate sense-data", and so on); when this boundary disappears, when it can no longer be constructed, we find ourselves in the vicious circle that defines a differential order. A signifier is only its difference towards other signifiers, and since the same goes for all others, they can never form a consistent Whole – the signifying set is doomed to turn in a circle, striving in vain to attain – what? *Itself* as pure difference. The inaccessible for it is not – as in the case of a sign – the "external reality" but the pure signifier itself, the difference separating and thus constituting signifiers, their inter-diction. The boundary of the sign is the "thing"; the limit of the signifier is the "pure" signifier itself.[12]

And the Real – where is it in this circular movement of llanguage? Here the distinction between reality and the Real can be brought into use: reality, as we have just seen, serves as the external boundary which enables us to totalize language, to make out of it a close and coherent system, whereas the Real is its inherent limit, the unfathomable fold which prevents it from achieving its identity with itself. Therein consists the fundamental paradox of the relation between the Symbolic and the Real: the bar which separates them is *strictly internal to the Symbolic*, since it prevents the Symbolic from "becoming itself". The problem for the signifier is not its impossibility to touch the Real but its impossibility to "attain itself" – what the signifier lacks is not the extra-linguistic object but the Signifier itself, a non-barred, non-hindered One. Or, to put it in Hegelese: the signifier does not simply miss the object, it always-already "goes wrong" *in relation to itself*, and the object inscribes itself in the blank opened by this failure. The very positivity of the object is nothing but a positivization, an incarnation, of the bar which prevents the signifier from fully "becoming itself". This is what Lacan means when he says that "Woman doesn't exist": Woman *qua* object is nothing but the materialization of a certain bar in the symbolic universe – witness Don Giovanni.

The squabble about All

The figure of Don Giovanni (in Mozart's opera, of course) is usually conceived as the embodiment of the wild, demonic lust which overwhelms every obstacle, undermines every social convention including the bounds of language – in short, a kind of primordial force that threatens the very consistency of the social edifice. This view found its supreme expression in the famous Kierkegaard reading of *Don Giovanni* in his *Either–Or*, where Don Giovanni personifies the "aesthetical stage", the attitude of a subject living out his nature in self-consuming momentary enjoyment; the proper medium of this mode of life regulated by the "pleasure principle" is, of course, *music*, a Dionysiac dance best exemplified by the "champagne aria" from Mozart's opera. To this "aesthetical stage" Kierkegaard opposes the "ethical stage" where the subject rises up to the universal moral norm whose proper medium is *word* (as Hegel pointed out, the meaning of words is always universal: even "here and now" means *every* "here and now"); a mode of life regulated by the "reality principle".

Yet such an interpretation fails to take into account the crucial dimension of Don Giovanni: he is as far as possible from a self-infatuated, ruthless Narcissus enjoying the orgy of the moment, undermining every codified structure, and so on. In the very heart of his impetus, we encounter a relationship to the (signifying) *structure*. True, Don Giovanni wants to "have them *all*" – but problems arise as soon as he is no longer content with taking women "one by one", as soon as he endeavours to arrange them into species and sub-species, thus changing their dispersed collection into a structured All.

Suffice it to recall the symptomatic fact that the most famous piece from *Don Giovanni*, Leporello's aria "*Madamina, il catalogo è questo* . . .", deals with *cataloguing* Don Giovanni's conquests; it entangles itself into different deadlocks precisely when it attempts to seize them "all" on the basis of a single principle, so that it is forced to resort to different criteria of classification: first, the *national* criterion (in Italy six hundred and forty, etc., up to the "*mille e tre*" in Spain alone); then, the criterion of *social* strata (countrywomen, housemaids, townswomen, countesses . . .); finally, a kind of "reflection-into-itself" of the procedure, the *enumeration of the criteria themselves* (women of every grade, form and age . . .). After this first moment of satiation, Leporello so to speak changes the register and passes to the enumeration of the women's "immanent", "natural" characteristics, disposed in couples of opposites (blonde/brunette, corpulent/slim, tall/small) and described with reference to their "use-value" (when Don Giovanni is cold in winter, he seduces a fat lady; when he needs tenderness, he approaches a delicate blonde, and so on). The last couple in this series (old woman/young virgin) again introduces a level of "reflection-into-itself": "He conquers old women / for the pure pleasure of adding them to the list / whereas his predominating passion / is the young virgin". It is not difficult to locate the paradox of this last opposition: as if *all* his conquests are not accomplished out of passion and for the sake of the list! In other words, it is as if the last couple holds the place, within the different species, of their genus as such:

> as if, next to and other than lions, tigers, hares, and all the other real animals that constitute in a group the different races, species, sub-species, families, etc., of *the* animal kingdom, existed, furthermore, *the* Animal, the individual incarnation of the animal kingdom.[13]

– or, as Leporello would put it, as if, next to and other than women who embody different qualities satisfying different needs, existed, furthermore, *the* Woman, the individual incarnation of the feminine kingdom – *this* is the woman who, according to Lacan, "doesn't exist", which is why Don Giovanni is condemned to eternal flight from one woman to another. Why then is this Woman, the general equivalent of women, *split* into "old" and "young"? As we have just seen, the "use-value" of the "old" woman is that she adds yet another name to the list: precisely in so far as she is of no particular use, she exhibits and personifies the "exchange-value" of all other women; whereas the "young" incarnates its opposite, "usefulness" as such, in its non-specific, universal aspect. It is therefore the homology with the world of commodities which provides the answer: the split is simply that into "exchange-value" (the symbolic equivalence of all women in so far as they are inscribed in the catalogue) and "use-value" (the property they must have to satisfy Don Giovanni's passion).

The crucial point here, however, is that the very existence of this split implies the predominance of the "exchange-value" (the signifier) over the "use-value" (the passion) – as with commodities, we have to do with a fetishistic inversion; "use-value" is a mere form of appearance of "exchange-value". In other words, the ultimate driving force of Don Giovanni's conquest is not passion but *adding to the list*, as is openly ascertained in the above-mentioned "champagne aria". This aria is usually taken as the purest display of Don Giovanni's alleged attitude of all-consuming enjoyment which devours everything in its chaotic whirlpool, and the progression of the aria seems to confirm this; however, at its very peak, at this climactic moment of the formless Dionysiac frenzy, we so to speak all of a sudden find ourselves on the other side of the Moebius band – Don Giovanni associates supreme enjoyment with the *list*: "Ah! To my list / tomorrow morning / you will have to add / a round dozen!" he exclaims to Leporello, his servant in charge of the catalogue – a fact that is by no means insignificant: this reference to the "list" that determines Don Giovanni's innermost passion makes his subjective position dependent on his servant.

The general conclusion to be drawn is thus clear enough: since "Woman doesn't exist", Don Giovanni is condemned to an unending metonymic movement; his potency is nothing but a form of appearance of its very opposite: of a fundamental *impotence* designated by Lacan as the "impossibility of the sexual relationship". This impossibility takes effect the moment sexuality is caught in the cobweb of language – sexuality clearly *is* possible for animals led by their unmistakable sense of smell, whereas we all know what cruel tricks smell plays on Don Giovanni: when, in the first act, he smells the *odor di femina* and sets to seduce the veiled unknown, he soon learns that the mysterious belle is Donna Elvira, his wife, whom he wanted to avoid at any price!

This answer, however, still leaves open the question of the concrete historical conditions of the appearance of a figure like Don Giovanni. Apropos of *Antigone*, Lacan wrote that it presents a paradoxical case of a refusal of humanism before its very advent – isn't it somehow the same with Mozart's *Don Giovanni*, which articulates a refusal of the bourgeois ideology of the love couple prior to its hegemony in the course of the nineteenth century? (Even within the *œuvre* of Mozart himself, the glorification of the harmonious couple in *The Magic Flute follows* its refusal in *Don Giovanni*!) An implicit quasi-Marxist answer was provided by Joseph Losey's film version of the opera: Don Giovanni's escape into debauchery expresses the hopeless social perspective of the feudal ruling class in decline . . . . Although Don Giovanni undoubtedly does belong to the ruling class, it none the less seems that such a quick "sociologization" fails to take into account the concrete historical mediation that conditioned its emergence.

Let us indicate its contours by means of a comparison between Don

Giovanni and Casanova. That is to say, Casanova is Don Giovanni's exact opposite: a merry swindler and impostor, an epicure who irradiates simple pleasure and leaves behind no bitter taste of revenge, and whose libertinage presents no serious threat to the environs. He is a kind of correlate to the eighteenth-century freethinkers from the bourgeois *salon*: full of irony and wit, calling into question every established view; yet his trespassing of what is socially acceptable never assumes the shape of a firm position which would pose a serious threat to the existing order. His libertinage lacks the fanatic-methodical note, his spirit is that of permisiveness, not of purges; it is "freedom for all", not yet "no freedom for the enemies of freedom". Casanova remains a parasite feeding on the decaying body of his enemy and as such deeply attached to it: no wonder he condemned the "horrors" of the French Revolution, since it swept away the only universe in which he could prosper. It was only Don Giovanni who brought libertinage to the point of its "self-negation" and transformed resistance to Duty into the Duty to resist: his conquests are not a matter of enjoying simple life-pleasures but *stricto sensu* a matter of a compulsive Duty. To use Kantian terms: they are strictly "non-pathological", he is driven by an inner compulsion which is "beyond the pleasure principle".

In short, if Casanova was a correlate to the pre-revolutionary free-thinking *salon*, (Mozart's) Don Giovanni is a correlate to *Jacobinism*, a kind of "Jacobin of the libidinal economy" – the paradox of a *puritan débauché*. The Jacobins cut off the heads of citizens who yielded to decadent pleasures and never fully assumed the ideal of Citizen; Don Giovanni rejected with contempt women who never lived up to Woman. This homology is, however, *mediated by an impossibility*: Don Giovanni's "Jacobinism of the libidinal economy" can never meet the "real", political Jacobinism. Because of his social position (a member of the ruling class in decay) Don Giovanni carried out Jacobinism in the only field open to him, that of sexuality.[14] This is why his ultimate fate was the same as that of the Jacobins: an annoying "excess", a "vanishing mediator" shoved away as soon as the ideological hegemony of the bourgeois intimate love couple was established.

II Judgement by Default

"The word is an elephant"

"Lack of identity" as a key component of speculative identity finds its clearest expression in Hegel's theory of judgement, in the fact – surprising for those who always expect the same infamous "triad" from Hegel – that there are *four* types of judgement and not three: the judgement of existence, the judgement of reflection, the judgement of necessity and the judgement of the Notion. Let us immediately show our cards: the three judgements actually acquire the fourth because "Substance is Subject"; in other words, the "lack of identity" between subject and predicate is posited as such in the fourth judgement (that of the Notion).[15]

Let us begin with the first form, the judgement of existence. This form derives directly from the Individual as the last (third) moment of the Notion. Hegel starts the section on judgement with the proposition: "The judgement is the *determinatedness* of the Notion *posited* in the *Notion* itself."[16] The judgement [*Urteil*] originally divides [*ur-teilen*] the Notion (yet another of Hegel's famous wordplays) into subject and predicate – that is, the determinatedness of an individuality (of a self-subsistent, substantial entity as the final moment of the notional triad Universal–Particular–Individual) is externalized, opposed to individuality, and thereby posited as such: the individual subject is that predicate (this or that abstract-universal determination). In Hegel's example: "The rose is red."

We must be careful here on two points. First, that all the substantial content is here on the side of the subject: that which is presupposed as having "actual existence" (and for this reason we speak of the "judgement of existence") is the subject, the individual, and the predicate is only some abstract-universal property which it acquires; it has no self-subsistent existence. The obverse of it is that the relationship between subject and predicate is here completely external: the predicate is some completely indifferent abstract-universal property, acquired by the subject, not something dependent on the subject's inner nature.

The second form of the judgement of existence which follows the first (positive judgement), negative judgement, posits that indifferent external relationship as such by negating the first form: if the substantial nature of the rose is entirely indifferent to whether or not the rose is red, then we could just as reasonably posit the claim "The rose is not red". As Hegel stresses, we do not negate the relationship of subject and predicate as such: the claim "The rose is not red" is considered only against the background of the rose having *some (other) colour*, say blue. The negative judgement thus proceeds from the universal into the particular: the determinatedness of the predicate that was initially posited as an abstract universal is now specified as something particular, as a particular determination – the positive expression of the negative judgement is "the subject (this individual) is a particularity", the rose, for example, has some particular colour (it is blue or yellow or red . . .).

The third form of the judgement, the infinite judgement, redoubles the negation already at work in the negative judgement, or rather brings it to its self-reference: it negates not only some (particular) predicate but the universal domain itself which was present in the negation of the particular predicate. The infinite judgement is thus *senseless* in its form: a (particular) predicate is negated, whose (universal) genus itself is incompatible with the subject – so we get such empty-wisdom sentences as "The rose is not an elephant", "The spirit is not red", "Reason is not a table", and so on. These judgements are, as Hegel says, accurate or true, but nevertheless "senseless and tasteless". Hegel adduces *crime* as an example of infinite judgement, and we can understand why precisely from what has been mentioned: in contrast to a legal conflict before the courts where both sides invoke particular laws one after another, yet both admit universal law (legality) as the obligatory medium, the criminal act calls into question the general sphere of law itself, the law as such.[17]

The positive form of the infinite judgement – precisely because it negates not only the particular predicate but the genus itself in which the predicate could meet with the subject – is no longer a particular judgement implied by the negation: from "The rose is not red" it follows that the rose is some other colour; yet from "The rose is not an elephant" follows no positive particular determination. So the positive opposite pole of the infinite judgement can only be a tautology: from "The rose is not an elephant" follows only that "The rose is a rose". The tautology expresses in the positive form only the radical *externality* to the subject of the predicate; this "truth" of the whole sphere of the judgement of existence is what comes forth in the infinite judgement: because subject and predicate are completely external, no predicate can adequately determine the subject – or rather, the only adequate predicate for the subject is the *subject itself*.

What remains enigmatic here is only that Hegel, next to "tasteless" negation and tautology, does not mention the *third* form of the infinite judgement, the apparently "senseless" affirmative form ("The rose is an elephant", let us say). What we have here is not a kind of empty possibility, since such a form of the infinite judgement bears the speculative content of the dialectic of phrenology in the *Phenomenology of Spirit*: "The Spirit is a bone". It is only this judgement that fully expresses the speculative "lack of identity" by means of affirming the impossible identity of two mutually exclusive moments: this judgement is – if we read it immediately – experienced as patently absurd, the discrepancy between the moments is absolute; however, the "Spirit" as power of absolute negativity is none other than this absolute discrepancy.[18] One must read the thesis "The Substance is Subject" as exactly such a kind of "infinite judgement": it does not mean that the Substance is "really Subject" – that the Subject (self-consciousness) is the "ground", the "Substance" of all existence – but draws us into an absolute contradiction between Substance and Subject – substance can never "catch up with" the Subject, can never encompass in itself the negative power of the Subject; and the "Subject" is none other than this inability of the Substance to "contain" the Subject within itself, this internal self-split of the Substance, the lack of its identity-with-itself.

Therein consists the speculative reversal which gives us the key to the logic of the infinite judgement: it is not enough to say that there is a "lack of identity" between Substance and Subject – if we do only that, we still presuppose Substance and Subject as two (positive, identical) entities between which there is no identity; the point is rather that *one of the two moments (Subject) is none other than the non-identity-with-itself of the other moment (Substance)*. "The Spirit is a bone" *means that* bone itself can never achieve complete identity with itself, and "Spirit" is none other than that "force of negativity" which prevents bone from fully "becoming itself".[19]

Infinite judgement is thus internally ramified into the triad "The rose is not an elephant", "The rose is a rose", and "The rose is an elephant". The speculative truth of this last form is demonstrated by Lacan when, in his first *Seminar*, he evokes a similar paradox ("The word is an elephant") in order to exemplify the dialectical–negative relationship between word and thing; the fact that the word implies the symbolic murder of the thing: "The word is an elephant" means that an elephant is "more present" in the word which evokes it than in its immediate physical being – it is present (as Lacan points out by means of a reference to Hegel) in its Notion:

> To be sure, the notion is not the thing as it is, for the simple reason that the notion is always where the thing isn't, it is there so as to replace the thing, like the elephant that I brought into the room the other day by means of the word *elephant*. If that was so striking for some of you, it was because it was clear that the elephant was really there as soon as we named it. Of the thing, what is it that can be there? Neither its form, nor its reality, since, in the actual state of affairs, all the seats are taken. Hegel puts it with extreme rigour – the notion is what makes the thing be there, while, all the while, it isn't.[20]

"The word is an elephant" thus expresses the speculative identity of "word" and "elephant", the fact that an elephant is present in the word "elephant" as *aufgehoben*, internalized-sublated.

Where, then, does the result of the dialectic of the judgement of existence lead? To absolute contradiction, to a breakdown of any common medium between subject and predicate, which culminates in the subject being reduced to a tautology – in being able to be predicated only by itself. We can say nothing about the subject as such, we can attribute nothing to it, no determination; it is reduced to a null "this". This is where the transition to the following form of judgement, the judgement of reflection, occurs: the judgement of reflection takes cognizance of the result of the judgement of existence – that the subject of the judgement is a null, empty "this", lacking any substantial content – and so transposes the centre of gravity to the other side, to the *predicate* which now appears as the substantial moment.

The crucial feature of the judgement of reflection is therefore that within it, some contingent individuality is posited in relation to some determination which is no longer its indifferent, abstract-universal property, but its *essential determination*. Universality here is not the abstract "property" of a substantial thing, but some encompassing essence which subsumes individualities. Judgements of reflection are, as Hegel says, judgements of subsumption: an ever-wider circle of subjects is subsumed under the predicate as an essential determination which exists in itself. Examples of reflective judgement are "Men are mortal", "Things are transient", and so on. That all (material, finite) things are transient is their essential determination: it derives from their notion itself, from their having negativity *outside* themselves (in the form of the power of time, to which they are subject). The fact that these judgements are "reflective" is revealed even on a superficial first glance which here does not deceive: judgements of the type "Things are transient", "Men are mortal", and so on, express what we also mean by "reflection" in everyday speech – namely, deeper thoughts about the nature of things.

However, Hegel uses the term in a stricter technical sense: in reflective judgements the subject – who was conceived previously, in the judgement of existence, as a self-subsistent substantial entity – is posited as something transient-insubstantial, as something which only "reflects", whose contingent reality only "mirrors", the In-itself of a permanent essence, expressed in the predicate. "Reflection" should here be understood in the sense of external reflection: the finite world is posited as transient, indifferent appearance which reflects some transcendental, universal essence.

As we have seen, in the judgement of existence all "movement" is on the side of the predicate: the subject is posited as a permanent, substantial entity, and the predicate passes from the Universal through the Particular to the Individual. In the judgement of reflection, on the contrary, all "movement" is on the side of the subject, whereas the predicate remains a firm substantial content; the direction of movement is also contrary: from the Individual through the Particular to the Universal. This reversal of direction is easy to grasp: the predicate of a judgement of existence gradually conforms to the (individual) subject, until it coincides with it in an impossible identity; whereas in the judgement of reflection, the subject gradually conforms to the universal predicate by expanding from the Individual to the Universal. The three forms of the judgement of reflection are therefore singular, particular and universal judgements: for example, say, "This man is mortal", "Many men are mortal", "All men are mortal".

The paradoxes of sexuation

We have thus set the passage from the judgement of reflection to the following form, the judgement of necessity: all we have to do is expressly posit the determination of universality which in itself is contained in the universal judgement; in concrete terms, instead of

"*All men* are mortal" we have only to say "*Man* is mortal". The shift thus concerns the sole form, although it is essential: even on the intuitive level it is not difficult to sense how the statements "All men are mortal" and "Man is mortal" do not have the same weight – with the shift from the first to the second, we move from the empirical set of "all men" – from what all men have in common – to *universality*, to the necessary determination of the notion of man as such. In other words, whereas in the judgement of reflection we are still concerned with the relationship of the notional determination (predicate) to the contingent, non-notional set of empirical entities ("this"), in the judgement of necessity we enter the domain of necessary relationships of Notion – of the immanent self-determinations of Notion as such. "Mortality" is no longer the predicate of an extra-notional entity but the immanent determination of "man".

The entire reach of this shift could be more closely determined through the well-known paradox of the relationship between universal and existential judgement in the classical Aristotelian syllogism: existential judgement implies the existence of the subject, whereas universal judgement is also true even if its subject does not exist, since it concerns only the notion of the subject. If, for example, one says "At least one man is (or: some men are) mortal", this judgement is true only if at least one man exists; if, on the contrary, one says "Unicorn has only one horn", this judgement remains true even if there are no unicorns, since it concerns solely the immanent determinatedness of the notion of "unicorn".

In so far as this distinction seems too hairsplitting, it should only be recalled how much weight the difference between the universal and the particular can have in the "logic of emotions": if I know in general, without any particular details, that my wife sleeps around with other men, this need not affect me very deeply; the world comes crashing down only when someone brings me concrete details which confirm her adultery (a picture of her in bed with another man, and so on) – the passage from the universal to the existential particularity makes all the difference. In short, if I know, in general, that my wife is deceiving me, I in a way suspend the reality of it, I treat it as not serious – it becomes "serious" only with the passage to the particular. It is precisely this imbalance between existence and universality which provides the key to the paradoxes of the Lacanian "formulae of sexuation", in which on the "masculine" side the universal function ($\forall x.\Phi x$: all x are submitted to the function Φ) implies the existence of an exception (Ex.nonΦx: there is at least one x which is exempted from the function Φ), whereas on the feminine side a particular negation (nonVx.Φx: non-all x are submitted to the function Φ) implies that there is no exception (nonEx.nonΦx: there is no x which could be exempted from the function Φ):

$$\exists x.\overline{\Phi x} \qquad \overline{\exists x}.\overline{\Phi x}$$

$$\forall x.\Phi x \qquad \overline{\forall x}.\Phi x$$

Common sense would suggest that the formulae, if linked in two diagonal pairs, are equivalent: is not "all x are submitted to the function Φ" strictly equivalent to "there is no x which could be exempted from the function Φ"? And, on the other hand, is "non-all x are submitted to the function Φ" not strictly equivalent to "there is (at least) one x which is exempted from the function Φ"? Yet, as we have just seen, for Lacan the equivalence runs vertically! We approach the solution if we do not read the universal quantifier from the lower pair of the formulae on the level of reflective judgement but on the level of the judgement of necessity: not "*all x* are submitted to the function Φ" but "*x as such* is submitted to the function Φ".

Lacan's Φ, of course, means the function of (symbolic) castration: "man is submitted to castration" implies the exception of "at least one", the primordial father of the Freudian myth in *Totem and Taboo*, a mythical being who has had all women and was capable of achieving complete satisfaction. Yet we are better remaining with our example of mortality: true, "There is no man who is immortal" is equivalent to "All men are mortal", but not – as we have already seen – the equivalent of "man is mortal": in the first case, we are concerned with the empirical set of men, in which we take them "one by one" and thus establish that there is no one who is immortal; whereas in the second, we are concerned with the very notion of man. And Lacan's basic premiss is that the leap from the *general* set of "all men" into the *universal* "man" is possible only through an exception: the universal (in its difference to the empirical generality) is constituted through the exception; we do not pass from the general set to the universality of One-Notion by way of *adding* something to the set but, on the contrary, by way of *subtracting* something from it, namely the "unary feature" [trait unaire] which totalizes the general set, which makes out of it a universality.

There is an abundance of examples here for the "masculine" side of totalization-through-exception as well as for the "feminine" side of non-all collection without exception. Was it not Marx who – in the first chapter of *Capital*, in the dialectic of commodity-form (in the articulation of the three forms by which a commodity expresses its value in some other commodity which serves as its equivalent) – was the first to develop the logic of totalization-through-exemption? The "expanded" form passes into the "general" form when some commodity is excluded, exempted from the collection of commodities, and thus appears as the general equivalent of all commodities, as the immediate embodiment of Commodity as such, as if, by the side of all real animals, "there existed *the* Animal, the individual incarnation of the entire animal kingdom."[21]

It is only through this totalization-through-exemption that, from the empirical set of "all commodities", we arrive at the universality of Commodity, incarnated in individual commodities. On another level, Hegel repeats the same operation apropos of the Monarch: the set of men becomes a rational totality (the State) only when their unity as such is incarnated in some non-rational, "biologically" defined individual – the monarch. What is of special interest to us here is the way Hegel determines the exceptional character of the monarch: all other men are not by their nature what they are, but must be "made", educated, formed, whereas the monarch is unique in being by his nature that which is his symbolic mandate – we have here in clear form the exemplification of the "masculine" side of Lacan's formulae of sexuation: all men are submitted to the function of "castration" (they are not directly that which is their symbolic mandate, they arrive at their positive social role only through the hard work of "negativity", through inhibition, training . . .) on condition that there is the One who is exempt from it – who is by nature that which he is (the king).

This paradox simultaneously helps in understanding the Hegelian logic of the "negative self-relationship of the Notion": a universal Notion arrives at its being-for-itself, it is posited as Notion, only when, in the very domain of particularity, it reflects itself in the form of its opposite (in some element which negates the very fundamental feature of its notional universality). The notion of Man (as an active being, a being which is not by nature that which it is, but must create itself, "define" itself, through hard work) arrives at its being-for-itself by reflecting itself in an exception, in an individual who appears as the embodiment of Man in general, as such, precisely in so far as he is already by his nature what he is (the monarch). Value in its contrast to use-value (that is to say, value as the expression of a *social* relationship) is posited as such when it is embodied in some particular commodity; when it appears as a quasi-"*natural*" property of some particular commodity (money: gold).

As far as the other, "feminine", side of the formulae of sexuation is concerned, it is sufficient to recall how the notion of class struggle works in historical materialism. The good old leftist slogan (today, in the supposedly "post-ideological" world, more valid than ever) "there is nothing that is not political" must be read not as the universal judgement "everything (society as a whole) is political" but on the level of the "feminine" logic of a non-all set: "there is nothing that is not political" means precisely that the social field is irreducibly marked by a political split; that there is no neutral "zero-point" from which society could be conceived as a Whole. In other words, "there is nothing that is not political" means that in politics also "there is no metalanguage": any kind of description or attempt at conceiving society by definition implies a partial position of enunciation; in some radical sense it is already "political", we have always-already "taken sides". And the class struggle is none other than the name for this unfathomable limit, split, which cannot be objectivized, located within the social totality, since it is itself that limit which prevents us from conceiving society in general as a totality. So it is precisely the fact that "there is nothing that is not political" which prevents Society from being conceived as a Whole – even if we determine this Whole with the predicate "political" and say "All is political".[22]

Is this logic of non-all, however, compatible with Hegelian dialectics? Does it not rely on one of the key topics of traditional criticism of Hegel: that of the irreducible gap separating Universality and the reality of particular existence? Is not the Hegelian illusion that the Particular can be deduced from (and absorbed without any remnant into) the self-movement of the universal Notion? And is it not precisely in opposition to the lesson of the Aristotelian logical square: that there is an irreducible gap between the Universal and existence, that existence cannot be deduced from the Universal? Lacan actually tries to demonstrate from this gap the anxiety to which Hegel's "pan-logicism" gave rise with Schelling and Kierkegaard: anxiety that our entire existence would be subsumed into the self-movement of the Notion and thus lose its uniqueness, its paradox of bottomless freedom. As Freud put it, anxiety is the only affect which does not deceive; by means of which we encounter the real: the real of a lost object which cannot be absorbed into a circular movement of symbolization.

However, if we admit the paradox of the Hegelian rational totality that can be discerned, for example, apropos of the king as the condition of the State *qua* rational totality, the entire perspective changes. In so far as anxiety demonstrates the *proximity*, not the loss, of the object *qua* real – as Lacan inverts Freud – one should ask *which* object we have come too close to with the establishment of a rational totality. This object is of course precisely that absolutely contingent object, the "little piece of the real", which emerges as an incarnation of the rational totality itself – through which the rational totality arrives at its being-for-itself, at its actuality – in the case of the State, the king as biological, contingent individual. This is the object whose existence is implied with the universality itself, since only through it is the Universal "posited", does it arrive at its being-for-itself. Hegel is therefore far from transcending the gap between the Universal and particular existence by way of "deducing the Particular from the self-movement of the universal notion"; he rather exposes the contingent particularity to which the Universal itself is linked as with an umbilical cord (in the language of the formulae of sexuation: he exposes the particular exception which must exist if the universal function is to remain in force).

How necessity arises out of contingency

Let us then return to the judgement of necessity. As we have seen, the predicate in it is posited as a necessary, inherent specification, as a self-determination of the subject. So we come to the first form of the judgement of necessity, to the categorical judgement, by which the "categorical" – the notionally necessary – relationship between subject and predicate is posited as the relationship between a species and its genus: "A rose is a plant", "Woman is human", for example. However, this judgement is inadequate in so far as it leaves aside the fact that the content of the genus is not only this species – the genus articulates within it a series of species. The other form of the judgement of necessity, hypothetical judgement, thus posits a particular content (species) of the genus in its necessary relationship with another species: let us say, in our case, "Where there are women, there are also men"; or rather, "The being of woman is not only its own but also the being of another, of man". In the third form, the disjunctive judgement, the particular content of the judgement is explicitly posited as self-articulation, self-specification, of the universal Notion: "A human is either a man or a woman".

Here, at this precise point, we encounter the greatest surprise of Hegel's theory of judgement. That is to say, from the stereotyped view of Hegel we would expect now to be at the end: does not the triad of judgements (existence, reflection, necessity) encapsulate the triad of being–essence–notion? Is not the judgement of existence condemned to dissolution into an empty tautology precisely in so far as it remains on the level of being and as such is not able to render the reflective relationship between subject and predicate? Is not the judgement of reflection, as the name itself suggests, a judgement which articulates the relationship of some contingent, phenomenal entity to its essential determination, a relationship in which this essential determination is reflected in the plurality of contingent entities? And, finally, does the judgement of necessity not deliver us from contingent externality, is the entire content within it not explicitly posited as a result of the self-movement of the universal notion – that is to say, as its immanent self-specification? What can possibly follow? Hegel's answer is: *contingency*.

The judgement of necessity is followed by a fourth form, the judgement of the Notion. Only with this does the judgement actually become that which the word suggests: an appraisal of something. Predicates which contain this judgement are not predicates on the same level as predicates of the former forms of judgement; notional judgement is literally judgement on the Notion: the content of the predicate here is *the very relationship of the Subject to its Notion* (so to that which was the predicate in the previous forms of judgement) – it is a predicate of the type "good, bad, beautiful, righteous, true". According to Hegel, truth is not simply the adequacy or correspondence of some proposition to the object or to the state of things which the proposition describes, but the adequacy of the object itself to its own Notion: in this sense we could say about some "real" object – a table, for example – that it is "true" (in so far as it conforms to the Notion of table, the function it must perform as a table).

Notional judgement has to be located on this level: we evaluate with it the extent to which something is "true", how far it corresponds to its Notion. The first, immediate form of notional judgement, assertoric judgement, therefore comprises propositions of the type "This house is good". The problem which of course immediately arises is that not every house is good – some houses are and some are not; it depends on a series of contingent circumstances – the house must be built in a predetermined way, and so on. The second form of notional judgement, problematic judgement, problematizes precisely these conditions of the "truth" of the object (the subject of the judgement): whether a house is good or not depends on the circumstances, on what kind of house it is . . . . The third form, apodeictic judgement, displays in a positive form the conditions of "truth" of the subject of the judgement: such and such a construction of a house is good, such and such an act is lawful, and so forth.

It is not difficult to work out the passage here from judgement into syllogism, since one already finds oneself within the syllogism as soon as the elements contained in the notional judgement are posited as such: "Such and such a construction of a house is good; this house is built in such a way; this house is good." It is also not hard to guess how the fourth form of judgement affirms the moment of contingency: the circumstances on which whether or not the house is good are dependent – whether it is really a house, whether it corresponds to its Notion – are irreducibly contingent, or rather are posited as such by the very form of the judgement of the Notion. Therein consists the crucial shift from the second to the third form of the judgement of the Notion, from problematic to apodeictic judgement: problematic judgement opposes in an external way the inner, necessary Notion of the object (what a house must be to be really a house) and the external contingent conditions on which it is dependent whether some empirical house is really a house; apodeictic judgement surpasses this external relationship between contingency and necessity, between the contingent conditions and the Inner of the Notion – how?

The traditional answer has of course been: by way of conceiving the Notion as teleological necessity which prevails through inherent logic and regulates the apparent external set of circumstances, in accordance with the usual idea that in "dialectics" the necessity realizes itself through a set of contingencies. Examples that immediately come to mind are those of great historical personalities like Caesar or Napoleon: in the course of the French Revolution, its own immanent logic brought about the necessity of a passage from the republican form into that of personal dictatorship – that is, the necessity of a person *like* Napoleon; the fact that this necessity realized itself precisely in the person of Napoleon was, however, due to a series of contingencies. . . . This is how Hegel's theory of contingency is usually conceived: contingency is not abstractly opposed to necessity but its very form of appearance – necessity is the encompassing unity of itself and its opposite. Yet Hegel's theory on how a given phenomenon ascertains its necessity by positing itself its contingent presuppositions opens up the possibility of a rather different reading:

> The Possible which became Actual is not contingent but necessary, since it posits itself its own conditions. . . . Necessity posits itself its conditions, but it posits them as contingent.[23]

In other words, when, out of the contingent external conditions, their Result takes shape, these conditions are retroactively – from the viewpoint of the final Result itself – perceived as its necessary conditions. "Dialectics" is ultimately a teaching on how necessity emerges out of contingency: on how a contingent *bricolage* produces a result which "transcodes" its initial conditions into internal necessary moments of its self-reproduction. It is therefore Necessity itself which depends on contingency: the very gesture which changes necessity into contingency is radically contingent.

To make this point clear, let us recall how, at some turning point of the subject's (or collective) history, an act of interpretation which is in itself thoroughly contingent – non-deducible from the preceding series – renders the preceding chaos readable anew by introducing into it order and meaning, that is to say: necessity. John Irving's unjustifiably underrated novel *A Prayer for Owen Meany* is a kind of Lacanian "*roman à thèse*", a tract on this theme of how necessity arises out of a traumatic contingency. Its hero, Owen Meany, accidentally strikes with a baseball bat and kills his best friend's mother; in order to endure this trauma, to integrate it into his symbolic universe, he conceives himself as an instrument of God, whose actions have been preordained and can be considered God's intervention in the world. Even his death itself is a beautiful obsessive reversal of the customary process of trying to evade an evil prophecy (whereby one unwittingly brings about its realization): when Owen takes some accident as a prophecy that he will die in Vietnam, he does all he can to make the prophecy come true – he is terrified by the prospect of *missing his death*, since in that case all sense would be lost and he himself would be guilty of the death of his friend's mother . . .

Although this retroactive necessity seems to be limited to symbolic processes, it is of extreme interest to psychoanalysis that the same logic can be discerned even in today's biology – in the work of Stephen Jay Gould, for example, who freed Darwinism of evolutionary teleology and exhibited the radical contingency of the formation of new natural kinds. The Burgess Shale, which he analyses in *Wonderful Life*,[24] is unique because the fossils preserved in it belong to the moment when development could have taken an entirely different course: it captures nature, so to speak, at the point of its *undecidability*, at the point when a number of possibilities coexist which today, in retrospect, from an already established line of evolution, seem absurd, unthinkable; at the point when we have before us an excess wealth of (today) unthinkable forms, of complex, "highly developed" organisms which are constructed according to different plans to those of today and became extinct not because of their inherent lesser value or unadaptability, but above all because of their contingent discordance with a particular environment. We could even venture to say that the Burgess Shale is a "symptom" of nature: a monument which cannot be located within the line of evolution, as it had then developed, since it represents the outline of a possible alternative history – a monument which allows us to see what was sacrificed, consumed; what was lost so that the evolution we know today could take place.

It is essential to grasp how this kind of relationship of contingency to necessity, where necessity derives from the retroactive effect of contingency – where necessity is always a "backwards-necessity" (which is why Minerva's owl flies only at dusk) – is just another variation on the Substance-as-Subject motif. That is to say, as long as contingency is reduced to the form of appearance of an underlying necessity, to an appearance through which a deeper necessity is realized, we are still on the level of Substance: the substantial necessity is that which prevails. "Substance conceived as Subject", on the contrary, is that moment when this substantial necessity reveals itself to be the retroactive effect of a contingent process. We have thus also answered the question of why four and not three types of judgement: if the development of the judgements had been resolved with the judgement of necessity, it would have remained on the level of Substance, on the level of the substantial necessity of the Notion which, by means of its partition, develops its particular content from within itself. Such an image of the "self-movement of the Notion" which posits its own particular content may appear very "Hegelian"; it corresponds to the conventional idea about Hegel's "work of the Notion"; yet we are actually as far as possible from the Hegelian Subject which retroactively posits its own presuppositions. Only with the fourth type of judgement is the fact fully affirmed that "the truth of the Substance is the Subject"; only here does the Subject posit its own substantial presupposition (it retroactively posits the contingent conditions of its notional necessity). The core of Hegel's "positing the presupposition" consists precisely in this retroactive conversion of contingency into necessity, in this conferring of a form of necessity on the contingent circumstances.

Yet to discern the fact that with the fourth type of judgement we achieve the level of the Subject, one does not even need a sophisticated conceptual apparatus: it suffices to remind oneself that this type contains what we – inadequately – call evaluation, evaluative judgement which (according to philosophical common sense) concerns the Subject ("subjective valuation"). It is not enough, here, just to draw attention to the elementary fact that, with Hegel, judgement is not "subjective" in the customary meaning of the term but a matter of the relationship of the object itself to its own Notion – the radical conclusion to be drawn that *there is no Subject without a gap separating the object from its Notion* – that this gap between the object and its Notion is the ontological condition of the Subject's emergence. The Subject is nothing but the gap in the Substance, the inadequacy of the Substance to itself: what we call "Subject" is the perspective illusion by means of which the Substance perceives itself in distorted ("subjective") form. More crucially, the fact is here generally overlooked that such a type of judgement on the correspondence of an object to its own Notion implies a kind of reflective *redoubling* of the Subject's will and desire.

It is in this precise sense that one has to conceive Lacan's *dialectic* of desire – his basic thesis that desire is always *desire of a desire*: desire is never directly aimed at some object but is always desire "squared" – the subject finds in himself a multitude of heterogeneous, even mutually exclusive, desires, and the question with which he is thus faced is: Which desire should I choose? Which desire should I desire? This constitutive reflectivity of desire is revealed in the paradoxical sentiment of being angry or ashamed at oneself when one desires something that one considers unworthy of one's desire – a deadlock which could be described precisely in the words *I don't (want to) desire my desire*. What we call "valuation" is thus always based in this reflectivity of desire, which is of course possible only within the symbolic order: the fact that desire is always-already "symbolically mediated" means nothing but that it is always the desire of a desire. This reflectivity of desire opens up the dimension of symbolic deception: if the subject wants X, it does not follow from this that he also wants this desire; or rather it is possible for him to feign his desire for X, precisely in order to hide the fact that he does *not* want X.

The way this reflectivity is connected with the motive of contingency is also not difficult to grasp. Let us take, for example, the philosophical motif of "values": it is mistaken to say of people in so-called "traditional" societies – societies which are based on unreflected acceptance of a system of values – that they "possess" values; what we call from our external perspective "their values" the people themselves accept as an unquestioned framework of which they are not conscious as such; they entirely lack the reflective attitude to it implied by the notion of "value". As soon as we start to talk about "values", we have a priori posited values as something relative, contingent, whose preserve is not unquestionable, as something which it is necessary to discuss – that is to say, precisely to *value*: we cannot evade the question of whether these values are "true values", of whether they "correspond to their notion". In Hegelese: in so far as the notion of value is "posited", explicated, in so far as this notion arrives at its being-for-itself, value is experienced as something contingent, bound to the "problem of value": have we chosen the right values? How do we evaluate them? and so on.

The same can be said about the notion of "profession": in pre-capitalist society, in which the position of an individual is primarily decided by a set of traditional organic links, it is anachronistic to talk about a "profession" (even on an immediate level one can sense how inadequate it is to say that in the Middle Ages someone had the "profession" of serf) – the very notion of "profession" presupposes an indifferent, abstract individual, delivered from his determinatedness by substantial-organic links, who can "freely" decide on his profession, choose it. On yet another, third, level, it is the same with the notion of artistic style: it is anachronistic to talk about medieval or even classical styles; we can talk about them only when the possibility of choice of different styles is posited as such; when, therefore, style is perceived as something basically arbitrary.

"In father more than father himself"

The split which the judgement of the Notion brings, despite the deceptive first impression, is therefore not simply a split between the Notion and its empirical actualization (for example, between the Notion of a table and empirical tables, which indeed, dependent on circumstances, more or less correspond to their Notion); if it were simply that, then we would be concerned with a simple tension between the ideal, the ideal Notion, and its always-incomplete realization – in the end finding ourselves again on the level of reflective judgement, since the ideal–real relationship is a typical relationship of reflection. The movement with which we are actually concerned in the judgement of the Notion is more subtle: *the split is borne within the Notion itself.*

The reflectivity of which we have just spoken is indicated by the question: is the Notion itself something "adequate to itself"? True, Hegel talks of the circumstances on which it depends whether the house is good (say: "really a house"); however, the point here is not that no empirical house can completely correspond to its Notion, but that *in what appears as "external circumstances" in which is actualized the Notion of a house, yet another Notion is already at work, which is no longer that of a house although it corresponds to the house more than House itself* – here we are alluding to the dialectic which is displayed in the well-known paradox of saying about some non-X that it is "more X than X itself" (for example, about some skinflint: "He's more Scots than the Scots themselves"; about a loving stepmother that she is "more motherly than the mother herself"; about a fanatical Janissary that he is "more Turk than the Turks themselves").

The lack of identity which impels movement in judgement of the Notion is thus not the lack of identity between the Notion and its realization, but extends to the fact that the Notion can never correspond to itself, be adequate to itself, because as soon as it fully realizes itself it passes into another Notion: an X which is fully realized as X is "more X than X itself", and so *no longer X*. In the lack of identity between the Notion and its actualization, the surplus is therefore on the side of actualization, not on the side of the Notion: the actualization of a Notion produces some *notional* surplus over the Notion itself.

This kind of split is at work in the paintings of the American "realist" Edward Hopper; Hopper has claimed in some of his well-known statements that he does not like people, that people are uninteresting, that they are strange to him; and one can actually sense in his pictures how the human figure is depicted neutrally, without interest, whereas there is a very much more intense feeling for particular types of objects, above all his famous empty sunlit windows. In a very precise sense, one could say that in these objects – although, or rather just because, man is absent from them – the human dimension is intensely striking, that (if we could hazard a Heideggerian formula) this dimension is presented by means of the very absence of man. A man is more present in these traces than in his direct physical presence; only through such traces (a half-raised curtain in the window, and so on) is the authentic "human" dimension effectively rendered – as in the well-known experience after somebody's death when it is by going over his remaining everyday personal objects – his writing-table, little objects in his bedroom – that we become aware of who the deceased really was; that is to say, in Hegelese, of his Notion.

Hopper's paintings thus depict some non-X (inanimate, "dead" objects: empty streets, fragments of apartment buildings) which is "more X than X itself"; in which human dimensions are revealed more than in man himself. And, as we have already seen, the supreme case, the case which is the very exemplar of this paradoxical reversal, is the *signifier* itself: as soon as we enter the symbolic order, the "thing" is more present in the word that designates it than in its immediate presence – the weight of an elephant is more conspicuous when we pronounce the word "elephant" than when a real elephant enters the room.

Therein consists the enigma of the status of the father in psychoanalytic theory: the non-coincidence of symbolic and real father means precisely that some "non-father" (maternal uncle, the supposed common ancestor, totem, spirit – ultimately the *signifier* "father" itself) is "more father" than the (real) father. It is for this reason that Lacan designates the Name-of-the-Father, this ideal agency that regulates legal, symbolic exchange, as the "paternal *metaphor*": the symbolic father is a metaphor, a metaphoric substitute, a sublation [*Aufhebung*] of the real father in its Name which is "more father than father himself", whereas the "non-sublated" part of the father appears as the obscene, cruel and oddly impotent agency of the superego. In a way, Freud was already aware of it when, in *Totem and Taboo*, he wrote that, following the primordial parricide, the dead father "returns stronger than when he was alive" – the crucial word here is "returns", which indicates how we should conceive another mysterious sounding proposition of Lacan – that father is a symptom: the symbolic father is a symptom in so far as it is the "return of the repressed" primordial father, the obscene and traumatic Father-Enjoyment that terrorized his horde.[25]

What, however, we have to bear in mind apropos of the primordial Father-Enjoyment is again the logic of the "deferred action"; the fact that the non-symbolized father changes into the horrifying spectre of the Father-Enjoyment only backwards, retroactively, after the symbolic network is already here: "Father-Enjoyment" ultimately just fills out a structural insufficiency of the symbolic function of the Name-of-the-Father, its original status is that of a leftover produced by the failure of the operation of sublation [*Aufhebung*] which establishes the rule of the Name-of-the-Father; its allegedly "original" status ("primordial father") results from an illusion of perspective by means of which we perceive the remainder as the point of origins.[26]

In another approach, Lacan determines the Name-of-the-Father as the metaphoric substitute of the desire of the mother – that is to say:

$$\frac{\text{Name-of-the-Father}}{\text{desire of the mother}}$$

To grasp it, one has only to recall Hitchcock's *North by Northwest*, the precise moment in the film when Roger O. Thornhill is "mistakenly identified" as the mysterious "George Kaplan" and thus hooked on his Name-of-the-Father, his Master-Signifier: it is the very moment when he raises his hand in order to comply with his mother's desire by phoning her. What he gets in return from the Other – that is to say, what he gets *in the place* of the mother's desire he wants to comply with – is "Kaplan", his paternal metaphor. *North by Northwest* thus presents a case of "successful" substitution of the paternal metaphor for the mother's desire. One is even tempted to risk the hypothesis that *North by Northwest* presents a kind of spectral analysis of the figure of the father, separating it into its three components: the *imaginary* father (the United Nations official whose stabbing in the lobby of the General Assembly – the parricide – is attributed to Thornhill); the *symbolic* father ("Professor", the CIA official who concocted the nonexistent "George Kaplan") and the *real* father (the tragic, obscene and impotent figure of Van Damm, Thornhill's principal adversary).

A film like *Shadow of a Doubt*, on the contrary, displays the dire consequences of the *failure* of this metaphoric substitution: the analysis of this film is usually centred on the dual relationship of the two Charlies (the young niece and her murderous uncle); what is thus left out of consideration is the presence of the crucial third element which brought them together – namely, the *mother's desire*: Uncle Charlie visited the family in response to the mother's (his sister's) desire. In other words, the lesson of the film is that the dual relationship ends in a murderous impasse when the third element that mediates between its poles remains mother's desire and is not "sublated" in the paternal metaphor.

The ultimate proof that Hegel's articulation of the four species of judgement does follow an inherent logic lies in the fact that its consistency is that of the Greimasian "semiotic square" of necessity/possibility/impossibility/contingency:

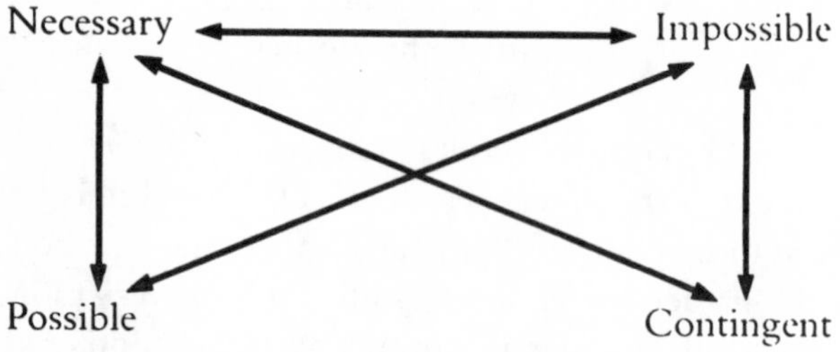

The fundamental category of the judgement of existence is that of *impossibility* (its "truth" is the infinite judgement where the relationship between subject and predicate is posited as impossible); the judgement of reflection is characterized by *possibility* (namely, the possibility of the ever-more-comprehensible correspondence between subject and predicate); the judgement of necessity asserts a *necessary* relationship between subject and predicate (as is evident from its very name), whereas the judgement of Notion exhibits the ultimate *contingency* upon which necessity itself depends. Do we have to add how this notional apparatus is related to the Lacanian triad of ISR? The status of impossibility is *real* ("real as impossible"); every necessity is ultimately a *symbolic* one; *imaginary* is the domain of what is "possible", whereas the emergence of the *symptom* which links together the three dimensions of ISR is radically *contingent*.

NOTES

1. From this perspective, even the theory that epitomizes the horror and imbecility of Stalinist "dialectical materialism" – the infamous "theory of reflection" – could be given a new twist in so far as one interprets it on the level of "squared reflection". An ideological edifice fails by definition, of course, to "reflect correctly" the social reality in which it is embedded; yet this very "surplus" of distortion is in itself socially determined, so that *an ideology "reflects" its social context through the very way its "reflection" is distorted.*

2. In passing, the same is true of the various popular Heideggerian "histories of Being" where the history of the West is reduced to a succession of episodes as ways of disclosure of Being (the Greek epoch, Cartesian subjectivity, post-Hegelian "will to power", and so on): what is lost here is the way each epochal experience of the truth of Being is a failure, a defeat of thought's endeavour to capture the Thing. Heidegger himself – at least in his great moments – never fell into this: so, for example, the emphasis of his interpretation of Schelling's *Treatise on Human Freedom* is that Schelling had a presentiment of a certain kernel which remained unthought in all previous metaphysical tradition, yet about which he simultaneously blinded himself when he formulated it in the categories of Aristotelian metaphysics (Hölderlin put this kernel into words more appropriately in his poems).

3. So it is actually much less "racist" than the kind of "understanding the Other in its diversity" – by which we preserve a safe distance from the Other and erase everything from our experience of the Other that could "disturb" our subjective position – a direct, rude resentment of the Other, which some years ago an English anthropologist exemplified when he wrote, after studying a Nigerian tribe for some years, that he had never seen a more corrupt tribe, that they instinctively and systematically tried to exploit and deceive him, and so on.

4. See Theodor W. Adorno and Max Horkheimer, *Dialectic of Enlightenment*, New York: Herder & Herder 1972.

5. See Gillian Rose, *Hegel contra Sociology*, London: Athlone 1981, pp. 48 ff.

6. On a different conceptual level, it is the same with what Lacan designates as the "subject of the signifier" (as opposed to the "subject of the signified"). Every signifier by definition misrepresents the subject, distorts it; yet the subject does not possess any ontological consistency outside this series of signifying (mis)representations – its entire "identity" consists in its *lack of identity*, in the distance that separates it from the identity that could have been conferred upon it by an "adequate" signifying representation. In short, the "subject of the signifier" is ultimately nothing but the name for a certain limit

missed by every signifying representation, a limit constituted retroactively by the very failure of representation.

7. See Michel Silvestre, *Demain la psychanalyse*, Paris: Navarin Éditeur 1987, p. 93. There is, however, one precise point at which we disagree with Silvestre: for Silvestre, the "sentiment of guilt" is deceitful in so far as it serves to elude the real guilt of parricide, while it seems to us that in a Lacanian perspective, even this radical guilt is already a deceptive stratagem by means of which the subject eludes the traumatic fact that the big Other is from the very beginning "dead" (that is, an inconsistent, impotent impostor) – we didn't kill Him, He is always-already dead, and the idea that we are responsible for His death enables us to sustain the illusion that once upon a time, before our Crime, He was alive and well (in the form of the primal Father-Enjoyment, for example).

8. G.W.F. Hegel, *Phenomenology of Spirit*, Oxford: Oxford University Press 1977, p. 10.

9. Ibid., p. 21.

10. This illusion enables us to avoid a lethal look into the Other's eyes: when we confront the Other eye to eye, we meet death.

11. As to the arguments for translating "*lalangue*" as "llanguage", compare Russell Grigg's translation of Jacques Lacan, "Geneva lecture on the symptom", *Analysis* 1, Melbourne 1989.

12. Let us recall how Marx produced the same formula apropos of capital: the limit of capital is capital itself; the capitalist mode of production.

13. Paul-Dominique Dognin, *Les "sentiers escarpés" de Karl Marx* I, Paris: CERF 1977.

14. The relationship here is the same as that between French politics and German philosophy in the epoch of the French Revolution: the great German idealists thought out the philosophical foundations of the French Revolution not *in spite of* the German political backwardness but precisely *because* the political blockage left open only the path of theory.

15. Let us recall that in the last section of his *Science of Logic*, Hegel says that we can consider the moments of the dialectic process to be three or four – the subject is actually that fourth surplus-moment, that "nothing", self-referential negativity, which none the less counts as "something". (See also Chapter 5 below.)

16. *Hegel's Science of Logic*, London: Allen & Unwin, 1978, p. 623.

17. Actually the passage from the negative into the infinite judgement epitomizes the logic of the infamous "negation of the negation": it reveals how the "negation of the negation" is not simply a return to the immediate identity but the negation which negates the universal field itself left untouched by the simple negation of the predicate.

18. See Slavoj Žižek, *The Sublime Object of Ideology*, London: Verso 1989, pp. 207–9.

19. This paradox of the "infinite judgement" is the clearest proof of how wrong is the (mis)reading of Hegel according to which he considers our "ordinary" language a rude tool inappropriate to express the finesse of dialectical self-mediation; limited to the level of Understanding, of "abstract" determinations. Such a (mis)reading of course arouses a dream of another, ethereal language that would avoid the clumsiness of our ordinary language and immediately give adequate expression to speculative movement – perhaps such a language is accessible to gods, whereas we common mortals are unfortunately condemned to the vulgar instrument at our disposal, forced to think, to

express ourselves, "in language against language itself" . . . . To anyone versed in Hegelian procedure, it should be clear that such a notion completely misses his point, which is that in order to capture the speculative movement we do not need any other, more adequate language: our "ordinary" language is more than sufficient – all we have to do is, so to speak, to take it more literally than it takes itself; to become aware of how even the most crude judgements succeed *by means of their very failure*.

To put it succinctly: "speculative judgement" is the same thing as an ordinary judgement of Understanding, only *read over twice* – the failure of the first reading forces us to accomplish the dialectical shift of perspective and to discern success in failure itself. "The Spirit is a bone", for example: the first reading results in utter dismay, failure, a sense of absurd incompatibility between the subject and its predicate – yet all we have to do is to observe how the *speculative* notion of "subject" consists precisely in this radical incompatibility, split, negativity. Or, to put it another way: all we have to do to arrive at the speculative truth of a proposition of Understanding is *to comprise in its meaning our subjective position of enunciation*: to realize that what we first take for our "subjective" reaction to it – the sense of failure, incompatibility, discord – *defines the "thing itself"*. So, contrary to the expanded doxa, Hegel does not speak a kind of esoteric "private language": he speaks the same language as we all do, *only more so*.

20. *The Seminar of Jacques Lacan, Book I*, Cambridge: Cambridge University Press 1988, pp. 242–3.

21. Quoted from P.-D. Dognin, *Les "sentiers escarpés" de Karl Marx* I, p. 72.

22. There is much talk today about the obsolescence of the difference between Right and Left; in order not to be deceived it is useful to remember the asymmetry of these notions: a leftist is somebody who *can* say "I am a left-winger" – that is, recognize the split, the Left/Right distinction; whereas a right-winger can invariably be recognized by the way he positions himself in the centre and condemns all "extremism" as "old-fashioned". In other words, the Right/Left distinction is perceived as such (in Hegelese: posited) only from a Left perspective, whereas the Right perceives itself as being in the "centre"; it speaks in the name of the "Whole"; it rejects the split. The articulation of the political space is thus a paradox well exemplified by the deadlocks of sexuation: it is not simply the articulation into two poles of the Whole, but one pole (the Left) represents the split as such; the other (the Right) denies it, so that the political split Left/Right necessarily assumes the form of the opposition between "Left" and "centre", with the place of the "Right" remaining empty – the Right is defined by the fact that its adherents can never say of themselves in the first person "I am a right-winger"; they appear as such only from a Left perspective.

23. Dieter Henrich, *Hegel im Kontext*, Frankfurt: Suhrkamp Verlag 1971, p. 163.

24. Stephen Jay Gould, *Wonderful Life*, London: Hutchinson Radius 1990.

25. Apropos of Joyce, Lacan speaks of the symptom ["*sinthome*"] as a substitute-formation that enables the psychotic to elude the disintegration of his symbolic universe; as an agency that the subject builds up to supplement the failure of the Name-of-the-Father as "quilting point" [*point de capiton*] of his discourse; in the case of Joyce, this "*sinthome*" was, of course, literature itself. (See Jacques Lacan, "Joyce le symptôme" I-II, in *Joyce avec Lacan*, Paris: Navarin Éditeur 1987.) What one has to do here is to *reverse* and at the same time *universalize* this logic of substitution: it is not just that the "*sinthome*" acts as a substitute for the defective symbolic Father; the point is rather that *father as such* is already a symptom covering up a certain defectiveness, inconsistency, of

the symbolic universe. In other words, the step one has to make is from the *symptom of the father* to the *father itself as symptom.*

26. This is why Lacan designates the spectre of the Father-Enjoyment as the neurotic's fantasy-construction; as his attempt to fill out the impasse of his relationship towards the symbolic father.

4

On the Other

I Hysteria, Certainty and Doubt

Wittgenstein as a Hegelian

In *Logic*, Hegel "stages" identity (imagines a subject saying "Plant is . . . a plant") and thus arrives at its truth – that is to say, demonstrates that identity-with-itself consists in the absolute contradiction, in the coincidence of the (logical) subject with the void at the place of the expected, but failed, predicate. By translating the identity of an object with itself into the satirical scene of a subject's procedure, Wittgenstein of the *Philosophical Investigations* is here extremely close to Hegel:

> "A thing is identical with itself." – There is no finer example of a useless proposition, which yet is connected with a certain play of the imagination. It is as if in imagination we put a thing into its own shape and saw that it fitted. [We might also say: "Every thing fits into itself." Or again: "Every thing fits into its own shape." At the same time we look at a thing and imagine that there was a blank left for it, and that now it fits into it exactly.] Does this spot • "*fit*" into its white surrounding? – *But that is just how it would look* if there had been a hole in its place and it then fitted into the hole . . . [1]

Like Hegel, Wittgenstein determines identity-with-itself as the paradoxical coincidence of a thing with its own empty place: the notion of "identity-with-itself" has no sense outside this "play of the imagination" in which a thing occupies its space; outside this procedure of "staging".

The crucial point here is that such a notion of identity implies the presence of the *symbolic order*: for an object to "coincide" with its empty place, we must in advance "abstract" it from its place – only in this way are we able to perceive the place without the object. In other words, the object's absence can be perceived *as such* only within a differential order in which absence as such acquires positive value (which is why, according to Lacan, the experience of castration equals the introduction of the symbolic order: by way of this experience, the phallus is, so to speak, "abstracted" from its place).[2] To determine more closely this uncanny proximity of Hegel and Wittgenstein, let us take as our starting point Lacan's designation of Hegel as "the most sublime of all hysterics" – is it just an empty witticism or does it stand rigorous theoretical examination? Let us answer this dilemma by starting with the most basic question: What characterizes the subjective position of a hysteric?

Hegel's hysterical theatre

The elementary form of hysteria, hysteria *par excellence*, is the so-called "conversion hysteria" [*Konversionshysterie*], where the subject "gives body" to his deadlock, to the kernel that he is unable to put in words, by means of a hysterical symptom, the abnormality of a part of his body or bodily functions (he starts to cough without any apparent physical reason; he repeats compulsive gestures; his leg or hand stiffens, although there is nothing medically wrong with it, and so on). In this precise sense we speak of hysterical *conversion*: the impeded traumatic kernel is "converted" into a bodily symptom; the psychic content that cannot be signified in the medium of common language makes itself heard in a distorted form of "body language".

From this brief sketch, one can already guess where the connection with Hegel lies: a homologous conversion is what defines "figures of consciousness" in Hegel's *Phenomenology of Spirit*. "Lordship and Bondage", "Unhappy Consciousness", "Law of the Heart", "Absolute Freedom", and so on, are not just abstract theoretical positions; what they name is always also a kind of "existential dramatization" of a theoretical position whereby a certain *surplus* is produced: the "dramatization" gives the lie to the theoretical position by bringing out its implicit presuppositions.[3]

In "dramatizing" his position, the subject renders manifest what remains unspoken in it, what *must* remain unspoken for this position to maintain its consistency. In other words, the "dramatization" reflects the conditions of a theoretical position overlooked by the subject who holds to it: the "figure of consciousness" stages ("figures") the concealed truth of a position – in this sense, every "figure of consciousness" implies a kind of hysterical theatre. We can see already how the logic of this dramatization subverts the classical idealist relationship of a theoretical Notion and its exemplification: far from reducing exemplification to an imperfect illustration of the Idea, the staging produces "examples" which, paradoxically, *subvert the very Idea they exemplify* – or, as Hegel would say, the imperfection of the example with regard to the Idea is an index of the imperfection proper to the Idea itself.

What we have here is quite literally a "conversion": the *figuration* ("acting out") of a theoretical impasse (of the "unthought" of a theoretical position) and at the same time the *inversion* best rendered by one of Hegel's constant rhetorical figures: when, for example, Hegel deals with the ascetic's position, he says that the ascetic converts the *denial of the body* into the *embodied denial*. Here, we must take care not to mistake this inversion for the simple mirror-reversal that just turns the elements round within the confines of the same configuration: the crucial point is that the Hegelian conversion is "mediated" by an *impossibility* – since the ascetic is unable to deny the body (this would simply mean death), the only thing that remains to him is to *embody denial itself* – to organize his *bodily* life as a standing disavowal and renunciation. His own practice thereby subverts the theoretical position according to which the earthly, bodily life is inherently null and worthless: all the time he is preoccupied with his body, inventing new ways of mortifying and pacifying it, instead of assuming an indifferent distance towards it. The passage from one "figure of consciousness" to the next occurs when the subject takes cognizance of this gap separating his "enunciated" (his theoretical position) from his position of enunciation and assumes thereby what he unknowingly staged as his new explicit theoretical position: each "figure of consciousness", so to speak, stages in advance what will become the next position.

And what is hysteria if not the bodily staging of the same rhetorical figure? According to Lacan, the fundamental experience of man *qua* being-of-language is that his desire is impeded, constitutively dissatisfied: he "doesn't know what he really wants". What the hysterical "conversion" accomplishes is precisely an inversion of this impediment: by means of it, the impeded desire converts into a *desire for impediment*; the unsatisfied desire converts into a *desire for unsatisfaction*; a desire to keep our desire "open"; the fact that we "don't know what we really want" – what to desire – converts into a *desire not to know*, a desire for ignorance . . . . Therein consists the basic paradox of the hysteric's desire: what he desires is above all that his desire itself should remain unsatisfied, hindered – in other words: alive as a desire. Lacan demonstrated this with brilliance apropos of the dream of the "merry butcher's wife" quoted by Freud:[4] as a defiance to Freud, to his theory that a dream is a fulfilled wish, she proposed a dream in which the wish is *not* fulfilled; the solution to this enigma, of course, is that her true desire was precisely that her too-compliant husband should for once *not* satisfy her whim, thus keeping her desire open and alive. This conversion confirms the "reflective" nature of desire: desire is always also *a desire for desire itself*, a desire to desire or not to desire something.

Do we need to add that the same conversion is at work already in the Kantian notion of the Sublime?[5] The paradox of the Sublime, in other words, is in the conversion of the impossibility of presentation into the presentation of impossibility: it is not possible to present the transphenomenal Thing-in-itself within the domain of phenomena, so what we can do is *present this very impossibility* and thus "render palpable" the transcendent dimension of the Thing-in-itself. Furthermore, do we not encounter the same mechanism in the most notorious formal aspect of the Hegelian dialectics, that of the "concrete", "determinate" negation – negation the result of which is not an empty nothingness but a new positivity? What we have here, then, is the same reflective inversion of "negation of [determinate] being" into "[determinate] being of negation": the determinate being *qua* negation's outcome is nothing but *a form in which negation as such assumes positive existence.*

This aspect is lost in the usual comprehension of "concrete" negation, where negativity is grasped as the intermediary, passing moment of the Notion's self-mediation; it is wrong to say that the final Result "sublates" negativity by making it a subordinate moment of the concrete totality – the point is rather that the new positivity of the Result is nothing but positivized power of the Negative. This is how one has to read the much-quoted propositions from the Preface to *Phenomenology of Spirit* defining Spirit as the power to look the negative in the face and convert it into being: one "tarries with the negative" not by abstractly opposing it to the positive but by conceiving positive being itself as materialization of Negativity – as "metonymy of Nothing", to use the Lacanian expression.

As we have already seen, the only philosophical counterpart to this Hegelian strategy of subverting a theoretical position by means of its "staging", its "conversion" into a determinate existential attitude, is the " 'scenic' character of Wittgenstein's presentation"[6] – of Wittgenstein-II, the Wittgenstein of *Philosophical Investigations*, of course. That is to say, how does Wittgenstein proceed in solving a philosophical problem which – when approached directly, in its immediate, abstract form – appears to be a dark, insoluble deadlock? By withdrawing from the "thing itself" (the problem in its general philosophical form) and concentrating on its "exemplifications" – on the "uses" of the notions that define the problem within our everyday "life-form".

Let us take, for example, the basic notion of the philosophy of mind, such as remembering, imagining, calculating: if we tackle the problem directly and ask "What is *the real nature* of remembering, imagining, calculating?", we are sooner or later drawn into the blind alley of fruitless ruminations about different kinds of "mental events", and so on. What Wittgenstein proposes we do is to replace our original question with the question "What are *the circumstances we presuppose when we say of someone* 'He suddenly *remembered* where he had left his hat', 'He *imagined* the house he wanted', or 'He *calculated* the number in his head?' " To philosophical common sense, such a procedure appears, of course, like "evading the real issue"; whereas the dialectical approach recognizes in the scenic dramatization which displaces the question, replacing the abstract form of the problem with concrete scenes of its actualization within a life-form, the only possible access to its truth – we gain admittance to the domain of Truth only by stepping back, by resisting the temptation to penetrate it directly.

In other (Hegelian) words, the only solution of a philosophical problem is its displacement – a reformulation of its terms which makes it disappear as a problem. Far from implying a common-sense attitude usually (and wrongly) associated with Wittgenstein-II, such a strategy is the very heart of the Hegelian procedure: *a problem disappears when we take into account (when we "stage") its context of enunciation.* Therein Wittgenstein's "A method will now be shown by means of examples":[7] as with Hegel's "staging", what is at stake here is not an "illustration" of general propositions – examples here are not "mere examples" but "scenic presentations" which render manifest its unspoken presuppositions. These Wittgensteinian "stagings" are not without satirical sting, as in *Philosophical Investigations* 38, where he ironizes over the philosophical problem of naming – of hooking "words" on to "objects" – by imagining a solitary scene with a philosopher in the immediate presence of an object, at which he stares, compulsively repeating its name or even the word "This! This!" – do we have to add that (unknowingly, probably) Wittgenstein resumes here the dialectic of "sense certainty" from Chapter I of *Phenomenology of Spirit*, where Hegel likewise subverts sense certainty by means of "staging" a subject pointing at an object and repeating over and over "This! Here! Now!" . . .

The content of Wittgenstein's "behaviourism" is therefore the endeavour to translate, to transpose, "meaning" as fetishistic, "reified" given entity, a "property of the word", into a series of the ways we use this word – or, to refer to Wittgenstein's own example, if I say "The king in chess is *the* piece that one can check", this "can mean no more than that in our game of chess we only check the king".[8] Henry Staten adds a keen comment to this: "Notice the precise distinction Wittgenstein makes here. What looks like a property of the king is being translated into a remark about *how we do something*."[9] In Hegelese: the property of an object is found to be its "determination of reflection" [*Reflexionsbestimmung*]; the reflection-into-the-object of our own, the subject's, dealing with it.[10]

Cogito and the forced choice

What is the dimension, the common medium, enabling us to "compare" – to conceive as part of the same lineage – Hegel and Wittgenstein? The Heideggerian answer here would be quick and unambiguous: both belong to the tradition of Cartesian subjectivity. What we will try to bring out is, on the contrary, the way both Wittgenstein and Hegel call into question the Cartesian tradition of certainty through radical doubt.

Let us start with the paradoxes of the Cartesian *cogito* itself as they are exhibited by Lacan. The crucial fact which, as a rule, is passed over in silence is that there are two different, even mutually exclusive, interpretations of the Cartesian *cogito* in Lacan's teaching. One usually considers only the interpretation from *Seminar XI* which conceives *cogito* as resulting from a forced choice of thought: the subject is confronted with a choice "to think or to be"; if he chooses being, he loses all (including being itself, since he has being only as thinking); if he chooses thought, he gets it, but truncated of the part where thought intersects with being – this lost part of thought, this "un-thought" inherent to thought itself, is the Unconscious. Descartes's error was to assume that by choosing thought the subject secured himself a small piece of being; obtained the certainty of "I" as "thinking substance" [*res cogitans*]. According to Lacan, Descartes thereby misrecognized the proper dimension of his own gesture: the subject which is left as a remainder of the radical doubt is not a substance, a "thing which thinks", but a pure point of substanceless subjectivity, a point which is nothing but a kind of vanishing gap baptized by Lacan "subject of the signifier" (in opposition to the "subject of the signified"), the subject lacking any support in positive, determinate being.[11]

In the shadow of these renowned theses from *Seminar XI*, one usually forgets the fact that two years later, in the seminar on *Logic of Fantasy* (1966–7), Lacan accomplished one of the reversals of his previous position so characteristic of his procedure and proposed the opposite reading of Cartesian doubt. While he still maintains that the terms of *cogito* are defined by a forced choice between thought and being, he now claims that the subject is condemned to a choice of *being*: the Unconscious is precisely the thought lost by this choice of being. Lacan's new paraphrase of *cogito ergo sum* is therefore: *I* (the subject) *am in so far as it* (*Es*, the Unconscious) *thinks*. The Unconscious is literally the "thing which thinks" and as such inaccessible to the subject: in so far as I am, I am never where "it thinks". In other words, I am only in so far as something is left unthought: as soon as I encroach too deeply into this domain of the forbidden/impossible thought, my very being disintegrates.

What we have here is the fundamental Lacanian paradox of a being founded upon misrecognition: the "unconscious" is a knowledge which must remain unknown, the "repression" of which is an ontological condition for the very constitution of being.[12] The being chosen by the subject has of course its support in *fantasy*: the choice of being is the choice of fantasy which procures frame and consistency to what we call "reality", whereas the "unconscious" designates scraps of knowledge which subverts this fantasy-frame.

The consequences of this shift are more far-reaching than they may appear: through it, the emphasis of the notion of *transference* is radically displaced. In *Seminar XI*, Lacan defines transference as a supposed knowledge relying upon being (that is, upon the "*objet petit a*" *qua* remainder-semblance of being lost in the forced choice of meaning), whereas in the *Logic of Fantasy*, transference is conceived as a breakthrough into the domain of knowledge (thought) lost in the forced choice of being. Transference emerges when knowledge lost in the choice of being is "transferred" to an object (the subject towards which we maintain a relationship of transference) – that is to say, when we presuppose that this object (subject) possesses knowledge the loss of which is a condition of our very being. First, we had knowledge that relied on the remainder-semblance of being; now, we have being (of the subject towards which we maintain a relationship of transference) on to which some impossible/real knowledge is hooked.

In the background of this shift we find one of the crucial changes between the Lacanian teaching of the 1950s and his teaching of the 1970s: the change of emphasis in the relationship between subject and object. In the heyday of the 1950s, the object was *devalorized* and the aim of the psychoanalytic process was consequently defined as "(re)-subjectivization": translation of the "reified" content into the terms of the intersubjective dialectic; whereas in the 1970s, the *object within subject* comes to the fore: what procures dignity for the subject is *agalma*, what is "in him more than himself", the *object* in him.[13] More precisely: in the 1950s, the object is reduced to a medium, a pawn, in the intersubjective dialectic of recognition (an object becomes object in the strict psychoanalytic sense in so far as the subject discerns in it the other's desire: I desire it not for its own sake but because it is desired by the other); in the 1970s, on the contrary, the object which comes to the fore is the *objet petit a*, the object which renders possible the transferential structuring of the relation between subjects (I suppose a knowledge in another subject in so far as "there is in him something more than himself", *a*). This is why, from the 1960s onwards, Lacan avoids speaking of "intersubjectivity", preferring the term "discourse" (in clear opposition to the 1950s, when he repeated again and again that the domain of psychoanalysis is that of intersubjectivity): what distinguishes "discourse" from "intersubjectivity" is precisely the addition of the object as fourth element to the triad of the (two) subjects and the big Other as medium of their relationship.

To return to the Lacanian reading of the Cartesian *cogito*, however: what both versions of it have in common is that Lacan, in opposition to Descartes, insists on the irreducible gap separating thought from being: as a subject, I never *am* where I *think*. Taking this gap into account renders it possible to formulate what Lacan, in his *Seminar XI*, calls "the Freudian *cogito*": the Freudian step from doubt to certainty;

the Freudian way to confirm our certainty by means of the doubt itself.

According to Lacan, Freud's variation on "I think, therefore I am" is "where the subject [analysand] has doubts, we can be sure that there is unconscious": the analysand's doubts, his hesitation and resistance to accepting an interpretation proposed by the analyst, are the best possible proof that the analyst's intervention has stirred up some traumatic unconscious nerve. As long as the subject accepts the analyst's interpretations without disturbance and uneasiness, we have not yet touched "it"; a sudden emergence of resistance (ranging from ironic doubt to horrified refusal) confirms that we are finally on the right track.

In spite of their formal resemblance, the inherent logic of this Freudian mode of using doubt as a lever to reach certainty differs radically from the Cartesian reversal of doubt into certainty: here, doubt is used not as a hyperbolic gesture of suspending every content heterogeneous to it, but on the contrary as the ultimate proof that there *is* some traumatic, insistent kernel eluding the reach of our thought. Again, the only philosophical homology to this procedure is that of the Hegelian strategy of recognizing heteronomy in the very way a consciousness asserts its autonomy (like the ascetic who exhibits his dependence on the material world by his very obsession with getting rid of it).

Lacan's last word, however, is not certainty about the unconscious: he does not reduce the subject's doubt to his resistance to the unconscious truth. As to the problem of "scepticism", of calling into question our most assured everyday certitudes, Lacan is far more radical than Descartes: his "scepticism" concerns what the late Wittgenstein defined as the field of "objective certainty", the field which Lacan baptized "the big Other".

"Objective certainty"

Wittgenstein's reference to the "objective certainty" embedded in the very "life-form" is an answer to a doubt which goes even a step further than the Cartesian one. That is to say, Wittgenstein calls into question the very coherence and consistency of our thinking: How do I know that I think at all? How can I be sure that the words I use mean what I think they do? By means of a reference to the "life-form",

Wittgenstein endeavours to discern a foothold always-already presupposed in our language games, including the game of philosophical doubt. Here, we must be precise in order to avoid missing his crucial emphasis: "life-form" is – unlike the Cartesian *cogito* – *not* a remainder that withstands even the most radical doubt; it is simultaneously less and more: it is the agency that makes every kind of radical scepticism simply *meaningless* by wearing away its very ground. In other words, it is not the agency which stands the test, which solves the question, an answer to it, but the agency which forces us to *renounce the very question as false*.

In a first approach, Wittgenstein's solution seems to be to rely on a fundamental level of belief, acceptance, trust – *by the very act of speaking, we partake in the basic social pact*, we presuppose the consistency of the language order: "Our learning is based on believing."[14]/ "Knowledge is in the end based on acceptance-recognition" [*Anerkennung*].[15]/"A language game is only possible, if one trusts something."[16] However, we must be careful here not to mistake the subject of this acceptance-recognition for the Cartesian subject: the "big Other" on whose consistency the subject relies here is *not* the Cartesian God who does not deceive. Wittgenstein's point is that our knowing, thinking, speaking, make sense only as moments of a determinate "life-form" within the frame of which individuals relate practically to each other and to the world that surrounds them. "To speak" *means* to relate to objects in the world, to address our neighbours, and so on; which is why questions like "How can I be sure that objects in the world actually correspond to the meaning of my words?" are strictly *beside the point*: they presuppose a gap which, were it to exist, would make the very act of speaking impossible.

In order to isolate the specific level of this pact in which we partake by the very act of speaking, Wittgenstein introduces the difference between "subjective" and "objective" certainty. "Subjective certainty" is a certainty subjected to doubt, it concerns states of things where the usual criteria of accuracy and falsity, of knowledge and ignorance, apply. The attitudes and beliefs that constitute "objective certainty" are on the contrary a priori not submitted to test and doubt: the act of calling them into question would undermine the very frame of our "life-form" and entail what psychoanalysis calls "loss of reality". It is therefore superfluous and wrong even to say that "objective certainty" concerns things about which "we undoubtedly know they are true": such an affirmation introduces a reflective distance which is totally out of place, since the attitudes and beliefs of "objective certainty" form the very background against which we may consistently doubt something, test it, and so on. Let us say that I have doubts about the presence of a table in the room next door: I enter it and see that the table *is* there; if, now, somebody asks me, "But how do you know that it was *you* who entered the room? How can you be sure that what you saw was a *table*?", it would be totally inappropriate to answer: "I know it, I was fully aware of myself when I entered it, I saw the table with my own eyes" . . . such questions (and answers which implicitly accept their validity) simply do not make sense within the frame of our "life-form".

What Wittgenstein calls "objective certainty" is therefore his counterpart to the Lacanian "big Other": the field of a symbolic pact which is "always-already" here, which we "always-already" accept and recognize. The one who does *not* recognize it, the one whose attitude is that of *disbelief* in the big Other, has a precise name in psychoanalysis: a *psychotic*. A psychotic is "mad" precisely in so far as he holds to attitudes and beliefs excluded by the existing "life-form": it is not accidental that Wittgenstein's examples of propositions which call into question "objective certainty" (Wittgenstein maintaining that his name is not Ludwig Wittgenstein but Napoleon; somebody in the middle of a Scottish bog claiming he is in Trafalgar Square, and so on) read like caricatural statements from jokes about madmen. So it seems that, after all, Wittgenstein does endorse his attachment to the Cartesian procedure in the very gesture of undercutting the abstract status of *cogito*: does not "objective certainty" play the role of the ultimate foothold and horizon enabling us to get rid of the very possibility of doubt?

Wittgenstein's last word, however, is *not* "objective certainty": in a collection of his last fragments which bears somewhat of a Cartesian-sounding title – *On Certainty* – he asserts an irreducible – albeit imperceptible and ineffable – *gap* separating "objective certainty" from "truth". "Objective certainty" does not concern "truth"; on the contrary, it is "a matter of attitude", a stance implied by the existing life-form, where there is no assurance that "something *really unheard-of*"[17] will not emerge which will undermine "objective certainty", upon which our "sense of reality" is grounded. Let us just recall the worn-out case of a primitive Stone Age tribe confronted all of a sudden with television: this "box with living men in it" cannot but wear away their "objective certainty", as an encounter with extra-terrestrial life would do for us (or, as a matter of fact, as is already the case with contemporary particle physics, with its theses on the time–space continuum, on curved space, and so on).

In other words, Wittgenstein is well aware that life-forms ultimately, so to speak, "float in empty space"; that they possess no "firm ground under their feet" – or, to use Lacanian terms, that they form self-referring symbolic vicious circles maintaining an unnameable distance from the Real. This distance is empty; we cannot pinpoint any positive, determinate fact that would call "objective certainty" into question since all such facts always-already appear against the unquestionable background of "objective certainty"; yet it attests to the lack of support of the "big Other", to its ultimate impotence, to the fact that, as Lacan would put it, "the big Other doesn't exist", that its status is that of an impostor, of pure pretence. And it is only here that Wittgenstein effectively breaks out of the Cartesian confines: by means of affirming a radical discontinuity between certitude and "truth"; of positing a certainty which, although unquestionable, does not guarantee its "truth".[18]

From Ⱥ to S̸

In his *Philosophical Investigations*, Wittgenstein already came across the "nonexistence of the big Other" as guarantee of the consistency of our symbolic universe in the form of his "sceptical paradox": "no course of action could be determined by a rule, because every course of action can be made out to accord with the rule."[19] In short: every course of action that appears to infringe the established set of rules can retroactively be interpreted as an action in accordance with another set of rules. We all know the mathematical function of addition denoted by the word "plus". Let us say, for example, that "68 + 57" is a computation that I have never performed before; when, finally, I perform it, I ascertain that "68 + 57 = 5". Let us, further, suppose that the word "quus" designates a rule of addition which gives the same result as "plus", with the only exception that for "68 + 57", it gives "5"; so, to the protestations of my bewildered companion, I answer: "How do you know this is a mistake? I simply followed another rule: for me, 'plus' means and has always meant 'quus', and '68 + 57 = 5' is a correct application of quus!"[20]

It would of course be simple enough to refute this paradox within a *hermeneutical* approach by way of pointing out how it presupposes a certain distance towards "rule" which is not present in our everyday attitude: when, in our everyday life, we add up, we do not "follow" some rule external to the act – the "rule" is inherent to the act itself; it constitutes the very horizon within which it is possible to speak only of "adding", which is why, when we add up, we cannot first make an abstraction from its "rule" and then ask ourselves which was the rule we followed. This hermeneutical horizon of meaning which is always-already present as the inherent background of our operations – and, as such, constitutes the very place *from which* we speak and which therefore cannot be called into question in a consistent way – is one of the dimensions of what Lacan designates as "the big Other": the big Other is always-already here; by means of our very act of speaking, we attest to our "belief" in it.

Yet the field of psychoanalysis is not confined to this dimension of the big Other – witness the crucial role the interpretation of *slips of the tongue* plays in it: they cannot be accounted for by the hermeneutical horizon. That is to say, is not a slip of the tongue precisely an act we did not succeed in performing in accordance with its inherent rule, yet where our very failure to follow the rule, our deviation from it, occurred in accordance with another, unknown rule (namely, the rule unearthed by its interpretation)? Is not the aim of interpretation precisely to discern a rule followed unknowingly where "common sense" sees nothing but meaningless chaos – *in other words, to discern "quus" where "common sense" sees a simple mistake, a simple failure of our effort to follow "plus"*? The analyst as "subject supposed to know" is supposed to know precisely the "quus", the hidden rule we followed unknowingly, the rule that will retroactively confer meaning and consistency upon our slips . . . . In this way, however, we have just replaced the "big Other" of the hermeneutical horizon with another "big Other", with another "rule" guaranteeing consistency of our speech: the "big Other" still exists, the analyst still functions as the guarantee that all our slips and errancies follow some hidden Rule.

The ultimate conclusion to be drawn from the "sceptical paradox" is far more radical – it consists in the exact counterpart to Lacan's late thesis that "the big Other doesn't exist": if every infringement can be made out to accord with the rule, then, as Kripke puts it succinctly, "the ladder must finally be kicked away":[21] strictly speaking we never know what – if any – rule we are following. The consistency of our language, of our field of meaning, on which we rely in our everyday life, is always a precarious, contingent *bricolage* that can, at any given moment, explode into a lawless series of singularities. "Wittgenstein-II", the Wittgenstein of *Philosophical Investigations*, still thought it possible to elude this radical conclusion by means of a reference to the unquestionable foothold of "life-form"; it was only in *On Certainty* that he articulated his version of the "nonexistence of the big Other".

On Certainty therefore compels us to distinguish another Wittgenstein, "Wittgenstein-III", from "Wittgenstein-II": what "Wittgenstein-II" leaves out of consideration is the abyss, the "empty" distance, which forever separates a "life-form" from the non-symbolizable Real. The "unheard-of occurrences" the emergence of which undermine "objective certainty" are – to use Lacanian terms – precisely the intrusions of some traumatic Real which entail a "loss of reality". In *On Certainty*, Wittgenstein sketches three possible modes of the subject's answer to such an "unheard-of occurrence"; let us exemplify them by the already-mentioned case of contemporary physics.

First, I can behave "rationally" and replace the previous certainty with doubt ("maybe particles *do* behave in this strange way, maybe matter *is* just curved space, although my common sense tells me this is absurd"); the second possibility is that such a shock completely undermines my capacity to think and to judge ("if nature behaves this way, then the universe is mad and nothing really consistent can be said about anything"); finally, I can simply refuse the new evidence and stick to my previous certainty ("all the ruminations about time–space continuum, about curved space, etc., are plain nonsense, you just have to open your eyes and experience how the world really is . . . "). And what is "traumatism" in psychoanalysis if not such an "unheard-of occurrence" which, when fully assumed, undercuts the "objective certainty" that pertains to our "life-form"?

In other words, do not the three modes articulated by Wittgenstein correspond to three possible reactions of the subject to the intrusion of psychic traumatism: its assumption into the psychic apparatus, the disintegration of the apparatus, the refusal of the apparatus to take into account the traumatic occurrence? What is of special interest to us here, however, is that this inconsistency of the "big Other" (of the field of "objective certainty", of "common knowledge") has its reverse in the splitting of the subject itself, in its division into S1, a signifier that represents it within the symbolic order, and the leftover of the signifying representation, the pure void whose counterpart is the non-symbolized object (*a*). Wittgenstein traced out this splitting through his refined observations upon the way the pronoun "I" functions; he resolutely refuses the idea that "I" is a demonstrative pronoun by means of which a phrase self-referentially points towards its subject of enunciation:

> When I say "I am in pain", I do not point to a person who is in pain, since in a certain sense I don't know at all *who* is in pain. And this can be justified. For the main point is: I did not say that such-and-such a person is in pain, but "I am . . . ". . . . What does it mean to know *who* is in pain? It means, for example, to know which man in this room is in pain: for instance, the one who is sitting there, or the one who is standing in that corner . . . . What am I getting at? At this, that there are many different criteria for the "*identity*" of a person.[22]

The crucial point here is that, contrary to philosophical common sense, "I" does *not* ensure the subject's identity: "I" is nothing but an empty vanishing point of the "subject of the enunciation" which arrives at its identity only by means of its identification with a place in the symbolic network that structures social reality; it is only here that the subject becomes "somebody"; that we can answer the question "*Who* is in pain?". It is because of this distance between the "subject of the enunciation" and the "subject of the enunciated" that phrases like "I, Ludwig Wittgenstein, thereby engage myself . . . " are not pleonastic: the function of "Ludwig Wittgenstein" is precisely to supply an answer to the question "Who am I?". When, instead of simply saying "I maintain . . . ", I say "I, Ludwig Wittgenstein, maintain . . . ", I identify with a place in the symbolic intersubjective network.

As Lacan points out in his analysis of *Hamlet*,[23] phrases like "I, Ludwig Wittgenstein, . . . " attest the subject's ability to "pass to the act", founded in the certainty of symbolic identification – of fully assuming a symbolic mandate. Hamlet himself, the very embodiment of obsessive procrastination, unable to "pass to the act", becomes capable of acting at the exact moment when, in the last act of the play, he answers the rhetorical question "Who am I?": "What is he whose grief / Bears such an emphasis? . . . / . . . this is I, Hamlet the Dane." It is the split between "I" and "Hamlet the Dane", between the vanishing point of the subject of the enunciation and his support in symbolic identification, which is primordial: the moment of "passage to the act" is nothing but an illusory moment of decision when the subject's being seems to coincide without remainder with his symbolic mandate. Wittgenstein is quite clear and univocal in his insistence on the primordial character of this split: "The word 'I' does not mean the same as 'L.W.' even if I am L.W., nor does it mean the same as the expression 'the person who is now speaking'."[24]

So we find ourselves back at the beginning, since it is precisely this split – the resistance, the hesitation of the subject fully to assume his symbolic mandate – which defines the position of a hysteric: what is a hysteric if not an "I" who resists full identification with the mandate "Ludwig Wittgenstein" ("father", "wife", "son", "leader", "pupil" . . .)? And what is hysterical theatre if not a staging of this resistance? This is the ultimate domain of doubt and certainty: a certainty that "I" am my symbolic mandate, a doubt if "I" really am that.

II The "Formal Aspect"

History of an apparition

What is the first "materialist reversal" of Hegel? One can locate it exactly: it occurred on 26 May 1828, in the central square of Nuremberg. On this day a young man appeared there, singularly dressed, of stiff, unnatural gestures; his entire language consisted of a few fragments of the Lord's Prayer learnt by heart and pronounced with grammatical errors, and of the enigmatic phrase "I want to become such a knight as was my father", the design of an identification with the Ego-Ideal; in his left hand, he carried a paper with his name – Kaspar Hauser – and the address of a Captain of the Nuremberg cavalry. Later, when he learnt to speak "properly", Kaspar told his story: he had spent all his life alone in a "dark cave" where a mysterious "black man" procured food and drink for him, until the very day when he dressed him and took him to Nuremberg, teaching him a few phrases on the way . . . . He was entrusted to the Daumer family, quickly "humanized" himself and became a celebrity: an object of philosophical, psychological, pedagogical and medical research, even the object of political speculation about his origin (was he the missing Prince of Baden?). After a couple of quiet years, on the afternoon of 14 December 1833, he was found mortally wounded with a knife; on his deathbed, he announced that his murderer was the same "black man" who had brought him to the central square of Nuremberg five years earlier . . .

Although the sudden apparition of Kaspar Hauser provoked a shock that pertains to this kind of brutal encounter with a real–impossible which seems to interrupt the symbolic circuit of cause and effect, the most surprising thing about it was that, in a sense, *his arrival was awaited*: precisely as a surprise, he arrived on time. It is not only that Kaspar realized the millenary myth of a child of royal origins abandoned in a wild place and then found at the age of adolescence (remember the rumour that he was the Prince of Baden), or that the fact that the only objects in his "dark cave" were a couple of wooden animal figures pathetically realizes the myth of a hero saved by the animals who take care of him. The point is rather that towards the end of the eighteenth century, the theme of a child living excluded from human community became the object of numerous literary and scientific texts: it staged in a pure, "experimental" way the theoretical question of how to distinguish in man the part that belongs to Culture from the part that belongs to Nature.

"Materially", the emergence of Kaspar resulted from a series of unforeseen and improbable accidents, yet from the *formal* standpoint, it was *necessary*: the epoch's structure of Knowledge prepared the place for it in advance. His apparition caused such a sensation precisely because the empty place waiting to be filled was already there: a century earlier or later, it would have passed unnoticed. To grasp this *form*, this empty place preceding the content which fills it out – therein consists the objective of Hegelian *Reason*; that is to say, of Reason in so far as it is opposed to Understanding where a form expresses some positive, previous content. In other words: far from being surpassed by his "materialist reversals", Hegel *accounted* for them in advance .

Saying and meaning-to-say

According to the dialectical Vulgate, Understanding is supposed to treat categories, notional determinations, as abstract, coagulated moments, cut off from their living totality, reduced to the particularity of their fixed identity; whereas Reason surpasses this level of Understanding by means of exhibiting the live process of subjective (self-)mediation whose abstract, "dead" moments, whose "objectivizations", are the categories of Understanding. Where Understanding sees only rigid determinations, Reason sees the living movement which engenders them. The distinction between Understanding and Reason is thus conceived as a kind of Bergsonian opposition between the flexible *élan vital* and inert matter, its product, accessible to Understanding.

Such a conception misses entirely what is at stake in the Hegelian distinction between Reason and Understanding: Reason is in no way something "more" in relation to Understanding, it is definitely *not* a living movement which would elude the dead skeleton of the categories of Understanding; on the contrary, Reason is Understanding itself in so far as it lacks nothing, in so far as there is nothing "beyond" it – the absolute Form beyond which there is no transcendent Content eluding its grasp. We remain stuck at the level of Understanding as long as we continue to believe that there is something beyond it, some unknown quantity above its reach – *even though (and especially when) we call this Beyond "Reason"!* By accomplishing the pass to Reason, we do not "add" anything to Understanding; rather, we *subtract* something from it (the spectre of an Object persisting in its Beyond) – that is to say, we reduce it to its formal procedure: one "surpasses" Understanding the moment one becomes aware of how it is already Understanding itself which is the living movement of self-mediation one was looking for in vain in its Beyond.

An awareness of this may help us to dispel a current misunderstanding as to the Hegelian critique of "abstract thought". Habitually, one retains from it the idea that common sense (or Understanding) "thinks abstractly" in so far as it subsumes the entire richness of an object in a particular determination: one isolates from the concrete network of determinations that constitute a living totality one single feature – a man, for example, is identified with, reduced to, the determination "thief" or "traitor" . . . and the dialectical approach is supposed to compensate for this loss by helping us to rejoin the wealth of the concrete living totality. However, as Gérard Lebrun pointed out,[25] such a notion totally misrepresents the dialectical approach: as soon as one enters *Logos*, loss is irredeemable, what is lost is lost once and for all; or, to use Lacan's terms, as soon as one speaks, the gap separating the Symbolic from the Real is irreducible. Far from lamenting this loss, Hegel rather praises the immense power of Understanding capable of "abstracting" – that is, of dismembering – the immediate unity of Life:

> The activity of dissolution is the power and work of the *Understanding*, the most astonishing and mightiest of powers, or rather the absolute power. The circle that remains self-enclosed and, like substance, holds its moments together, is an immediate relationship, one therefore which has nothing astonishing about it. But that an accident as such, detached from what circumscribes it, what is bound and is actual only in its context with others, should attain an existence of its own and a separate freedom – this is the tremendous power of the negative; it is the energy of thought, of the pure "I".[26]

In other words, the concrete-of-thought is totally incommensurable with the immediate concretion that pertains to the fullness of Life: the "progress" of dialectical thought in relation to Understanding in no way consists in a "reappropriation" of this pre-discursive fullness – rather, it entails the experience of its ultimate nullity; of how the richness that disappears on the way to symbolization is already in itself something disappearing. To put it succinctly: we pass from Understanding to Reason when we experience how the loss of immediacy by Understanding is actually a *loss of a loss*, a loss of something without proper ontological consistency.

The error of Understanding does not consist in its striving to reduce the wealth of Life to abstract notional determinations: its supreme error is rather this very opposition between the concrete wealth of the Real and the abstract network of symbolic determinations – its belief in an original fullness of Life supposedly eluding the network of symbolic determinations. When, consequently, one bemoans the negative power of Understanding which dismembers the living, organic totality, and contrasts it with the synthetic, healing capacity of Reason, one usually misses the crucial point: the operation of Reason does *not* consist in re-establishing the lost unity on a "higher" level, as a Whole which maintains the inner difference by positing it as its sublated moment, or some similar pseudo-Hegelian prattle. The passage from Understanding to Reason occurs when the subject becomes aware of how the organic Whole lost by Understanding "*comes to be* through being *left behind*"; of how there is *nothing* beyond or previous to Understanding, of how this Beyond of an idyllic organic Whole is retroactively posited (presupposed) by Understanding itself. The fundamental illusion of Understanding is precisely that there is a Beyond eluding its grasp, so, to put it succinctly, Reason is simply Understanding *minus* what it is supposed to be lacking, what is supposed to elude its grasp – in short: what appears to it as its inaccessible Beyond.[27]

The worn-out formulae according to which Reason "sets in motion" the rigid categories of Understanding, introducing the dynamism of dialectical Life in them, thus fall prey to a misapprehension: far from "surpassing the limits of Understanding", Reason marks the moment of reduction of all content of thought to the immanence of Understanding. The categories of Understanding "become fluid", put in motion by dialectics, when one renounces the conception of them as fixed moments, "objectivizations", of a dynamic process that surpasses them – that is to say, *when one locates the impetus of their movement in the immanence of their own contradiction*. "Contradiction as the impetus of dialectical movement": again a commonplace whose function is, in most cases, to spare us the effort of determining the precise nature of this "contradiction". What then is, *stricto sensu*, this "contradiction" which sets in motion the dialectical process?

On a first approach, one could determine it as the contradiction of a Universal *with itself*, with its own particular content: every universal totality, posited as "thesis", necessarily contains within its particular elements "at least one" which *negates* the universal feature that defines it. Therein is its "symptomatic point"; the element which – within the field of universality – holds the place of its constitutive Outside, of what has to be "repressed" for the universality to constitute itself. Consequently, one does not compare the universality of a "thesis" with some Truth-in-itself to which it is supposed to correspond: one compares it *to itself*, to its concrete content. One undermines a universal "thesis" by way of exhibiting the "stain" of its constitutive exception – let us just recall Marx's *Capital*: the inherent logic of private ownership of the means of production (the logic of societies where producers themselves own their means of production) leads to capitalism – to a society where the majority of the producers own *no* means of production and are thus forced to sell on the market themselves – their labour – instead of their products.

Furthermore, one has to specify further the character of this comparison of a Universal with itself, with its own concrete content: it consists, ultimately, in a comparison of what the subject enouncing a universal thesis *wanted to say* with what he *actually said*. One subverts a universal thesis when one demonstrates to the subject who enounced it how, *by means of its very enunciation*, he said something entirely different from what he intended to say; as Hegel points out again and again, the most difficult thing in the world is to say exactly what one "wants to say". The most elementary form of such a dialectical subversion of a proposition by way of self-reference – that is, by relating it to its own process of enunciation – is found in Hegel's treatment of the "principle of identity": unknowingly, the subject who enounces it inscribes difference in the very heart of identity, in its very identity:

> It is thus the empty identity that is rigidly adhered to by those who take it, as such, to be something true and are given to saying that identity is not difference, but that identity and difference are different. They do not see that in this very assertion they are themselves saying that *identity is different*; for they are saying that *identity is different* from difference.[28]

This is why, with Hegel, truth is always on the side of what is *said* and not on the side of what one "meant to say"; let us articulate this distinction – which, incidentally, coincides with the Lacanian distinction between *significance* [*signifiance*] and *signification* – apropos of the dialectic of essence and appearance. "For us", for the dialectical consciousness which observes the process afterwards, essence is "appearance *qua* appearance": the very movement of self-sublation of appearance, the movement by means of which appearance is posited as such – that is to say, as "mere appearance". However, "for the consciousness", for the subject caught in the process, essence is something beyond appearance, some substantial entity hidden beneath the delusive appearance. The "signification" of essence, what the subject "wants to say" when he speaks of an essence, is thus a transcendent entity beyond appearance, whereas what he "actually says", the "significance" of his words, is reduced to the movement of self-sublation of the appearance: appearance does not possess any ontological consistency, it is an entity whose very being coincides with its own disintegration. The crucial point here is how the "significance" of the essence consists in the movement performed by the subject, in the procedure by way of which he posits an entity as the appearance of some essence.

This dialectic may be exemplified by a consideration of Hegel's interpretation of the paradoxes by means of which Zeno attempted to prove the nonexistence of Movement and of the Multiple. Zeno, of course, "wanted to say" that Movement "doesn't exist" – that only the One, the immovable and indivisible Being, truly exists; yet what he actually did was to demonstrate the contradictory nature of Movement: Movement exists only as the movement of its own self-sublation, self-surpassing. Here we can see how erroneous is the current understanding of the Hegelian category of In-itself [*An-sich*] which conceives it as a substantial-transcendent content still eluding the grasp of consciousness, not yet "mediated" by it – that is to say, which models it upon the Kantian notion of the "Thing-in-itself".

What, however, is the "In-itself" of Zeno's argumentation? Zeno took his argumentative procedure as an *a contrario* proof of the immovable Being which persists in itself, beyond the false appearance of Movement – in other words, *a difference between what is only "for the consciousness" and what exists "in itself" is there already "for the consciousness"* (for Zeno himself): Zeno's view is that Movement is a false appearance which exists for the naive consciousness, whereas only the immovable One truly exists. This therefore is the first correction to be introduced into the above-mentioned current understanding: the difference between what is only "for it" (for the consciousness) and what exists "in itself" is a difference inherent to the "naive" consciousness itself. The Hegelian move consists only in *displacing* this difference by way of demonstrating that its place is not where the "naive" consciousness (or the "critical" consciousness as the supreme form of naivety) posits it.

"For the consciousness", for Zeno, we are dealing with a distinction between the contradictory, self-sublating appearance of Movement and the immovable Being which persists in its identity with itself; the "truth" of Zeno, *his* "In-itself or For-us", is that the entire content of this immovable Being, all that Zeno actually says about it, consists in the Movement of the self-sublation of Movement – the immovable Being beyond appearance *coincides with* the auto-dissolution process of Movement. The crucial point here is that "for the consciousness", for Zeno, this procedure, this argumentative movement, is conceived as something *external to the "thing itself"*, as *our* path towards the One which persists in its In-itself, unperturbed by our procedure – to resort to a well-known metaphor, this procedure is like a ladder that one pushes away after climbing up it. "For us", on the contrary, the content of Being *is* the path of argumentation which leads towards it; the immovable Being is nothing but a kind of "coagulation" of the procedure by means of which Movement is posited as false appearance.

The passage from what is only "for the consciousness" to what is "in itself or for us" thus in no way corresponds to the passage from a delusive appearance to its substantial Beyond supposed to exist in itself: it consists, on the contrary, in the experience of how what the consciousness took only for a path towards the truth, and as such external to it (Zeno's argumentative procedure, for example), *is already truth itself*. In a sense, "all is in the consciousness", the true In-itself is by no means hidden in some transcendent Beyond: the entire error of the consciousness is to mistake the "thing itself" for the external procedure leading to it. It is here that the category of "the formal aspect" [*das Formelle*] from the Introduction to Hegel's *Phenomenology of Spirit* assumes all its weight: the "truth" of a moment or a stage of the dialectical process is to be sought in its very form – in the formal procedure, in the way the consciousness arrived at it:

> . . . in the movement of consciousness there occurs a moment of *being-in-itself* or *being-for-us* which is not present to the consciousness comprehended in the experience itself. The *content*, however, of what presents itself to us does exist *for it*; we comprehend only the formal aspect of that content, or its pure origination. *For it*, what has thus arisen exists only as an object; *for us*, it appears at the same time as movement and a process of becoming.[29]

Contrary to the usual idea of the external form supposed to conceal the true content, the dialectical approach conceives content itself as a kind of "fetish", as an object whose inert presence *conceals its own form* (its network of dialectical mediations): the truth of the Eleatic Being is the formal procedure by means of which one demonstrates the ontological inconsistency of Movement. It is for this reason that Hegelian dialectics implies the experience of the ultimate nullity of "content" in the sense of some kernel of In-itself one is supposed to approach via the formal procedure: this kernel is, on the contrary, nothing but the inverted way consciousness (mis)perceives its own formal procedure. When Hegel reproaches Kant with "formalism", it is because Kant *is not "formalist" enough* – that is to say, because he still clings to the postulate of an In-itself supposed to elude the transcendental form and fails to recognize in it a pure "thing-of-thought" [*Gedankending*]. The reverse of the dialectical passage to the "truth" of an object is thus its *loss*: the object, its fixed identity, is dissolved in the network of "mediations". By conceiving the movement of the self-sublation of Movement as the "truth" of Zeno's Being, we *lose* Being as substantial entity that exists in itself: all that remains is the abyssal whirlpool of the self-sublation of Movement – Heraclitus as the truth of Parmenides.

Apropos of the notion of truth, Hegel accomplished his famous reversal: truth does not consist in the correspondence of our thought (proposition, notion) with an object, but in the correspondence of the object itself to its notion; as is well known, Heidegger retorted that this reversal remains within the confines of the same metaphysical notion of truth as correspondence.[30] What, however, eludes this Heideggerian reproach is the radically *asymmetric* character of the Hegelian reversal: with Hegel, we have *three* and not two elements – the dual relationship of "knowledge" between "thought" and its "object" is replaced by the triangle of (subjective) thought, the object and its notion *which in no way coincides with thought*. We could say that Notion is the *form of thought*, form in the strict dialectical sense of the "formal aspect" *qua* truth of the content: the "unthought" of a thought is not some transcendent content eluding its grasp but its form itself. The encounter between an object and its Notion is for that reason necessarily a *failed* one: the object can never fully correspond to its Notion since *its very existence, its ontological consistency, hangs on this non-correspondence*. The "object" itself is in a sense *the incarnated non-truth*; its inert presence fills out a hole in the field of "truth", which is why the passage to the "truth" of an object entails its loss, the dissolution of its ontological consistency.

The Hegelian performative

It is this necessary discord between an object and its "truth" that accounts for the fundamental Hegelian paradox of "retroactive performativity" – that is to say, for the fact that the dialectical process is characterized by two features which seem to be mutually exclusive. The principal motif of Hegel's critique of the "naive", commonsensical theory of knowledge is that it conceives the process of knowledge after the model of penetrating some previously unknown domain: the "spontaneous" idea is that one discovers, discloses, some reality that already existed prior to our process of knowing it; this "naive" theory overlooks the constitutive character of the process of knowledge with regard to its object: the way knowledge itself modifies its object, confers upon it the form it has as an "object of knowledge".

This constitutive character of knowledge seems to be what Kant had in mind when he spoke of transcendental subjectivity; yet Hegel's emphasis lies elsewhere and is directed precisely against Kant. That is to say, with Kant, the subject procures universal form for the substantial content of transcendent provenance (the "Thing-in-itself"); we thus remain within the frame of the opposition between subject (the transcendental network of the possible forms of experience) and substance (the transcendent "Thing-in-itself"), whereas Hegel endeavours to grasp Substance itself as Subject. In the process of knowledge, we do not penetrate some substantial content which would be in itself indifferent to our knowing it; it is rather that our act of knowledge is included in advance in its substantial content – as Hegel puts it, the path towards truth partakes in truth itself. To clarify this point, let us recall an example which confirms Lacan's thesis that Marxism is not a "world view",[31] – namely, the idea that the proletariat becomes an *actual* revolutionary subject by way of integrating the *knowledge* of its historical role:[32] historical materialism is not a neutral "objective knowledge" of historical development, since it is an act of self-knowledge of a historical subject; as such, it implies the proletarian subjective position. In other words, the "knowledge" proper to historical materialism is self-referential, it changes its "object" – it is only through the act of knowledge that the object becomes what it truly "is".

This accent on the "performativity" of the Hegelian process of knowing, on the way it changes and creates its object, is of course a commonplace; what is usually passed over in silence, however, is its *reverse*. That is to say, when Hegel describes the dialectical process, its crucial inversion, he always resorts to figures of speech which ascertain an already-given state of things: "already here", "always-already", and so on. The passage from scission to "synthesis" consists not in some productive act of reconciliation but in a simple shift of perspective by means of which we become aware of how what we mistook for scission is already in itself reconciliation: the scission is not "overcome" but rather retroactively "undone".[33]

How, then, are we to think together these two aspects of the dialectical process which seem to be mutually exclusive – namely its "performative" character and the fact that, in the course of a dialectical process, an obstacle is removed by way of ascertaining that it never was one at all? Therein consists the ultimate proof that Hegelian logic is a logic of the signifier, since it is precisely this unity of the two opposed features, this paradox of *retroactive performativity*, which defines the notion of signifier: a signifying mark "makes" a thing what it "always-already was". In a crucial passage in *Encyclopaedia*, Hegel articulates the link between this retroactive performativity and the dialectics of truth and deception:

> The consummation of the infinite End, therefore, consists merely in removing the deception which makes it seem yet unaccomplished. The Good, the absolutely Good, is eternally accomplishing itself in the world: and the result is that it need not wait upon us, but is already by implication, as well as in full actuality, accomplished. This is the deception under which we live. It alone supplies at the same time the actualizing force on which the interest in the world reposes. In the course of its process the Idea creates that deception, by setting an antithesis to confront it; and its action consists in getting rid of the deception which it has created. Only out of this error does the truth arise. In this fact lies the reconciliation with error and with finitude. Error or other-being, when sublated, is still a necessary dynamic element of truth: for truth can only be where it makes itself its own result.[34]

At first sight, things seem to be as clear as they can be: does not this passage confirm the commonplace on Hegel? Idea, the absolutely Good, is the Substance–Subject of the entire process, and the fissure, the deception, is just a game Idea plays with itself. Idea realizes its true ends by means of the "cunning of Reason": it allows individuals to follow their finite ends, whilst it accomplishes its infinite End through the mutual "wear and tear" and failure of the finite ends. The "deception" thus consists in the fact that individual agents pursue their interests, strive for wealth, power, pleasure, glory and other ideological values, whilst unknowingly they are nothing but Idea's unconscious tools.

Let us take the case of the market economy. Individual producers who appear on the market, led by the endeavour to satisfy their egotistical lust for profit, are unaware of the way historical Reason uses the interplay of their passions to realize the true End of social production, the development of productive forces, the growth of society's productive potential in which Spirit achieves "objective" existence. In this sense, deception is a "necessary dynamic element of truth": historical Reason can accomplish its true End only by means of deception: by means of the cunning exploitation of individual interests and passions – rudely speaking, nobody works "for the development of productive forces", individuals necessarily perceive this true End as a means to satisfy their needs . . .

Such a commonplace conception of the "cunning of Reason", however, implies a notion of Reason as substantial entity external to the historical process, elevated above it, "manipulating" its agents (active individuals), "playing" deception while keeping itself undamaged behind the scenes, at a safe distance from historical turmoil, like the God of traditional teleology who uses history to accomplish His incomprehensible goals. If we subscribe to this reading, we assign to individuals the position of a tool of God's inconceivable will – in other words, "substance" is not effectively "subject", since subjects are reduced to the means of a transcendent substantial End. So, is there another possible reading of the quoted passage from *Encyclopaedia*?

"Cunning of Reason" revisited

A quite different possibility presents itself if we read this passage against the background of Hegel's logic of reflection – the reflective "positing of presuppositions".[35] The commonplace as regards this logic is that the dialectical process runs from the immediate starting point through its reflective mediation to the restored, mediated immediacy of the result. What gets lost here is Hegel's crucial insight according to which the very initial immediacy is always-already "posited" retroactively, so that its emergence *coincides with its loss*:

> Reflection therefore *finds before it* an immediate which it transcends and from which it is the return. But this return is only the presupposing of what reflection finds before it. What is thus found only *comes to be* through being *left behind*; its immediacy is sublated immediacy.[36]

Herewith, the "deception" proper to the dialectical process appears in a new light. We are "deceived" in so far as we think that *what is "found" has already existed prior to being "left behind"* – in so far as we think that *once, before the loss, we possessed* what is lost by reflection. In other words, what we are deluded about is the fact that *we never had what we lost by reflection*. It is precisely this paradox which enables us to formulate a concise delimitation of "external" and "absolute" reflection. "External" reflection exercises its activity upon an object which it perceives as a substantial entity, given in advance – that is, independently of its activity. Its problem is that the very activity of reflection entails the loss of the object's immediate, full presence – in reflection, the object is lost "as such"; it is mortified, dissected by means of analytic-reflective categories. What the network of reflection retains are just partial aspects, instead of the live totality, we are stuck with a dead abstraction. In this sense, the philosopher of "external reflection" *par excellence* is Kant – for example, his theory of how the Thing-in-itself eludes subjective reflection.

The inversion of "external" into "absolute" reflection occurs when we experience how the object in its immediate, pre-reflective givenness "only *comes to be* through being *left behind*"; how, then, there is nothing that precedes the movement of reflection since this movement itself "posits its presuppositions"; produces the retroactive illusion according to which its object was given in advance.[37] Therein consists the Hegelian "loss of the loss": not in the annulment of the loss, not in the reappropriation of the lost object in its full presence, but in the experience of how we never had what we have lost – in the experience that loss in a way *precedes* what is being lost. "In the beginning" there always-already was a loss, and this loss opens up the space to be filled out by objects. In the course of the passage of "external" into "absolute" reflection, loss is thus not abolished in the full presence-to-itself of the subject–object, it is only its *place* that shifts.[38]

The conclusions to be drawn from this displacement of the loss for the logic of the political space are far-reaching. Let us take just the case of the present disintegration of "real socialism". This disintegration is of course immediately perceived as a "loss" – loss of the quasi-idyllic stability that characterizes the social fabric of post-Stalinist "real socialism", the feeling that we have lost our footing. The crucial step that has to be taken here is to get rid of this nostalgic longing for the lost closed universe by recognizing that *we never had what we have lost*; the idyll was false from the very beginning, society was always-already ridden with fierce antagonisms. The most traumatic loss that occurs in the disintegration of "real socialism" is undoubtedly that of the "essential appearance" that kept society together:[39] the appearance according to which the entire society supports the Party and enthusiastically builds socialism – when this appearance falls apart, we have the purest possible case of the "loss of a loss". That is to say, by means of this disintegration, in a way we lose nothing (nobody really believed in the appearance), but the loss is none the less tremendous, experienced as traumatic. So, when the appearance of enthusiastic support for the Party disintegrates, the Party literally *loses what it never possessed* – namely, the support of the people.

With reference to the notion of social antagonism elaborated by Laclau and Mouffe,[40] we could also say that by way of the "loss of a loss", antagonism is acknowledged as "primordial", not as a mere secondary disruption of an original harmony. So, when we are faced with a breakdown of the hitherto stable social order, "loss of a loss" names the experience of how this preceding stability was itself false, masking internal strife. And, incidentally, this is what Hegelian "reconciliation" ultimately means: the exact opposite of what is usually assumed – a humble consent that "all is NOT rational", that the moment of contingent antagonism is irreducible, that notional Necessity itself hangs on and is "embedded" in an encompassing contingency. To be convinced, one has only to recall the exact place in *Phenomenology of Spirit* where the "word of reconciliation" occurs: at the end of the dialectics of Beautiful Soul, when the subject is forced to accept that the "way of the world" eludes the grasp of (his) Reason.

Now, it also seems clear how we should reread the quoted passage from Hegel's *Encyclopaedia*. We fall prey to deception precisely when we perceive the Good as something that "need not wait upon us, but is already by implication, as well as in full actuality, accomplished" – that is, when we overlook how the absolutely Good also "only *comes to be* through being *left behind*". We fall prey to deception when we assume the existence of a Substance–Subject, excluded from the vicissitudes of the historical process, which "stages" the deception of finite subjects, "plays" with them and exploits their activity for the accomplishment of its own ends. In short, the supreme deception is the very commonplace notion of the "cunning of Reason", the supposition of Reason as transcendent agency pulling the strings and "running the show" of history.

It would be totally misleading, however, simply to oppose these two deceptions (the deception of the everyday consciousness which follows its egotistical ends, unaware that it is a tool by means of which historical Reason accomplishes its infinite End; and the very deception of thinking that we are a tool of some transcendent Reason that, although unknown to us, guarantees the meaning and consistency of the historical process) and to proclaim the first an "illusion" and the second the "truth". This way, we would miss the moment of truth that pertains to the first conception. The experience of how the absolute End "need not wait upon us, but is already accomplished" gives expression to the "silent weaving of the Spirit"; to the necessary *delay* of the formal act of decision. The unconscious "weaving" indeed does not wait upon us, so that when the conflict is brought into the open it is illusory to think that now everything depends on us, on our decision – things are effectively "already accomplished".

The real problem is: how can both levels of deception be thought *together*? In other words: why is the illusory supposition of Reason as transcendent agency *necessary*? To exemplify this paradoxical conjunction, let us take the case of the October Revolution: today, it is clear that the ideology the Bolsheviks were guided by when they carried out the revolution – the ideology according to which they were mere executors of historical necessity, a "tool of History" fulfilling the prescribed historical Mission – was wrong. The crucial fact, however, is that they could not have brought about the revolution if they had not *believed* that they were mere tools of History – to recall the concise formulation of Leszek Kolakowski, Lenin's success was based on making the right mistakes at the right moment. Here, we have both levels of deception together: the Bolsheviks believed in the "cunning of Reason", they took themselves for instruments of historical Necessity, and this deception was in itself "productive", a positive condition of their accomplishment.

Such a paradoxical logic implies a kind of temporal paradox. What we are looking for is created by the very process of our search; it is at work in a series of jokes, like the one about the conscript who tries to evade military service by pretending to be mad. His symptom is that he compulsively checks all the pieces of paper he can lay his hands on, constantly repeating: "That's not it!" He is sent to the military psychiatrist, in whose office he also examines all the papers around, including those in the wastepaper basket, repeating all the time: "That's not it!" The psychiatrist, finally convinced that he really is mad, gives him a written warrant releasing him from military service. The conscript casts a look at it and says cheerfully: "*That's* it!"[41]

When Hegel speaks about "error" being "a necessary dynamic element of Truth", when he writes that "truth can only be where it makes itself its own result", and so forth, these strange-sounding propositions should be grasped against the background of the logic proper to the joke about the conscript: without error, without the illusion of the persons around the conscript that he was looking for an already-existing paper, this paper would not have been produced at the end (as with the October Revolution, which would not have taken place without its participants' illusion that they were fulfilling a historical necessity). In this precise sense, truth "makes itself its own result" – the paper which finally satisfies the conscript is not simply found but is literally the result of all the fuss about it: of the confusion the conscript has provoked by means of his "mad" search for it. This is how the ill-famed Hegelian "teleology of Reason" has to be grasped: the End towards which the movement tends is not given in advance, it is so to speak created by the movement itself – the necessary deception consists in the fact that for this movement to take place, the subjects must overlook how their own search created what they "find" at the end. The Lacanian name for this structural deception is *sujet supposé savoir*, "the subject supposed to know", and what Hegel calls "absolute knowledge" is precisely the *fall* of the subject supposed to know. That is to say, the starting point of the dialectical process is of course the presupposition of knowledge; the trust that the knowledge we are looking for is already present in the Other: as Hegel points out again and again, the dialectician does not apply an external method on the object, his sole presupposition is that "Reason governs actuality" – that actuality is already in itself "reasonable" (it is the same in psychoanalysis, where the presupposition of the so-called "free associations" is that there is a meaning hidden beneath their apparent chaos). This is why the dialectician can limit his role to that of a pure observer discovering the inherent rationality of the Real. At the end of the dialectical process, this presupposition loses ground: the subject discovers that *from the very beginning there was no support in the Other*, that he was himself producing the "discovered" meaning. And finally, one should not forget that in the case of the joke about the conscript, the object created through search is none other than a *letter*, an official communication, so that this joke is ultimately *a joke about how a letter always arrives at its destination.*

Notes

1. Ludwig Wittgenstein, *Philosophical Investigations*, Oxford: Blackwell 1976, para. 216.
2. The paradoxical *tautological* character of the Lacanian "definition" of the signifier

("the signifier represents the subject for another signifier") must be grasped precisely against the background of the Hegelian notion of identity-with-itself as supreme contradiction. "Subject" is nothing but the name for the contradiction implied by the self-identity; in its most elementary dimension, it emerges as a void that gapes in the middle of the tautology "X is . . . X".

3. See Judith Butler, *Subjects of Desire*, New York: Columbia University Press 1987.

4. Sigmund Freud, *The Interpretation of Dreams*, Harmondsworth: Penguin 1976, pp. 228–9.

5. As to this notion, see Chapter 6 of Slavoj Žižek, *The Sublime Object of Ideology*, London: Verso 1989.

6. Henry Staten, *Wittgenstein and Derrida*, Oxford: Blackwell 1985, p. 67.

7. Wittgenstein, *Philosophical Investigations*, para. 133.

8. Ibid., p. 136.

9. Staten, *Wittgenstein and Derrida*, p. 80.

10. Do we have to recall that in the long tradition that reaches from Pascal to Marx, "king" serves as the exemplary case of the "determination of reflection"? Here also, the properties of the king (his charismatic aura, etc.) are to be translated into a description of how his subjects treat him.

11. See Chapters 11 and 16 of Jacques Lacan, *The Four Fundamental Concepts of Psycho-Analysis*, London: Hogarth 1977. Descartes is to be opposed here to Husserl, who rightly pointed out that the remainder left over after the radical doubt is not a "small piece of reality", since its status is transcendental and not inner-worldly: the phenomenological *epohe* "derealizes" the entire "reality", suspends its existence.

12. See Chapter 2 of Žižek, *The Sublime Object of Ideology*.

13. One of the consequences of this change is of course the reversal in the balance of weight between the Universal and the Particular: in the 1950s, Lacan conceived symptoms as particular imaginary traces not yet integrated in the universal symbolic order, so the aim of psychoanalysis was precisely to effectuate this retarded universalization; in the 1970s, on the contrary, its aim is to isolate the object-cause of desire, the absolutely particular mode by which a subject organizes his enjoyment, the mode which resists unconditionally every attempt at its universalization.

14. Ludwig Wittgenstein, *On Certainty*, Oxford: Blackwell 1969, para. 170.

15. Ibid., para. 378.

16. Ibid., para. 509.

17. Ibid., para. 513.

18. This radical, unheard-of "scepticism" which undermines every kind of "evidence", especially that obtained by phenomenological experience, entails political consequences of extreme importance: it is quite possible to have a deeply authentic subjective position which can nevertheless be "wrong" – like, for example, the position of American Communists in the years of the McCarthy witch-hunt. On the level of factual truth, it is clear that – at least as far as the Soviet Union was concerned – the Cold Warriors were "right" (the Soviet Union *was* a vast kingdom of Terror with aggressive imperialist goals, and so on), yet our "spontaneous" feeling that the position of the victims of the McCarthy witch-hunt was "authentic", while the hunters themselves were scoundrels, is none the less totally justified. One of the lessons of psychoanalysis is precisely that we must assume this irreducible gap between "authenticity" and factual truth.

19. Wittgenstein, *Philosophical Investigations*, para. 201. As to the interpretation of the "sceptical paradox", we draw on Saul Kripke's *Wittgenstein on Rules and Private Language*, Oxford: Blackwell 1982.

20. Let us, in passing, be attentive to the homology between this "sceptical paradox" and the structure of a joke Lacan often refers to: "My fiancée never misses an appointment with me, since the moment she misses it, she is no longer my fiancée." – "I never make a mistake in applying a rule, since what I do defines the very rule." This homology, of course, conceals a radical opposition: in the case of following a rule, the rule in question is reduced to the factuality of what I do, whereas the unfortunate fiancée loses her very status of fiancée the moment she doesn't fulfil obligations that go with it. This opposition is at the basis of the conflict and at the same time uncanny similarity between Jacobins and the king: the Jacobins, who followed the logic of "A French Citizen never fails to accomplish his Duty, since the one who does not accomplish it is no more a French Citizen (and can as such be liquidated)!", were naturally forced to behead the king, who never broke the law, since what he did *was* the law.

21. Kripke, para. 21.

22. Wittgenstein, *Philosophical Investigations*, para. 404.

23. See his unpublished seminar *Désir et son interprétation* (1958–9).

24. Ludwig Wittgenstein, *The Blue and The Brown Books*, Oxford: Blackwell 1958, para. 67.

25. See Gérard Lebrun, *La Patience du concept*, Paris: Gallimard 1972.

26. G.W.F. Hegel, *Phenomenology of Spirit*, Oxford: Oxford University Press 1977, pp. 18–19.

27. This paradox of the relationship between Understanding and Reason is best exemplified by *analytical philosophy*, which is usually reproached with being confined to the level of abstract analysis and thereby missing some "real thing" (History, Dialectics, Life, Spirit). Such condescending criticism usually ends with a recommendation that analytical philosophy is quite acceptable on its own modest level – in so far as it does not extend its claim in an illegitimate way and leave no room for the "real thing". Although this criticism might appear "Hegelian", it is as far as possible from the proper Hegelian attitude: for a dialectical approach, the problem with analytical philosophy is, on the contrary, that it does not take *itself* seriously enough – that it believes in some X supposedly eluding it (which explains analytical philosophers' tendency to supplement their position with mysticism, Eastern wisdom, and so on). What analytical philosophy does not know is that *it already has* what it is desperately looking for elsewhere: its own paradoxes (self-referential vicious circles, and so on) already produce the "subject", the "unspeakable" . . .

Hegelian dialectics diverges here from the usual criticism according to which analytical philosophy is able to conceive its Beyond only in the negative form of paradoxes and contradictions with which it becomes entangled as soon as it penetrates the domain which is not its own, whereas proper philosophical thought (phenomenology, hermeneutics, and so on) can grasp this Beyond in its own positivity: "*all is already here" in the self-referential paradoxes*; it is the phenomenological etc., positivity which is on the contrary, strictly speaking, secondary – which supplants and conceals the abyss indicated by the paradoxes. The "subject", for example, is *nothing but* the void encircled by the self-relating movement of the signifier – as soon as we conceive it in its positive self-presence, we already misrecognize its proper dimension.

28. *Hegel's Science of Logic*, London: Allen & Unwin 1969, p. 413.

29. Hegel, *Phenomenology of Spirit*, p. 56.

30. Martin Heidegger, *Hegel's Concept of Experience*, New York: Harper & Row 1972.

31. Jacques Lacan, *Le Séminaire, livre XX: Encore*, Paris: Éditions du Seuil 1975, p. 32.

32. This point was articulated in all its philosophical weight by Georg Lukács in his *History and Class Consciousness*, London: NLB 1969.

33. See Chapter 2 above.

34. *Hegel's Science of Logic*, p. 274.

35. See Chapter 6 of Žižek, *The Sublime Object of Ideology*.

36. *Hegel's Science of Logic*, p. 402.

37. We could formulate this difference also through the relation between a Text and its interpretations. Within the logic of external reflection, different interpretations endeavour to approach the Text-in-itself which, however, remains inaccessible and eludes them, whereas we pass into "absolute" reflection when we experience how these interpretations are *part of the Text itself*; how it is not only the reader who, by means of interpretations, looks for the Text's meaning, attempts to penetrate it from an external position, but how, through our interpretations, the Text itself is in a way "in search of itself", reconstructs itself, acquires new dimensions. The "meaning of a Text" is not some hidden kernel, given in advance and waiting to be unearthed; it constitutes itself through the series of its historical "effectualities". To use "deconstructivist" jargon: by means of our reading of the Text, the Text itself reads and (re)writes itself.

38. From here, one should approach anew the Freudian problem of the fetishist disavowal [*Verleugnung*] of castration, following the path opened recently by Elizabeth Cowie (*Sexual Difference and Representation in the Cinema*, London: Macmillan 1991). Disavowal is of course in the first place disavowal of the lack of phallus: the fetishist cannot accept the traumatic fact that woman has no phallus, which is why he clings to the fetish-substitute (with the fundamental ambiguity this implies: by holding the place of the phallus, the fetish simultaneously conceals and points towards its lack). We must, however, go a step further: it is true that the fetishist disavows castration, but the crucial question is: Why is woman's lack of a phallus perceived as "castration" at all, as the lack of something? In other words: whence does the *expectation* arise that we should see a phallus there, since it is only against the background of this expectation that the simple fact of not having it can be perceived as "castration"? Is not, therefore, the very perception of "woman has not got it" as "castration" already a disavowal – a disavowal of the fact that woman, in contrast to man, did not "lose" it, since she never *had* it – in short, the disavowal of sexual difference? That is to say, the perception of "woman has not got it" as "castration" is possible only against the background of the surmise that women "should be like men" – that, in fact, they are "mutilated (castrated) men".

The disavowal in fetishism is thus double. The fetish disavows "castration"; by means of it, we avoid the traumatic experience that "she has not got it". But the very perception of this absence as "castration" is already an interpretation, an interpretation on the basis of the theory that she *should* have it. *The real, ultimate disavowal is therefore "castration" itself* (the experience of the sexual difference as woman's "castration"): the real traumatism is not the loss (of phallus) but the fact that woman *never had* what she "lost". The same formula applies to all experiences of the "Paradise Lost". The very experience of a "traumatic loss" of an idyllic fullness conceals the fact that this state of fullness never existed in the first place – that it "*comes to be* only through being *left behind*". Hegel says this explicitly in his lectures on the philosophy of religion: "Paradise" is strictly correlative to man's Fall, it is a retroactive projection, a way man (mis)perceives the previous, animal state.

There are, of course, two main possible readings of this double disavowal. The usual feminist reading would be to grasp sexual difference outside the category of "loss" – that is, outside the asymmetric logic where one element is the mutilated version of the other (woman is castrated man). Although this possibility sounds very "emancipated", Lacan refuses it: for him, the phallus remains the unique point of reference, the unique signifier of the sexual difference. What he does is simply to grasp "castration" as *symbolic*: he endeavours to locate it as a symbolic, signifying opposition. That is to say, for Lacan, the fact that we perceive the absence of phallus in woman as a lack presupposes the fundamental feature of the symbolic order, its differential character. Only within a differential order can the *absence* of an element *as such* acquire meaning, assume positive value, in so far as it is perceived against the background of the expected presence – in differential opposition to it. (Sometimes, for example, silence is more telling than words: if it appears against the background of expected words.) Lacan draws a radical conclusion: if, in woman, the absence of phallus is perceived as lack, then its presence in man should also be perceived against the background of its possible absence, in symbolic opposition to it – in other words, the very *presence* of phallus signifies *its possible absence*, "castration".

39. As to the notion of "essential appearance", see Žižek, *The Sublime Object of Ideology*, pp. 197–9.

40. Ernesto Laclau and Chantal Mouffe, *Hegemony and Socialist Strategy*, London: Verso 1985.

41. For a reading of this joke different from that proposed here, see Žižek, *The Sublime Object of Ideology*, pp. 160–61.

PART III

Cum Grano Praxis

5

All's Well That Ends Well?

I Why Should a Dialectician Learn to Count to Four?

The triad and its excess

How far must a Hegelian dialectician learn to count? Most of the interpreters of Hegel, not to mention his critics, try to convince us in unison that the right answer reads: to three (the dialectical triad, and so on). Moreover, they vie with each other in who will call our attention more convincingly to the "fourth side", the non-dialecticizable excess, the place of death (of the dummy – in French *le mort* – in bridge), supposedly eluding the dialectical grasp, although (or, more precisely, in so far as) it is the inherent condition of possibility of the dialectical movement: the negativity of a pure expenditure that cannot be sublated [*aufgehoben*], re-collected, in its Result.

Unfortunately, as is the custom with criticism of Hegel, the trouble with Hegel is here the same as the trouble with Harry in Alfred Hitchcock's film of the same title: he does not consent to his burial so easily – on a closer look, it soon becomes obvious that the supposedly annihilating reproach drawn by the critics from their hats actually forms the crucial aspect of the very dialectical movement. That is to say, a careful reader will immediately recall not only numerous particular cases like the four types of judgement from the first part of "subjective logic", but also the fact that Hegel thematizes a quadruplicity proper to the dialectical movement as such: the excess of the pure nothingness of self-relating negativity which vanishes, becomes invisible, in the final Result. In the last chapter of his *Logic*, apropos of the elementary matrix of the dialectical process, he points out that the moments of this process could be counted as three or as four, with the subject as the surplus-moment which "counts for nothing":

> In this turning point of the method, the course of cognition at the same time returns into itself. As self-sublating contradiction this negativity is the *restoration* of the *first immediacy*, of simple universality; for the other of the other, the negative of the negative, is immediately the *positive*, the *identical*, the *universal*. If one insists on *counting*, this *second* immediate is, in the course of the method as a whole, the *third* term to the first immediate and the mediated. It is also, however, the third term to the first or formal negative and to absolute negativity or the second negative; now as the first negative is already the second term, the term reckoned as *third* can also be reckoned as *fourth*, and instead of a *triplicity*, the abstract form may be taken as a *quadruplicity*; in this way, the negative or the difference is counted as a *duality*.[1]

The first moment is the immediate positivity of the starting point; the second moment, its mediation, is not simply its immediate contrary, its external opposite – it comes forth precisely when we endeavour to grasp the first moment, the immediate, *in and for itself, as such*: in this way, we already mediatize it and, imperceptibly, it turns into its own opposite. The second moment is thus not the negative of the first, its otherness; it is the first moment itself as *its own other*, as the negative of itself: as soon as we conceive the abstract-immediate starting point (as soon as we determine the concrete network of its presuppositions and implications, explicate its content), it changes into its own opposite. Even on the most abstract level, "nothingness" is not the external opposite of "being": we arrive at "nothingness" by simply trying to specify, to determine the content of the notion of "being". Herein consists the fundamental dialectical idea of "inner negativity": an entity is negated, passes over into its opposite, as a result of the development of its own potential.

Fascism, to take a worn-out example, is not an external opposite to liberal democracy but has its roots in liberal democracy's own inner antagonisms . . . . This is why negativity must be counted twice: effectively to negate the starting point, we must negate its own "inner negation" in which its content comes to its "truth" (Fascism, although opposed to liberal capitalism, is not its effective negation but only its "inner" negation: effectively to negate liberal capitalism, we must therefore negate its very negation). This second, self-relating negation, this (as Hegel would put it) otherness reflected into itself, is the vanishing point of absolute negativity, of "pure difference" – the paradoxical moment which is *third*, since it is already the *first* moment which "passes over" into its own *other*. What we have here could also be conceptualized as a case of retroactive determination: when opposed to its radical Negative, the first moment itself changes retroactively into its opposite. Capitalism-in-itself is not the same as capitalism-as-opposed-to-Communism: when confronted with the tendencies of its dissolution, capitalism is forced to negate itself "from within" (to pass into Fascism) if it is to survive. This dialectics was articulated by Adorno apropos of the history of music:

> The means and forms of musical composition discovered later concern and change the traditional means and above all the forms of interdependence that they constitute. Every tritone used today by a composer already sounds as the negation of the dissonances liberated in the meantime. It no longer possesses its former immediacy . . . , but is something historically mediated. Therein consists its own opposition. When this opposition, this negation, is passed over in silence, every tritone of this kind, every traditionalist move, becomes an affirmative, convulsively confirming lie, equal to the talking about a happy world customary in the other domains of culture. There is no primordial sense to be re-established in music . . . [2]

Here we have an exemplary case of what structuralism calls "determination-by-absence": after the advent of dissonances, the meaning of the tritone changes, since its further use implies the negation of dissonances – its new meaning results from the way the very *absence* of dissonances *is present* in the use of the tritone. In its immediate presence, the tritone remains the same; its historical mediation is revealed by the fact that *it changes precisely in so far as it remains the same.*[3] Herein consists also the falsity of today's calls for a return to traditional values: in so far as we re-establish them, they are no longer the same, since they legitimize the social order which is their very opposite.[4]

We can see, now, how the supplementary element emerges: as soon as we add to the immediate its negation, this negation retroactively changes the meaning of immediacy, so we must count to three, although what we effectively have are just two elements. Or, if we envisage the complete cycle of the dialectical process, there are just three "positive" moments to count over (the immediacy, its mediation and the final return to the mediated immediacy) – what we lose is the unfathomable surplus of the pure difference which "counts for nothing", although it makes the entire process go, this "void of the substance" which is at the same time the "receptacle" [*Rezeptakulum*] for all and everything", as Hegel put it.

Protestantism, Jacobinism . . .

Such ruminations, however, are of a purely formal nature, in the best tradition of the exasperating abstract reflections on "dialectical method"; what they lack is the inner relatedness to a concrete historical content. As soon as we move to this level, the idea of a fourth surplus-moment as "vanishing mediator" between the second moment (the split, the abstract opposition) and the final Result (reconciliation) immediately acquires concrete contours – one has only to think of the way Fredric Jameson, in his essay on Max Weber,[5] articulates the notion of "vanishing mediator" apropos of Weber's theory of the role of Protestantism in the rise of capitalism. This theory is usually read as (and was also meant by Weber himself to be) a criticism of the Marxist thesis of the primacy of economic infrastructure: ultimately, Weber's point *is* that Protestantism was a condition of capitalism. Jameson, on the contrary, interpretes Weber's theory as fully compatible with Marxism: as the elaboration of the dialectical necessity by means of which, in feudalism's passage into capitalism, the "normal" relationship of "base" and "superstructure" is inverted.

Wherein, *precisely*, consists this dialectical necessity? In other words: how, *specifically*, does Protestantism create conditions for the emergence of capitalism? Not, as one would expect, by limiting the reach of religious ideology, by undermining its all-pervasive presence characteristic of medieval society, but on the contrary by *universalizing* its relevance: Luther was opposed to cloisters and church as an institution apart, separated by a gap from the rest of society, because he wanted the Christian attitude to penetrate and determine our entire secular everyday life. Contrary to the traditional (pre-Protestant) stance which basically limits the relevance of religion to the aims towards which we must tend, while leaving the means – the domain of secular economic activity – to non-religious common judgement, the Protestant "work ethic" conceives the very secular activity (economic acquisitiveness) as the domain of the disclosure of God's Grace.

This shift can be exemplified by the changed place of asceticism: in the traditional Catholic universe, asceticism concerns a stratum of people separated from everyday secular life, devoted to representing in this world its Beyond, the Heaven on Earth (saints, monks with their abstinence); whereas Protestantism requires of every Christian to act ascetically in his secular life – to accumulate wealth instead of spending it thoughtlessly, to live in temperance and modesty – in short: to accomplish his instrumental-economic activity "with God in mind"; asceticism as the affair of a stratum apart thereby becomes superfluous.

This universalization of the Christian stance, the affirmation of its relevance for secular economic activity, generates the attributes of the "Protestant work ethic" (compulsive work and accumulation of wealth – renunciation to consumption – as an end-in-itself); simultaneously, yet unknowingly and unintentionally, following the "cunning of Reason", it opens the way to the devaluation of religion, to its confinement to the intimacy of a private sphere separated from state and public affairs. The Protestant universalization of the Christian stance is thus merely a transitory stage in the passage to the "normal" state of bourgeois society where religion is reduced to "means", to a medium enabling the subject to find new strength and perseverance in the economic fight for survival, like those techniques of "self-experience" which put the encounter of our "true Self" in the service of our "fitness".

It is of course easy to assume an ironic distance towards the Protestant illusion and to point out how the final result of Protestant endeavours to abolish the gap between religion and everyday life was the debasement of religion to a "therapeutic" mean; what is far more difficult is to conceive the *necessity* of Protestantism as the "vanishing mediator" between medieval corporatism and capitalist individualism. In other words, the point not to be missed is that one cannot pass from medieval "closed" society to bourgeois society immediately, without the intercession of Protestantism as "vanishing mediator": it is Protestantism which, by means of its universalization of Christianity, prepares the ground for its withdrawal into the sphere of privacy.

In the political domain, a similar role was played by Jacobinism which can even be determined as "political Protestantism": Jacobinism universalizes the democratic political-ideological project in the same way – it does not grasp it as a mere formal political principle without immediate bearing on economic, family, etc., relations, but endeavours to make the democratic-egalitarian project into a principle structuring the totality of social life. The trap into which Jacobinism fell is also the same: unknowingly, its political radicalism prepared the way for its opposite, for the bourgeois universe of egotistic and acquisitive individuals who care not a pin for egalitarian moralism.

Here, too, it is easy to assume an ironic distance and point out how the Jacobins, by means of their violent reduction of the social totality to the abstract principle of equality, necessarily finished in terrorism, since this reduction is resisted by the ramified network of concrete relations that characterize civil society (see Hegel's classical criticism of the Jacobins in the *Phenomenology of Spirit*); what is far more difficult to accomplish is to demonstrate why no immediate passage was possible from the *ancien régime* to the egotistic bourgeois everyday life – why, precisely because of their illusory reduction of social totality to the democratic political project, the Jacobins were a *necessary* "vanishing mediator" (therein, not in the commonplaces about the utopian-terrorist character of the Jacobinical project, consists the effective point of Hegel's criticism). In other words, it is easy to detect in Jacobinism the roots and the first form of modern "totalitarianism"; it is far more difficult and disquieting to acknowledge and assume fully the fact that, without the Jacobinical "excess", there would be no "normal" pluralist democracy.[6]

That is to say, the illusion into which Protestantism and Jacobinism are enmeshed is more complicated than may seem on a first approach: it does not consist simply in their naive-moralistic universalization of the Christian or egalitarian-democratic project – that is, in their overlooking the concrete wealth of social relations that resist such an immediate universalization. Their illusion is far more radical: it is of the same nature as the illusion of all historically relevant political utopias, the illusion to which Marx drew attention apropos of Plato's *State* when he remarked that Plato did not see how what he effectively described was not a not-yet-realized ideal but the very fundamental structure of the existing Greek state. In other words, utopias are "utopian" not because they depict an "impossible Ideal", a dream not for this world, but because they misrecognize the way their ideal state *is already realized* in its basic content ("in its notion", as Hegel would say).

Protestantism becomes superfluous, it can vanish as a mediator, the moment the very social reality is structured as a "Protestant universe": the notional structure of capitalist civil society is that of a world of atomized individuals defined by the paradox of "acquisitive asceticism" ("the more you possess, the more you must renounce consumption") – that is to say, the structure of the Protestant content without its positive religious form. And it is the same with Jacobinism: what the Jacobins overlooked is the fact that the ideal after which they strove was, in its notional structure, *already realized* in the "dirty" acquisitive activity which appeared to them as the betrayal of their high ideals. Vulgar, egotistic bourgeois everyday life is the actuality of freedom, equality and brotherhood: freedom of free trade, formal equality in the eyes of the law, and so on.

The illusion proper to the "vanishing mediators" – Protestants, Jacobins – is precisely that of the Hegelian "Beautiful Soul": they refuse to acknowledge, in the corrupted reality over which they lament, the ultimate consequence of their own act – as Lacan would put it, their own message in its true, inverted form. And our illusion, as "sobered" inheritors of Protestantism and Jacobinism, is no less: we perceive those "vanishing mediators" as aberrations or excesses, failing to notice how we are nothing but "Jacobins without the Jacobinical form", nothing but "Protestants without the Protestant form".

. . . and other "vanishing mediators"

This gap between the form and its notional content offers us also the key to the necessity of the "vanishing mediator": the passage from feudalism to Protestantism is not of the same nature as the passage from Protestantism to bourgeois everyday life with its privatized religion. The first passage concerns "content" (under the guise of preserving the religious form or even its strengthening, the crucial shift – the assertion of the ascetic-acquisitive stance in economic activity as the domain of the manifestation of Grace – takes place), whereas the second passage is a purely formal act, a change of form (as soon as Protestantism is realized as the ascetic-acquisitive stance, it can fall off as form).

The "vanishing mediator" therefore emerges because of the way, in a dialectical process, form stays behind content: first, the crucial shift occurs within the limits of the old form, even taking on the appearance of its renewed assertion (the universalization of Christianity, return to its "true content", and so on); then, once the "silent weaving of the spirit" finishes its work, the old form can fall off. The double scansion of this process enables us to grasp in a concrete way the worn-out formula of the "negation of negation": the first "negation" consists in the slow, underground, invisible change of substantial content which, paradoxically, takes place *in the name of its own form*; then, once the form has lost its substantial right, it falls to pieces by itself – the very form of negation is negated, or, to use the classic Hegelian couple, the change which took place "in itself" becomes "for itself".

The picture should be complicated even a step further: a closer look reveals the presence of *two* "vanishing mediators" in the passage from feudal to bourgeois political structure: the absolute monarchy and Jacobinism. The first is the sign, the embodiment of a paradoxical compromise: the political form enabling the rising bourgeoisie to strengthen its economic hegemony by breaking the economic power of feudalism, of its guilds and corporations – what is paradoxical about it, of course, is the fact that feudalism "digs its own grave" precisely by absolutizing its own crowning point – by giving absolute power to the monarch; the result of absolute monarchy is thus a political order "disconnected" from its economic foundation. And the same "disconnection" characterizes Jacobinism: it is already a commonplace to determine Jacobinism as a radical ideology which "takes literally" the bourgeois political programme (equality, freedom, brotherhood) and endeavours to realize it irrespective of the concrete articulation of civil society.

Both paid dearly for their illusion: the absolute monarch noticed too late that society praised him as almighty only to allow one class to oust another; the Jacobins also became superfluous once their job of destroying the apparatus of the *ancien régime* was done. Both were carried away by the illusion of the autonomy of the political sphere, both believed in their political mission: one in the unquestionable character of royal authority, the other in the pertinence of its political project. And could not the same be said , on another level, for Fascism and Communism, viz. "actually existing socialism"? Is not Fascism a kind of inherent self-negation of capitalism, an attempt to "change something so that nothing really changes" by means of an ideology which subordinates the economy to the ideological-political domain? Is not the Leninist "actually existing socialism" a kind of "socialist Jacobinism", an attempt to subordinate the whole of socioeconomic life to the immediate political regulation of the socialist state? Both are "vanishing mediators", but into what? The usual cynical answer, "from capitalism back to capitalism", seems a little bit too easy . . .

The inversion of the "normal" relationship of "content" ("economic basis") and its ideological "form" which renders possible the anti-Marxist reading of Weber consists therefore in the above-described "emancipation" of form from its content that characterizes the "vanishing mediator": the break of Protestantism with the medieval church does not "reflect" new social content, but is rather *the criticism of the old feudal content in the name of the radicalized version of its own ideological form*; it is this "emancipation" of the Christian form from its own social content that opens up the space for the gradual transformation of the old into the new (capitalist) content. It is easy for Jameson thus to demonstrate how Weber's theory of the crucial role of Protestantism in the emergence of capitalism affects only vulgar economism and is quite compatible with the *dialectic* of "base" and ideological "superstructure" according to which one passes from one social formation to another through a "vanishing mediator" which *inverts* the relationship between "base" and "superstructure": by emancipating itself from its own "base", the old "superstructure" prepares the terrain for the transformation of the "base". The classical Marxist theoretical edifice is thus saved, the "emancipation" of the ideological form is explained from the inner antagonism of the "base" itself: it emerges when these antagonisms become so violent that they can no longer be legitimized by their own ideological form.

There is an inherent *tragical* ethical dimension proper to this "emancipation" of the ideological superstructure: it presents a unique point at which an ideology "takes itself literally" and ceases to function as an "objectively cynical" (Marx) legitimization of the existing power relations. Let us mention another, more contemporary case: the "new social movements" that emerged during the last years of "actually existing socialism" in Eastern Europe, movements whose exemplary representative is *Neues Forum* in the former GDR: groups of passionate intellectuals who "took socialism seriously" and were prepared to stake everything in order to destroy the compromised system and replace it with the utopian "third way" beyond capitalism and "actually existing" socialism. Their sincere belief and insistence that they were not working for the restoration of Western capitalism of course proved to be nothing but an insubstantial illusion; however, we could say that precisely as such (as a thorough illusion without substance) it was strictly speaking *non-ideological*: it did not "reflect" in inverted-ideological form any actual relations of power.

At this point, we should correct the Marxist Vulgate: contrary to the commonplace according to which an ideology becomes "cynical" (accepts the gap between "words" and "acts", doesn't "believe in itself" any more, is no longer experienced as truth but treats itself as pure instrumental means of legitimizing power) in the period of the "decadence" of a social formation, it could be said that precisely the period of "decadence" opens up to the ruling ideology the possibility of "taking itself seriously" and effectively opposing itself to its own social base (with Protestantism, the Christian religion opposes feudalism as its social base, just as *Neues Forum* opposes the existing socialism in the name of "true socialism"). In this way, unknowingly, it unchains the forces of its own final destruction: once their job is done, they are "overrun by history" (*Neues Forum* polled 3 per cent at the elections) and a new "scoundrel time" sets in, with people in power who were mostly silent during the Communist repression and who none the less now abuse *Neues Forum* as "crypto-Communists" . . .

"A beat of your finger . . . "

Is, however, this reading whereby the "vanishing mediator" effectively appears as just a mediator, an intermediate figure between two "normal" states of things, the only one possible? The conceptual apparatus elaborated by "post-Marxist" political theory (Claude Lefort, Ernesto Laclau) allows for another reading which radically shifts the perspective. Within this field, the moment of "vanishing mediator" is the moment defined by Alain Badiou[7] as that of the "event" in relation to the established structure: the moment when its "truth" emerges, the moment of "openness" which, once the eruption of the "event" is institutionalized into a new positivity, is lost or, more precisely, becomes literally *invisible*.

According to the well-known commonplace (which, contrary to the usual pattern, is not a stupidity clothed as wisdom), "after the fact", backwards, History can always be read as a process governed by laws; as a meaningful succession of stages; however, in so far as we are its agents, embedded, caught in the process, the situation appears – at least during the turning points when "something is happening" –

open, undecidable, far from the exposition of an underlying necessity: we find ourselves confronted with responsibility, the burden of decision pressing upon our shoulders.

Let us just recall the October Revolution: retroactively, it is easy to locate it within the wider historical process, to show how it emerged out of the specific situation of Russia with its failed modernization and simultaneous presence of "islands of modernity" (highly developed working class in isolated places) – in short, it is not too difficult to compose a sociological treatise on this theme. However, it is sufficient to reread the passionate polemics between Lenin, Trotsky, the Mensheviks and other participants to find oneself face to face with what is lost in such an "objective" historical account: the burden of decision in a situation which, so to speak, *forced* the agents to invent new solutions and make unheard-of moves without any guarantee in "general laws of historical development".

This "impossible" moment of openness constitutes the moment of *subjectivity*: "subject" is a name for that unfathomable X called upon, suddenly made accountable, thrown into a position of responsibility, into the urgency of decision in such a moment of undecidability. This is the way one has to read Hegel's proposition that the True is to be grasped "not only as *Substance*, but equally as *Subject*":[8] not only as an objective process governed by some hidden rational Necessity (even if this necessity assumes the Hegelian shape of the "cunning of Reason") but also as a process punctuated, scanned by the moments of openness/undecidability when the subject's irreducibly contingent *act* establishes a new Necessity.

According to a well-known doxa, the dialectical approach enables us to penetrate the surface play of contingencies and reach the underlying rational necessity which "runs the show" behind the subject's back. A proper Hegelian dialectical move is almost the exact inversion of this procedure: it disperses the fetish of "objective historical process" and allows us to see its genesis: the way the very historical Necessity sprang up as a positivization, as a "coagulation" of a radically contingent *decision* of the subjects in an open, undecidable situation. "Dialectical Necessity" is always, by definition, a necessity *après coup*: a proper dialectical account calls into question the self-evidence of "what actually took place" and confronts it with what did *not* take place – that is, it considers what did not happen (a series of missed opportunities, of "alternative histories") a constituent part of what "effectively happened". The dialectical attitude towards the problematic of the "possible worlds" is therefore more paradoxical than it may seem: since what goes on now, in our reality, is the result of a series of radically contingent acts, the only way to define our actual world properly is to include in its definition the negation of the "possible worlds" contained in its position – our lost opportunities are part of what we are, they *qualify* it (in all meanings of the word).

Yet our horizon of reading the past is determined by the contingent acts we made and which enforce the retroactive illusion of Necessity; for this reason, it is impossible for us to occupy a neutral position of pure metalanguage from which we could overview all the "possible worlds". This means that, since the only way to define our own, actual world is in terms of its negative relationship to its alternatives, we cannot ever determine the world we actually live in. In other words, to carry the paradox to its extreme: of course, only one world was really possible, namely the one in which we actually live, but since the position of a neutral observer is not accessible to us, *we don't know which this world is*; we don't know in which of the "possible worlds" we actually live. The point is not that "we will never learn what opportunities we *lost*", but rather that we will never really know what we have *got*. Extreme as this position may appear, is it not discernible in the everyday phrase we use to designate somebody who is unaware of how lucky he was to miss a series of possible catastrophes: "he doesn't know his own luck"? If "dialectics" does not *also* mean this, then all the talk about "Substance as Subject" is ultimately null and we are back at Reason as substantial Necessity pulling the strings behind the stage . . .

It is against this background that we must conceive Hegel's thesis on "positing of presuppositions": this retroactive positing is precisely the way Necessity arises out of contingency. The moment when the subject "posits his presuppositions" is the very moment of his effacement as subject, *the moment he vanishes as a mediator*: the moment of closure when the subject's act of decision changes into its opposite; establishes a new symbolic network by means of which History again acquires the self-evidence of a linear evolution. Let us return to the October Revolution: its "presuppositions" were "posited" when, after its victory and the consolidation of the new power, the openness of the situation was again lost – when it was again possible to assume the position of an "objective observer" and narrate the linear progression of events, ascertaining how Soviet power broke the imperialist chain at its weakest link and thus started a new epoch of World

History, and so on. In this strict sense, the subject is a "vanishing mediator": its act succeeds by becoming invisible – by "positivizing" itself in a new symbolic network wherein it locates and explains itself as a result of historical process, thus reducing itself to a mere moment of the totality engendered by its own act. Witness the Stalinist position of pure metalanguage where (contrary to the commonplaces about "proletarian science", etc.) the very engagement of Marxist theory on the side of the proletariat, its "partisanship", its "taking sides", is not conceived as something *inherent* to the theory as such – Marxists did not speak *from* the subjective position of the proletariat, they "based their orientation on" the proletariat from an external, neutral, "objective" position:

> In the eighties of the past century, in the period of the struggle between the Marxists and the Narodniks, the proletariat in Russia constituted an insignificant minority of the population, whereas the individual peasants constituted the vast majority of the population. But the proletariat was developing as a class, whereas the peasantry as a class was disintegrating. And just because the proletariat was developing as a class the Marxists based their orientation on the proletariat. And they were not mistaken, for, as we know, the proletariat subsequently grew from an insignificant force into a first-rate historical and political force.[9]

The crucial question to be asked here, of course, is: at the time of their struggle againts the Narodniks, *where did the Marxists speak from* to be subject to mistake in their choice of the proletariat as the basis of their orientation? Obviously from an external point encompassing the historical process as a field of objective forces, where one must "be careful not to be mistaken", and "be guided by just forces" – those that will win: in short, where one must "bet on the right horse".

Read this way – that is, retroactively – the decision on how to act *follows* the "objective" evaluation: first, we view the situation from a neutral, "objective" position; then, after ascertaining which are the forces likely to win, we decide to "base our orientation on them" . . . . This retroactive narration, however, falls prey to a kind of illusion of perspective: it misrecognizes the crucial fact that "the true reason for deciding only becomes apparent once the decision has been taken".[10] In other words, reasons for "basing our orientation on" the proletariat become apparent only to those who *already speak from the proletarian subjective position* – or, as perspicacious theologians would put it, of course there are good reasons to believe in Jesus Christ, but these reasons are fully comprehensible only to those who already believe in him. And the same goes also for the famous Leninist theory of the "weakest link" in the chain of Imperialism: one does not first ascertain via an objective approach which is this weakest link and then take the decision to strike at this point – the very act of decision *defines* the "weakest link". This is what Lacan calls *act*: a move that, so to speak, *defines its own conditions*; retroactively produces grounds which justify it:

> What is impossible for [those who count on an objective appraisal of conditions] is that a gesture could create conditions which, retroactively, justify it and make it appropriate. It is, however, attested that this is what happens and that the aim is not to see [things correctly], but to blind oneself sufficiently to be able to strike the right way, i.e. the way that disperses.[11]

The act is thus "performative" in a way which exceeds the "speech act": its performativity is "retroactive": it redefines the network of its own presuppositions. This "excess" of the act's retroactive performativity can also be formulated in the terms of the Hegelian dialectics of Law and its transgression, Crime: from the perspective of the existing, positive Laws of a symbolic community, an act appears by definition as Crime, since it violates its symbolic limits and introduces an unheard-of element which turns everything topsy-turvy – there is neither rhyme nor reason in an act; an act is by its very nature scandalous, as was the very appearance of Christ in the eyes of the keepers of the existing Law – that is, before Christ was "Christianized", made part of the new Law of Christian Tradition. And the dialectical genesis renders visible again the "scandalous" origins of the existing Law – let us just recall again Chesterton's perspicacious remark about how the detective story

> keeps in some sense before the mind the fact that civilization itself is the most sensational of departures and the most romantic of rebellions. . . . It is based on the fact that morality is the most dark and daring of conspiracies.[12]

The dialectical approach brings to the light of day this forgotten reverse of Law: the way Law itself coincides with supreme criminal transgression. And an act "succeeds" the moment it "sutures" anew its own past, its own conditions, effacing its "scandalous" character – the act is the emergence of a new master-signifier, that supplementary "beat of your finger" which, miraculously, changes the previous chaos into "new harmony":

> A beat of your finger on the drum discharges the sounds and
> begins the new harmony.
> A step by you, and new men arise and set on their march.
> Your head turns away: the new love! Your head turns back:
> the new love!
> (Rimbaud, *A une raison*)

What is lost after the onset of the "new harmony" is the radically contingent, "scandalous", abyssal character of the new Master-Signifier – witness, for example, the transformation of Lenin into a wise figure who "saw it all and foresaw it all", Stalinism included, within the Leninist hagiography. This is why it is only today, after the breakdown of Leninism, that it becomes possible to approach Lenin as an actor in the historical drama, capable of making unforeseen moves that were, as Leszek Kolakowski put it so succinctly, the right mistakes at the right time.[13]

Why is Truth always political?

This notion of the act immediately bears on the relationship between Social and Political – on the difference between "the Political" and "politics", as elaborated by Lefort[14] and Laclau:[15] the difference between "politics" as a separate social complex, a positively determined sub-system of social relations in interaction with other sub-systems (economy, forms of culture . . .) and the "Political" [*le Politique*] as the moment of openness, of undecidability, when the very structuring principle of society, the fundamental form of the social pact, is called into question – in short, the moment of global crisis overcome by the act of founding a "new harmony". The "political" dimension is thus *doubly inscribed*: it is a moment of the social Whole, one among its sub-systems, *and* the very terrain in which the fate of the Whole is decided – in which the new Pact is designed and concluded.[16]

In social theory, one usually conceives the political dimension as secondary in relation to the Social as such: in positivist sociology, as a sub-system by means of which society organizes its self-regulation; in classical Marxism, as the separate sphere of alienated Universality which results from society's class division (with the underlying implication that a classless society would entail the end of the Political as a separate sphere); even in the ideology of some of the "new social movements", the Political is delimited as the domain of State Power against which civil society must organize its self-defensive regulatory mechanisms. Against these notions, one could risk the hypothesis that the very genesis of society is always "political": a positively existing social system is nothing but a form in which the negativity of a radically contingent Decision assumes positive, determinate existence.

It was no accident that the Jacobins, those "vanishing mediators" *par excellence*, "absolutized the political"; the reproach that they failed because they wanted to make of politics, one of the social sub-systems, the structuring principle of the entire social edifice overlooks the crucial fact that with the Jacobins, the political dimension was not one sub-system among many but designated the emergence of a radical negativity rendering possible a new foundation of the social fabric – *they vanished not because of their weakness but because of their very success* – that is, when their work was accomplished.

In more "semiotic" terms, we could say that politics as sub-system is a *metaphor* of the political subject, of the Political as subject: the element which, within the constituted social space, holds the place of the Political as negativity which suspends it and founds it anew. In other words, "politics" as "sub-system", as a separate sphere of society, represents *within* society its own forgotten foundation, its genesis in a violent, abyssal act – it represents, within the social space, what must *fall out* if this space is to constitute itself. Here, we can easily recognize the Lacanian definition of the signifier (that which "represents the subject for another signifier"): politics as sub-system represents the Political (subject) for all other social sub-systems. This is why positivist sociologists desperately attempt to convince us that politics is just a sub-system: it is as if the very desperate and urgent tone of this persuasion echoes an imminent danger of "explosion" whereby politics would again "be all" – change into "political". There is an unmistakable *normative* undertone to this persuasion, bestowing on it an air of conjuration: it *must remain* a mere sub-system . . .

What is at stake in the two possible readings of the paradox of "vanishing mediator" is therefore the very status of social antagonism viz. negativity: is the emergence of negativity in the social space a mere intermediary in the passage from one form of positivity to another, the "exception" that characterizes the transition from one "normality" to another, or is this very "normality" nothing but the aftermath, the "gentrification" of a forgotten excess of negativity? The second solution reverses the entire perspective: the stable network of "sub-systems" is the very form of hegemony of one pole in the social antagonism, the "class peace" the very index of the hegemony of one class in the class struggle . . . . What is lost once the network of "sub-systems" is stabilized – that is to say, once the "new harmony" is established, once the new Order "posits its presuppositions", "sutures" its field – is the *metaphoricity* of the element which represents its genesis: this element is reduced to being "one among the others"; it loses its character of *One which holds the place of Nothing* (of radical negativity).

Now we can return to the notorious Hegelian triad: the subject is this "vanishing mediator", the fourth moment which, so to speak, enacts its own disappearance; whose disappearance is the very measure of its "success", the void of self-relating negativity which becomes invisible once we look at the process "backwards", from its Result. The consideration of this excessive fourth moment at work in the Hegelian triad enables us to read it against the background of the Greimasian "semiotic square":

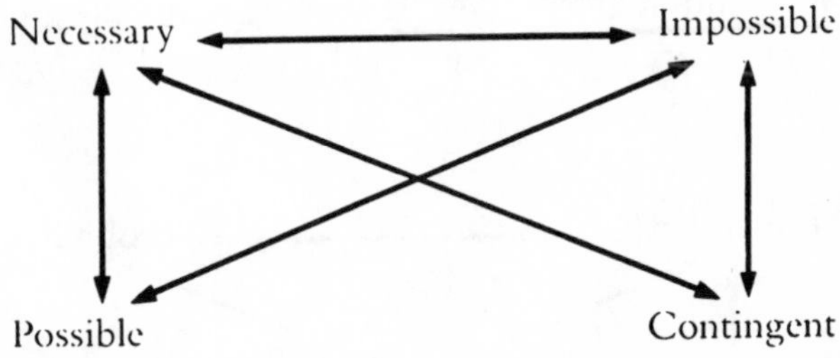

The opposition of necessity and impossibility dissolves itself into the domain of possibility (possibility is, so to speak, the "negation of negation" of necessity) – what disappears therewith is the fourth term, the Contingent which is in no way equal to Possible: there is always something of an "encounter with the Real" in contingency, something of the violent emergence of an unheard-of entity that defies the limits of the established field of what one holds for "possible", whereas "possible" is, so to speak, a "gentrified", pacified contingency, a contingency with its sting plucked out.

In psychoanalysis, for example, *truth* belongs to the order of contingency:[17] we vegetate in our everyday life, deep into the universal Lie that structures it, when, all of a sudden, some totally contingent encounter – a casual remark by a friend, an incident we witness – evokes the memory of an old repressed trauma and shatters our self-delusion. Psychoanalysis is here radically anti-Platonic: the Universal is the domain of Falsity *par excellence*, whereas truth emerges as a particular contingent encounter which renders visible its "repressed".[18] The dimension lost in "possibility" is precisely this traumatic, unwarranted character of the emergence of truth: when a truth becomes "possible", it loses the character of an "event", it changes into a mere factual accuracy and thereby becomes part of the ruling universal Lie.[19]

We can see, now, how far Lacanian psychoanalysis is from the pluralist-pragmatic "liberalism" of the Rortyan kind: Lacan's final lesson is not relativity and plurality of truths but the hard, traumatic fact that in every concrete constellation *truth is bound to emerge* in some contingent detail. In other words, although truth is context-dependent – although there is no truth in general, but always the truth *of* some situation – there is none the less in every plural field a particular point which articulates its truth and as such *cannot* be relativized; in this precise sense, truth is always *One*. What we are aiming at here comes to light more clearly if we replace the "ontological" square with the "deontological" one:

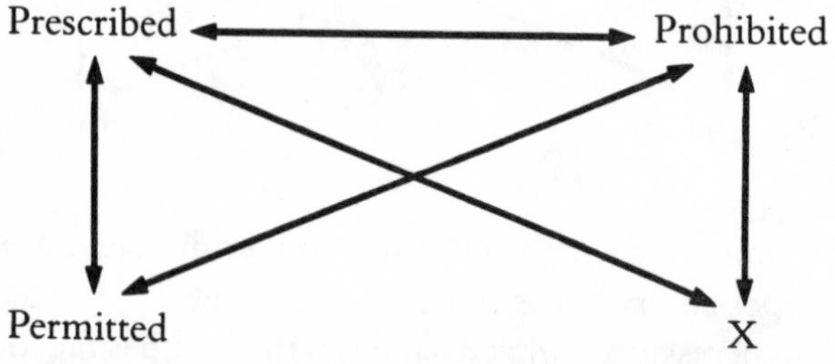

We even lack an appropriate term for this X, for the strange status of what is "not prescribed", "facultative", and yet not simply "permitted" – like, for example, the emergence of some hitherto forbidden knowledge in the psychoanalytic cure which holds up to ridicule the Prohibition, lays bare its hidden mechanism, without thereby changing into a neutral "permissiveness". The difference between the two pertains to the different relationship towards the universal Order: "permissiveness" is warranted by it, whereas this guarantee lacks in the case of "you may . . . " which Lacan designates as *scilicet*: you may know (the truth about your desire) – if you take the risk upon yourself. This *scilicet* is perhaps the ultimate recourse of the critical thought.

II The "Missing Link" of Ideology

The self-referring structure and its void

The basic paradox of the psychoanalytic notion of fantasy consists in a kind of time loop – the "original fantasy" is always the fantasy of the origins – that is to say, the elementary skeleton of the fantasy-scene is for the subject to be present as a pure gaze before its own conception or, more precisely, at the very act of its own conception. The Lacanian formula of fantasy ($\$ \diamond a$) denotes such a paradoxical conjunction of the subject and the object *qua* this impossible gaze: the "object" of fantasy is not the fantasy-scene itself, its content (the parental coitus, for example), but the impossible gaze witnessing it.

To exemplify the "travel in the past" constituent of the fantasy-constellation, let us just recall the famous scene from David Lynch's *Blue Velvet* in which the hero watches through a fissure in the closet door the sadomasochistic sexual play between Isabella Rossellini and Denis Hopper, games in which Hopper relates to Rossellini alternately as his mother and his daughter. This game is the "subject", the topic, the content of the fantasy, whereas its object is the hero himself reduced to the presence of a pure gaze.[20] The basic paradox of the fantasy consists precisely in this "nonsensical" temporal short circuit whereby the subject *qua* pure gaze so to speak *precedes itself* and witnesses its own origin.

A classical example is found in Mary Shelley's *Frankenstein*, where the most terrifying scenes depict Dr Frankenstein and his bride in their moments of greatest intimacy when, suddenly, they become aware that they are being watched by the artificially created monster (their "child"), a mute witness of its own conception: "It is therein that consists the enunciated of the fantasy which impregnates the text of *Frankenstein*: to be the gaze which reflects the enjoyment of one's own parents, a mortal enjoyment."[21]

Whence comes the tremendous impact of such a fantasy-scene? In other (and more precise) words: why does the subject supplant its lack of being (its "want to be") by means of such an impossible gaze? One has to look for the key to this enigma in the asymmetry between synchrony and diachrony: the very emergence of a synchronous symbolic order implies a gap, a discontinuity in the diachronous causal chain that led to it, a "missing link" in the chain. Fantasy is an *a contrario* proof that the status of the subject is that of a "missing link", of a void which, within the synchronous set, holds the place of its foreclosed diachronous genesis. The incompleteness of the linear causal chain is, consequently, a positive condition for the "subject-effect" to take place: if we were able to explain without remainder the advent of the subject from the positivity of some natural (or spiritual) process – to reconstruct the complete causal chain that led to its emergence – "subject" itself would be cancelled. The gap, the incompatibility between cause and effect, is therefore irreducible, since it is *constitutive of the very effect*: the moment we re-establish the complete chain of causes, we lose their effect.

In other words, the status of the "missing link" is not only epistemological but primarily ontological. The point is not to play the game of idealist obscurantism and preach the "inscrutable mystery of Man's origins", while simultaneously warning against curiosity that drives us to stir up this forbidden domain (by means of biogenetic experiments, etc.) in accordance with the paradoxical formula of prohibition of the impossible (it is *impossible* to penetrate the origins of Man, which is why one is *prohibited* from engaging in such research, for fear that one would discover too much and thus open the way to horrifying genetic, etc., manipulations). In its very being, the subject is constituted as the "missing link" of a causal chain – the chain in which no link is missing is the positivity of a substance without subject: "substance is subject" means that there is always a link missing in the substantial chain.

Abstract as they may sound, these propositions directly concern our most concrete phenomenological relationship towards the other: we can *recognize* the other, *acknowledge* him as person, only in so far as, in a radical sense, he remains *unknown* to us – *re*cognition implies the absence of *cognition*. A neighbour totally transparent and disclosed is no more a "person", we no longer relate to him as to another person: intersubjectivity is founded upon the fact that the other is phenomenologically experienced as an "unknown quantity", as a bottomless abyss which we can never fathom. The Lacanian "big Other" is usually conceived as the impersonal symbolic order, the structure that regulates symbolic exchanges; what is forgotten thereby is the crucial fact that the big Other (as opposed to the "small other" of the imaginary mirror-relationship) was first introduced to designate the radical alterity of the other person beyond our mirroring in it, beyond our recognition of it as our mirror-image. That is to say, in his *Seminar III*, Lacan put the reason for introducing the Other as follows:

> And why with a capital A [for *Autre*]? For a no doubt mad reason, in the same way as it is madness every time we are obliged to bring in signs supplementary to those given by language. Here the mad reason is the following. *You* are my *wife* – after all, what do you know about it? *You are my master* – in reality, are you so sure of that? What creates the founding value of those words is that what is aimed at in the message, as well as what is manifest in the pretence, is that the other is there *qua* absolute Other. Absolute, that is to say he is recognized, but is not known. In the same way, what constitutes pretence is that, in the end, you don't know whether it's a pretence or not. Essentially it is this unknown element in the alterity of the other which characterizes the speech relation on the level on which it is spoken to the other.[22]

In other words, our engagement, our commitment to the other and the other's engagement towards us, make sense only against the background of this absolute unknowableness: in so far as the other is perfectly known and disclosed, there is no sense in committing him to an action – what we encounter here is the "agnostic" foundation of language *qua* the order of symbolic engagement. The word given *engages* precisely because there is no factual guarantee that it will be *kept*.

From what we have just said, there is an inevitable, albeit surprising, conclusion to be drawn: the ultimate paradigm of the unknowable Thing, of its absolute alterity, is man himself, our neighbour – the other as person. Nature is simply unknown, its unknowableness is epistemological, whereas the Other *qua* another person is ontologically unknowable; its unknowableness is the way its very being is ontologically constituted, disclosed to us. Freud already had a presentiment of this when he wrote about a "foreign kernel" [*fremdes Kern*] in the very midst of our neighbour [*Nebenmensch*]: the Kantian unknowable "Thing-in-itself" is ultimately man himself.

Lacan baptized this subject *qua* "missing link" the "subject of the signifier": the signifying structure is defined by a central void (the "missing link") around which it is organized – it is precisely the *articulation of its void* (and, in *this* sense, the representation of the subject). The well-known structuralist principle of "priority of synchrony over diachrony" is ultimately nothing but the positive reverse of this impossibility of reaching its own origins that is constitutive of the symbolic structure: language as differential system turns in a kind of vicious circle, it so to speak endeavours to catch its own tail; it constitutes an abyss without any external point of reference serving as a support to it; each of its elements refers to all others, it "is" only its difference towards them, which is why it is a priori impossible to explain it "genetically" – language functions as a closed, involute circle which always-already presupposes itself. In other words, language emerges by definition *ex nihilo*: suddenly, it is "all here", suddenly, "everything has meaning".

This is what the "arbitrariness of the signifier" means: not the fact that we can "compare" from outside words and things and ascertain that their connection is arbitrary (table is called "table" or "*Tisch*" or . . .), but quite on the contrary the very *impossibility* of assuming such an external position from which we could "compare" words and things. Words mean what they mean only with regard to their place in the totality of language; this totality determines and structures the very horizon within which reality is disclosed to us; within which we can eventually "compare" individual words with things.

Recent analytical philosophy has arrived at the same result:[23] we can, of course, compare individual propositions with "reality" and ascertain their "correspondence" to the described state of things; it would, however, be an illusion to think that thereby we found a kind of immediate contact, a passage from "language" to "reality", a point at which words are directly "hooked" on to things – such an ascertaining of "correspondence" is, on the contrary, possible only within the already established global field of language. I can, of course, "compare" the proposition "There is a table in the room next door" with the factual state of things and thus ascertain its accuracy, but such a procedure already relies on the language-totality for the very meaning of the proposition "There is a table in the room next door".[24]

The very idea of a synchronous circular order therefore implies a gap, a discontinuity in its genesis: the synchronous "structure" can never be deduced from a diachronous "process" without committing a *petitio principii*. All of a sudden, by means of a miraculous leap, we find ourselves within a closed synchronous order which does not allow of any external support since it turns in its own vicious circle. This lack of support because of which language ultimately refers only to itself – in other words: this void that language encircles in its self-referring – *is* the subject as "missing link". *The "autonomy of the signifier" is strictly correlative to the "subjectivization" of the signifying chain*: "subjects" are not the "effective" presence of "flesh-and-blood" agents that make use of language as part of their social life-practice, filling out the abstract language schemes with actual content; "subject" is, on the contrary, the very abyss that forever *separates* language from the substantial life-process.

It is for this reason that the classical criticism of structural linguistics that reproaches it with treating language "idealistically", as an autonomous ideal order of differential relations – that is, with overlooking the way language is actual only as moment of a definite "life-form", embedded in the texture of concrete practices – misses the point completely: if we could reduce language to a moment of supralinguistic "life-form", the very "effect of meaning"ˣ would be lost, and with it the subjectivity that pertains to it.[25] The crucial point here is, again, that the self-referring vicious circle of a language-totality – the fact that the way it relates to "supralinguistic reality" is already overdetermined by language itself – functions as its positive ontological condition: far from displaying a kind of "default" to be compensated by means of a "concrete analysis" of the role of language within the totality of social practices or by means of a genetic presentation of the emergence of language from animal expressive behaviour, this vicious circle opens up the very space of meaning. In other words, the barrier separating the Symbolic from the Real is impossible to trespass, since the Symbolic *is* this very barrier.

What characterizes the symbolic order is the specific mode of causality, namely *retroactive* causality: positive, "substantial" causality runs in a linear-progressive way, the cause precedes its effect; whereas in the symbolic order "time runs backwards"; the "symbolic

ˣ the effect of meaning is a subjectivity – the latter creates the former – this dialectic is more ontological in nature than epistemological efficiency" (to borrow this expression from Claude Lévi-Strauss) consists in a continuous "rewriting of its own past", in including past signifying traces in new contexts which retroactively change their meaning. The most famous case of such retroactive causality within the field of psychoanalysis is of course that of the "Wolf Man", Freud's Russian analysand who as a child witnessed the parental *coitus a tergo*: all his later symptom-formations were nothing but so many endeavours to integrate this primal scene into the present, synchronous symbolic network, to confer meaning upon it and thus to contain its traumatic impact – or, to use Lacan's terminology from the 1950s, to locate it within the dimension of truth, to "realize it in the Symbolic". The originality of Lacan's reading of the Freudian notion of "deferred action" [*Nachträglichkeit*] specific to neurotic causality is precisely to link it with the motive of the "priority of synchrony over diachrony": what was originally a meaningless event later, retroactively, acquires meaningful impact, since it is only later that the traces of this event are included in a symbolic network that gives it its meaning. Psychoanalysis is therefore not concerned with the past "as such", in its factual purity, but in the way past events are included in the present, synchronous field of meaning – in other words, the proper dimension of psychoanalysis is not that of "reality" but that of "truth":

> It is not a question of reality in psychoanalytic anamnesis, but of truth, because it is the effect of full speech to reorder past contingencies in giving them the meaning of necessities to come, such that the little bit of freedom through which the subject makes them present constitutes them.[26]

In short: the true, the past (long-forgotten traumatic encounters) does determine the present, but the very mode of this determining is *overdetermined* by the present synchronous symbolic network. If the trace of an old encounter all of a sudden begins to exert impact, it is because the *present* symbolic universe of the subject is structured in a way that is susceptible to it.

Let us just recall the logic of artistic trends: when, for example, towards the end of the eighteenth century, the historical interest shifted from classicism to Shakespeare, when Shakespeare was suddenly "rediscovered", it is not appropriate to say that he "began to exert renewed influence" – the crucial event is the inner shift in the then "spirit of the age" so that suddenly it became susceptible to Shakespeare: the way it became possible to take cognizance of *present* traumas and antagonisms by means of reference to Shakespeare. What we must be careful not to overlook here is how *this retroactive causality, this symbolic "rewriting of the past", is inherently linked to the problematic of the "missing link"*: it is precisely because the chain of linear causality is always broken, because language as synchronous order is caught in a vicious circle, that it attempts to restore the "missing link" by retroactively reorganizing its past, by reconstituting its origins backwards. In other words, the very fact of incessant "rewriting of the past" attests to the presence of a certain gap, to the efficacy of a certain traumatic, foreign kernel that the system is trying to reintegrate "after the fact". If the passage from "genesis" into "structure" were to be continuous, there would be no inversion of the direction of causality: it is the "missing link" which opens the space for reordering the past.

Narrating the origins

Now we can return to our initial question concerning the function of the fantasy-object: this object as gaze fills out a void constitutive of the symbolic order, its vicious circle; it serves to obscure the fact that any given field of symbolically structured meaning in a way always presupposes and precedes itself. Once we are *within* a field of meaning, it is by definition impossible to adopt an external attitude towards it; there is no continuous passage from its outside to its inside – as Althusser put it, ideology has no outside. The hidden chasm of this vicious circle appears at its purest under the guise of *tautology*: "law is law", "God is God". Even a refined everyday sensitivity renders manifest the way such tautologies function: precisely in the Hegelian sense, as identity-with-itself which reveals the supreme contradiction. Does not the statement "God is God" forebode His ominous reverse: the first God ("God is . . . ") is the God of tranquillity, grace, and love, while the second God (" . . . God") is the God of an ungovernable rage and cruelty. And is it not the same with the tautology "law is law" – does it not display the illegal and illegitimate character of the very foundation of the reign of law? Blaise Pascal was probably the first to detect this subversive dimension of the tautology "law is law":

> Custom is the whole of equity for the sole reason that it is accepted. That is the mystic basis of its authority. Anyone who tries to bring it back to its first principle destroys it. Nothing is so defective as those laws which

x filmic realism

> correct defects. Anyone obeying them because they are just is obeying an imaginary justice, not the essence of law, which is completely self-contained: it is law and nothing more. . . . That is why the wisest of legislators used to say that men must often be deceived for their own good, and another sound politician: *When he asks about the truth that is to bring him freedom, it is a good thing that he should be deceived.* The truth about the usurpation must not be made apparent; it came about originally without reason and has become reasonable. We must see that it is regarded as authentic and eternal, and its origins must be hidden if we do not want it soon to end.[27]

It is almost superfluous to point out the scandalous character of these propositions: they undermine the foundations of power, of its authority, at the very moment when they give the impression of supporting them. "At the beginning" of the law, there is a certain "outlaw", a certain Real of violence which coincides with the act itself of the establishment of the reign of law: the ultimate truth about the reign of law is that of an usurpation, and all classical politico-philosophical thought rests on the disavowal of this violent act of foundation. The illegitimate violence by which law sustains itself must be concealed at any price, because this concealment is the positive condition of the functioning of law: it functions in so far as its subjects are deceived, in so far as they experience the authority of law as "authentic and eternal" and overlook "the truth about the usurpation".

This truth re-emerges in those rare moments in which philosophical reflection touches its limits – in Kant's *Metaphysics of Mores*, for example, where he expressly forbids probing into the obscure origins of legal power: through precisely such questioning the stain of illegitimate violence would appear which always soils, like some kind of original sin, the purity of the reign of law. It is not surprising, then, that this prohibition again assumes the paradoxical form well known in psychoanalysis: it *forbids* something which is already in itself posited as *impossible*:

> The origin of the supreme power, for all practical purposes, is *not discoverable* by the people who are subject to it. In other words, the subject *ought not* to indulge in *speculations* about its origin with a view to acting upon them . . . these are *completely futile* arguments for a people which is already subject to civil law, and they constitute a *menace* to the state.[28]

> It is *futile* to hunt for historical documentation of the origins of this mechanism. That is, we *cannot* reach back to the time at which civil society first emerged. . . . But it would be *quite culpable* to undertake such researches with a view to forcibly changing the constitution at present in existence.[29]

What we have here is a kind of ironic reversal of Kant's own famous ethical dictum "*Du kannst, denn du sollst!*" (You can because you must!): you cannot arrive at the obscure origins of the law, of the legitimate order, because you must not do it! That is to say, Kant formally prohibits the exploration of the origins of the legitimate order; arguing that such an exploration a priori puts us outside the legitimate order; it cancels its own validity by making it dependent on historico-empirical circumstances: we cannot at one and the same time assume the historical origins of the law in some lawless violence *and* remain its subjects. As soon as the law is reduced to its lawless origins, its full validity is suspended.

It is similar with the search for the historical origins of Christianity. True, we can explore Christianity as a "historical phenomenon", we can endeavour to explain it on the basis of social processes, and so on; but the point is that *we cannot do it as Christians*, because we thereby lose access to the Christian field of meaning. The mechanism of this closed loop is exposed in Bosch's famous depiction of the Crucifixion, where one of the two thieves executed together with Jesus Christ confesses before his death to a priest holding a Bible under his arm. This nonsensical short circuit exceeds by far a naive depiction of the closure of an ideological field unable to represent its exterior and thus obliged to presuppose its presence in its own genesis – it points towards an "ideology" proper to the symbolic order as such.

The fantasy constructed by bourgeois ideology in order to account for the origins of civil society – that is, of the reign of law – is of course the famous fiction of the "social contract" by means of which the subjects pass from a natural into a civil state. We find here the same self-referential vicious circle that defines fantasy: as Hegel pointed out, the fiction of a "social contract" *presupposes in advance* what is or should be its result, its final outcome – the presence of individuals who act according to the rules of a civilized rational order (as with the myth of "primitive accumulation", which presupposes the presence of a capitalist individual in order to explain the advent of capitalism). What is necessarily foreclosed here – the "forbidden" mediator which must vanish, become invisible, turn into a "missing link", if the reign of law is to be established – is of course the "pathological" act of violence out of which the "civil constitution" grew – the umbilical cord which links the social contract (the synchronous legal order) with "nature".[30]

This is what has to undergo a "primordial repression" if the reign of law is to take hold: not "nature as such" but rather the paradox of a violent act by means of which "nature" so to speak surpasses itself and grounds "culture" (the civil state); the "intersection" of nature and culture which is neither nature (since it is already perverted, derailed nature, nature "run amok") nor culture (since it is an excess of violence that is by definition foreclosed by culture). This uncanny third domain, the intersection of nature and culture, is that of the abyss of absolute freedom: the pure Evil of a violence which is "no longer" nature (it exceeds nature precisely by the "excessive nature" of its unconditional demand) and "not yet" culture. In other words, what the reign of law has to tame and subdue is not "nature" but the excess of Evil by means of which nature surpasses itself into culture – therein, in the taming of this radical "unruliness", consists the fundamental aim of education:

> Unruliness consists in independence of law. By discipline men are placed in subjection to the laws of mankind, and brought to feel their constraint. . . . The love of freedom is naturally so strong in man, that when once he has grown accustomed to freedom, he will sacrifice everything for its sake.[31]

What is crucial here is the radical gap separating this "unruliness" from the "animal impulses" in man – at this point Kant is quite unequivocal, when he directly opposes man's "unruliness" to animal instinctual stability:

> Owing to his natural love of freedom it is necessary that man should have his natural roughness smoothed down; with animals, their instinct renders this unnecessary.[32]

The Freudian name for this "unruliness", for this self-destructive freedom which marks the radical break from natural instincts, is of course *death-drive*. The condition of the passage from nature to culture is thus an uncanny inner split of nature itself into nature as balanced circuit regulated by instincts and nature as "unruliness" that has to be tamed by law. The ultimate "vanishing mediator" between nature and culture is the death-drive as this derailed, denaturalized nature – the point at which nature itself uncannily starts to resemble culture in its highest form, that of the "non-pathological" moral act. This resemblance can be discerned through what is perhaps the crucial passage of Kant's political writings, the long – even strangely overlong – remark on the already-quoted *General Remark on the Legal Consequences of the Nature of the Civil Union* which plays the part of a symptom: it is as if the double movement of the "remark on a remark" produces the truth-effect, as double mirroring produced the point of non-imaginary, symbolic identification. That is to say, in this remark Kant "says more than he intended to say" and reaches the very threshold of the link connecting him with de Sade; its topic is the difference between regicide and the execution of the king's death sentence.

This difference concerns the relationship between form and content: although regicide violates legal norms in an extremely grave way, it does not affect the form of legality as such – it retains towards it the relation of an excess to the norm. If, however, the insurgents organize a trial and sentence the king to death, this presents a far greater threat to the State, since it subverts the very form of legality and sovereignty – the legal execution of the king (of the person who embodies supreme power, who serves as the last guarantee for the legal order) is not just the death of the king as a person, it equals the death of the royal function itself – an "act of suicide by the State".[33] The king's death sentence is an abominable travesty in which *crime assumes the form of law* and, so to speak, undermines it from within; in it, the very subversion of the legal order puts on the mask of legality. This is therefore "a crime which must always remain as such and which can never be effaced [*crimen immortale, inexpiabile*]"[34] – or, to use Hegelian terminology, a crime which cannot be "*ungeschehengemacht*" (retroactively undone); which, to quote Kant again, "can never be forgiven either in this world or the next"[35] – why? Because it involves "a complete *reversal* of the principles which govern the relationship between the sovereign and the people. For it amounts to making the people, who owe their existence purely to the legislation of the sovereign, into rulers over the sovereign", and thus opens up "an abyss which engulfs everything beyond hope of return".[36]

Kant's mistake here is to conceive this "abyss which engulfs everything" only in its negative aspect: what he overlooks is that when the circle of self-destruction is over – when the snake swallows its own tail

– the result is not pure nothingness but precisely and simply *a (new) reign of law*. The absolute, self-referential crime which assumes the form of its opposite describes the very genesis of Law which is "forgotten" (repressed) the moment the reign of law is established. It is therefore against this background that one should locate the above-quoted Kantian thesis according to which one *cannot* arrive at the (historical) origin of legal power, since it is *forbidden* to search for it: the traumatic fact concealed by this paradoxical prohibition is precisely the fact of an absolute crime upon which legal power is founded. Every reign of law has its hidden roots in such an absolute – self-referential, self-negating – crime by means of which crime assumes the form of law, and if the law is to reign in its "normal" form, this reverse must be unconditionally repressed.

Here, one should recall Freud's thesis on the correlation between repression and (unconscious) memory: the absolute crime cannot be properly "forgotten" (undone, expiated and forgiven); it must persist as a repressed traumatic kernel, since it contains the founding gesture of the legal order – its eradication from the "unconscious memory" would entail the disintegration of the very reign of law; this reign would be deprived of its (repressed) founding force. The reason why even the absolute power of the Spirit that nothing can resist – namely, its capacity of *Ungeschehenmachen*, of retroactively "undoing" the past – is helpless in face of this supreme crime is that this crime literally *enforces* the reign of Spirit: it is the Negative of the Spirit itself, its hidden support and source.

The status of the Kantian absolute crime is thus exactly the same as that of the Freudian primordial parricide: an impossible Real that should be presupposed (reconstructed retroactively) if one is to account for the existing social order. *What Kant conceives as "impossible" (the unthinkable, unfathomable reality of the ultimate Evil) is actually the always-already realized (although repressed) foundation of the very reign of law* – and the aim of dialectical "recollection" is precisely to remind us of this absolute crime which is the necessary reverse of the reign of law. What is crucial here, however, is that Kant expressly defines this "crime for which there can be no atonement" as a formal and completely futile (non-profitable) – that is *non-pathological* – act:

> So far as can be seen, it is impossible for men to commit a crime of such formal and completely futile malice, although no system of morality

should omit to consider it, if only as a pure idea representing ultimate evil.[37]

We can see, now, why this impossible – that is, real – crime is uncannily close to the ethical act: it has the *form* of legality (that is to say, what we have is not a mere violent rebellion but a rightful procedure) and, furthermore, it is not guided by material, selfish, "pathological" motives. *This* paradox of "non-pathological", "ethical" Evil is what de Sade describes as the "absolute crime" which interrupts the circuit of nature: what, namely, is the advent of the human universe if not a break which introduces imbalance into the natural circuit? *From the standpoint of Nature, "Spirit" itself is "a crime which can never be effaced"*; this is why every positive law is in a way already its own mocking imitation, a violent overthrow of a previous "unwritten" law; a crime turned into law. This previous "unwritten" law of course never existed "as such", in the present: its status is again that of the Real – it is retroactively (presup)posited as that which was "violated" by means of the imposition of our, "human", reign of law.

In other words, there is no "original" law not based upon crime: the institution of law as such is an "illegitimate" usurpation. The Kantian unthinkable crime which subverts the form of law *by means of its very imitation* is thereby in itself already the self-sublation of crime, the foundation of a new law – what Kant takes for an obscene imitation of law is actually *law itself*. The absolute, self-relating crime is thus "uncanny" [*unheimlich*] in the strict Freudian sense: what is so horrifying about it is not its strangeness but rather its absolute *proximity* to the reign of law.

So-called "primitive accumulation"

The famous proposition from Marx's *Grundrisse* according to which "the anatomy of man offers us a key to the anatomy of monkey" also points in this direction. First, we have to dispose of an articulated concept of "man", the final stage of evolution, and it is only from this standpoint that we can, retroactively, reconstruct its diachronous genesis from "monkey". Consequently, when pursuing this genesis, we should not forget for a single moment that in truth, we do *not* "derive man from monkey": all we effectively do is reconstruct the process backwards, from the standpoint of the finished result. Marx formulates this proposition apropos of the genesis of capitalism, which is why it could also serve as a kind of guide for grasping the "primacy of synchrony over diachrony" in the functioning of capitalist ideology.

That is to say, according to the usual doxa of "historical materialism", we would expect Marx to search in its historical genesis for the key enabling him to articulate the logic of capitalism – to "derive" capitalism from the succession of preceding modes of production, from the dissolution of feudalism and the gradual assertion of market-orientated production of commodities. After all, is not the basic proposition of the "historical" method of explanation that to understand a given phenomenon theoretically equates to deploying its historical genesis? What Marx does, however, is the exact opposite of this standard procedure. First, he explores the "inner anatomy" of the capitalist system – he presents the "synchronous" cut of the universe of capital; and it is only then (in the last chapter of Volume I of *Capital*) that he confronts the question of its historical genesis, in the form of "so-called primitive accumulation".

Interpreters who think that the initial triad commodity– money–capital renders the matrix of historical development, reduced to its logical skeleton, condensed and purified of historical contingency, are deeply wrong. From the very beginning, the object of Marx's research is "developed" capitalism – to refer to his own formulation in the first line of the first chapter, societies in which the production of commodities predominates. It is only when the "synchronous" concept of the capitalist mode of production is developed that we can get to grips with its historical conditions, with the circumstances of its emergence; here, however, Marx's reasoning is far more interesting than may appear at first sight. The gist of his argument is that, once capitalism establishes itself as a fully articulated system, it is *indifferent* towards the conditions of its emergence. There were two main conditions: on the one hand a workforce freed from its "substantial" attachment to the objective conditions of production (means and objects of production) – reduced to the status of pure subjectivity; on the other a surplus of money (capital). How these two conditions originated is of no concern to dialectical deduction. It is simply a matter of empirical historical research – a dark story of violent expropriation and plunder, of merchant adventurers, and so on; a story with which we *do not* have to be acquainted in order to grasp the "synchronous" functioning of the capitalist system.

Within this framework, "so-called primitive accumulation" is nothing but the *ideological myth* produced by capitalism retroactively to explain its own genesis and, at the same time, to justify present exploitation: the myth of the "diligent saving worker" who did not immediately consume his surplus but wisely reinvested it in production and thus gradually became a capitalist, owner of the means of production, able to give employment to other workers possessing nothing but their ability to work. Like every myth, this is circular – it presupposes what it purports to explain: the notion of the capitalist. It "explains" the emergence of capitalism by presupposing the existence of an agent who "acts like a capitalist" from the very beginning. What we encounter here is thus again the logic of *fantasy*: the structure of the ideological myth of "primitive accumulation" corresponds exactly to that of the "voyage into the past"; the "capitalist" is present as a gaze at its own conception. In ideology, too, the fantasy-construct is a way for the subject to fill out the "missing link" of its genesis by assuring its presence in the character of pure gaze at its own conception – by enabling it to "jump into the past" and appear as its own cause.

The crucial point here is that the synchronous symbolic order fills out the void of its "origins" by means of a *narration*: fantasy has, by definition, the structure of a *story* to be narrated. Although this seems to be a minor point, it has its roots in the philosophical conflict between Hegel and Schelling concerning the way to present [*darstellen*] the Absolute: through *logos* or *mythos*, through logical deduction or through narration of God's "ages"? Hegel, to use Pascalian terms, stakes everything on *logos* (or so it appeared – wrongly – to Marx): the totality of the Absolute can be conceived and presented in the form of the Notion's logical development; "history" is reduced to the "external", temporal appearance of the inner, timeless logical articulation. Schelling, on the contrary, insists on *narration* as the appropriate medium of presentation of the Absolute: God cannot be reduced to *logos*, there is something in Him which is not Reason, Word, namely the obscure foundation of His existence, what is in God "more than Himself", the Real in God; this is why the presentation of the content of the Absolute must assume the form of a narration, of a story about God's "ages" that goes beyond rendering the inner necessity of a network of pure logical determinations.

With Marx, this problematic appears in the form of the relationship between "logical" and "historical" aspect: against Hegel, Marx insists on the inherent limitation of a purely dialectical presentation; on the necessity to supplement it with historical description. For him, the gap separating dialectical presentation and historical description is thus irreducible: their relationship is not that between "inner" and "external", between "essence" and "appearance"; historical description does not present the empirical wealth of the process whose notional structure, purified of contingent empirical content, would then be rendered by a dialectical deduction. What the historical description renders manifest is, on the contrary, the radically external historical presuppositions of the synchronous dialectical totality, its contingent starting point that eludes dialectical grasp, its "missing link" whose exclusion the dialectical totality endeavours to fill out by means of a fantasy-scene.

Let us return to the case of capitalism: what one can present dialectically is the "synchronous" functioning of the capitalist system in so far as this system has already "posited its presuppositions", reordered its external starting points so that they now function as inner moments of the closed circle of its self-reproduction. The role of historical description is, however, to "go through" the fantasy which masks this vicious circle: to denounce the mythical narration by means of which the synchronous system retroactively organizes its own past, its own origins, and to render visible the contingent reality full of blood and brute force:

> . . . the accumulation of capital presupposes surplus-value; surplus-value presupposes capitalist production; capitalist production presupposes the availability of considerable masses of capital and labour-power in the hands of commodity producers. The whole movement, therefore, seems to turn around in a vicious circle, which we can only get out of by assuming a primitive accumulation . . . which precedes capitalist accumulation; an accumulation which is not the result of the capitalist mode of production but its point of departure.
>
> This primitive accumulation plays approximately the same role in political economy as original sin does in theology. Adam bit the apple, and thereupon sin fell on the human race. Its origin is supposed to be explained when it is told as an anecdote about the past. Long, long ago there were two sorts of people; one, the diligent, intelligent and above all frugal elite; the other, lazy rascals, spending their substance, and more, in riotous living. The legend of theological original sin tells us certainly how man came to be condemned to eat his bread in the sweat of his brow; but the history of economic original sin reveals to us that there are people to whom this is by no means essential. . . . In actual history, it is a notorious fact that

> conquest, enslavement, robbery, murder, in short, force, play the greatest part. In the tender annals of political economy, the idyllic reigns from time immemorial. . . . As a matter of fact, the methods of primitive accumulation are anything but idyllic.[38]

In a first approach, these lines offer themselves with a deceitful self-evidence as a criticism of the Hegelian "closed circle": is not the "speculative" circulation of capital engendering itself the very paradigm of the dialectical "speculation", its notional self-movement? Is not therefore the implicit aim of the quoted passage from *Capital* to denounce the illusion of the immanent self-reproduction of capital *qua* "absolute Spirit" by exhibiting the irreducible trace of contingent materiality that cannot ever be "sublated", re-collected, made an internal moment posited by the Capital-Spirit itself? It would be a fatal misunderstanding, however, to succumb to this self-evidence: Hegel is thoroughly aware of the radically contingent and external starting points, "presuppositions", of a dialectical movement; he is thoroughly aware that the circle can never be closed by "sublating" these presuppositions without remainder – *the circle remains for ever a vicious one*; or, to use topological terms, its structure is that of a Moebius band.

What the dialectical presentation renders is not the closed circle but the very process of inversion – itself contingent – whereby the external, contingent presuppositions are retroactively "posited", re-ordered within a synchronous circle: *in other words, the very process that generates the illusion of a closed circle*. And what, accordingly, dialectical presentation unmasks is the "fetish" of an Origin by means of which the circle (the synchronous system) endeavours to conceal its vicious character – in the case of *Capital*, the myth of "primitive accumulation" by means of which capitalism generates the story of its origins. In this sense we could say that, ultimately, dialectical analysis is nothing but a repeated "going through the fantasy" which keeps the vicious character of the circle unconcealed.

Today, in the epoch of renewed national revival, the clearest cases of such fantasy-construction filling out the void of the "origins" are of course nationalist myths: there is no national identity before its (colonialist, etc.) "oppression"; national identity constitutes itself through resistance to its oppression – the fight for national revival is therefore *a defence of something which comes to be only through being experienced as lost or endangered*.[39] The nationalist ideology endeavours to elude this vicious circle by constructing a myth of Origins – of an epoch preceding oppression and exploitation when the Nation was *already there* (the Khmer kingdom in Cambodia, India before English colonialism, Ireland before the Protestant invasion, and so on) – the past is trans-coded as Nation that already existed and to which we are supposed to return through a liberation struggle.

The paradox of a finite totality

Contemporary systems theory has come up with just such a notion of a symbolic structure organized around a "missing link" as point of its ex-timacy (central externality, inherent limit): its main effort consists in formalizing the so-called "auto-poetic" systems – systems which afterwards, by means of a retroactive "trans-coding", transform their starting, initial conditions.[40] In its "prehistory", a system begins within conditions which determine it in an external way – that is, the signification of which is not determined by the system itself; this "prehistory" is over, the system finds its equilibrium and starts to run its own course, when it trans-codes its initial conditions by transforming them into inherent moments of its self-development.

Therein, in such a retroactive "positing of presuppositions", consists the fundamental matrix of the Hegelian "self-relating of the Notion": in the course of the dialectical "progress", the initial category "develops" into a "higher" category in such a manner that it is "trans-coded", posited as its subordinate-mediated moment; in the passage of "being" into "essence", the entire domain of "being" is retroactively determined as that of the "appearance", as the medium in which "essence" becomes manifest, appears to itself. At every "knot" of the logic, the emergence of a new category "trans-codes" (restructures, reorders) the entire precedent network, renders it visible in a new way;[41] or, to put it more pointedly, the new emerging category is *nothing but* the principle of trans-coding the preceding categories ("essence" is, as Hegel puts it, "appearance *qua* appearance" – *nothing but* the principle of the trans-coding of immediate being into a "mere appearance": the illusion of Understanding is precisely that "essence" is a positive entity *beyond* the negative movement of the appearance's self-sublation).

As we have already recalled, this involute process of retroactive "positing of presuppositions" has the structure of a Moebius band, of the "loopy", "inner" eight: towards the end of his *Logic*, Hegel himself determines the dialectical process as a "circle returned upon itself".[42] And as we have just seen, is not the presentation of the genesis of the capitalist system in Marx's *Capital* a description of such a retroactive "trans-coding"? Is not this the reason why Marx makes a distinction between the historical genesis of capitalism and the logic of its self-reproduction: capitalism reaches the level of self-reproduction once its external starting conditions are posited as moments of its immanent self-development. Money, for example, is at first the external presupposition not created by capitalism itself (it was accumulated through "non-capitalist" means – robbery, international trade, and so on); however, once the circle of capitalist reproduction is set in motion, money is posited as one of the "incarnations" of capital itself, as a moment of its movement Money–Commodity–Money.

These external presuppositions – the real of a violence *founding* the system and none the less *disavowed* once the system reaches the level of its self-reproduction – play the role of a "vanishing mediator": they must disappear, become invisible, if the system is to maintain its consistency and coherence. In other words, the gap separating the genesis of a structure from its self-reproduction is unbridgeable, the structure cannot "reflect into itself" the external conditions of its genesis since *it is constituted by means of their "repression"*; of a trans-coding which effaces their external, contingent character. It is clear, thereby, what is the use of this logic of "auto-poetic" trans-coding for the conceptualization of psychoanalytic praxis: trans-coding concerns the integration of some external, contingent traumatic kernel into the subject's symbolic universe, it is the way to "gentrify" a traumatic experience, to efface its traumatic impact by transforming it into a moment of meaningful totality.

Let us just recall the uneasiness of traditional democratic ideology when confronted with the "excess" of Jacobinism, with the fact that the so-called Jacobinical "horrors" were a necessary mediator in establishing a "normal" democratic order: the problem is solved by retroactively introducing into the process of the French Revolution a distinction between its liberal mainstream (human rights and freedoms, and so on) and its proto-totalitarian aberration – that is, by proclaiming Jacobinism a purely accidental exception.

Why is this "repression" of the "vanishing mediator" necessary? Because a symbolic system has by definition the character of *totality*: there is meaning only if *everything* has meaning. In the analysis of a dream, for example, one cannot simply distinguish among its elements those that can be interpreted as signifiers from those which result from purely physiological processes: if dreams are "structured like a language", then *all* their ingredients are to be treated as elements of a signifying network; even when the physiological causal link seems obvious (as in the caricatural case of a subject who dreams of a tap leaking when he feels a need to urinate) one must "put it in parentheses" and confine oneself to the signifying range of the dream's ingredients. What Freud called "primordial repression" [*Urverdrängung*] is precisely this radical rupture by means of which a symbolic system fractures its inclusion in the chain of material causality: if some signifier were not missing, we would not have a signifying structure but a positive network of causes and effects. In his *Seminar XI*, Lacan baptized this "primordially repressed" signifier – the "mising link" of the signifier's chain – the "binary signifier": because of its constitutive lack, the chain runs in a vicious circle, it produces again and again new "unary" signifiers (Master-Signifiers) which endeavour to close the circle by retroactively providing it with foundation.

It is the philosophical notion of the "transcendental" dimension which gives perhaps the clearest expression to this paradox of an order, the positive condition of which is that something – its very foundation – must be missing, must remain "repressed"; of an order which turns around its central void, an order *defined* by this void: if this void were to be filled out, the order itself would lose its consistency and dissolve itself. That is to say, the symbolic order is defined by the paradox of a *finite totality*: every language constitutes a "totality", a universe complete and closed in itself; it allows of no outside, everything can be said in it; yet this very totality is simultaneously marked by an irreducible finitude. The inner tension of a finite totality is attested by a loop that pertains to our basic attitude towards language: spontaneously, we somehow presuppose that language depends on "external" reality, that it "renders" an independent state of things, yet this "external" reality is always-already disclosed through language, mediated by it.

This enigmatic intermediary status of the symbolic order corresponds precisely to the Kantian notion of the "transcendental constitution": transcendental constitution is *more* than a mere subjective perspective upon reality, *more* than another name for the fact that we are condemned to perceive reality within the limits of our subjective horizon – the transcendental horizon is *ontologically constitutive* of what we call "reality"; yet transcendental constitution is in no way the same as ontic causation ("creation") of reality – it is decidedly *less*: namely, its ontological horizon.[43] In this precise sense, the notion of transcendental order coincides with that of the Symbolic: in both cases we have to do with a totality which, on the level of the ontic enchainment, implies a "missing link". Transcendental constitution takes place only within the confines of the ontic finitude – only in so far as the gap separating the phenomenal world of our experience from the suprasensible *noumenon* persists; only in so far as the *Ding an sich* remains inaccessible – as soon as this gap is leapt over, as soon as we gain access to the *Ding an sich*, this means the end of the transcendental as a specific intermediary domain. Therein consists the kernel of Kant's philosophical revolution: in conceiving finitude as ontologically constitutive.

And the crucial point not to be overlooked here is that *precisely on account of the notion of "absolute knowledge", Hegel remains entirely within this Kantian horizon of finitude as ontologically constitutive*. That is to say, the Hegelian "absolute knowledge" is usually adduced as a proof of his return to pre-critical metaphysics: as if the Kantian lesson was forgotten and the thought pretended again to grasp the Absolute itself . . . . Sometimes one even opposes this "absolute knowledge" to Hegel's alleged "historicism": how can we conceive ourselves as part of the historical process, as our (historical) time conceived in thought, and simultaneously pretend to pass the final judgement on history from a standpoint somehow exempted from it, as if history had come to an end?

Hegel's answer is, of course, that what is false and too pretentious is precisely the apparently modest relativistic standpoint *á la* Karl Popper which purports to be aware of its limitations ("the truth can only be approached in an asymptote, what is accessible to us are fragments of knowledge which could be proved false at any moment"): the very position of enunciation of such statements belies their modest enunciated, since it assumes a neutral, exempted standpoint from which it can pass a judgement on the limitation of its content. For Hegel, on the contrary, there is no contradiction between our absorption into the historical process and the fact that we not only can but are obliged to speak from the standpoint of the "end of history": precisely because we are absorbed into history *without remainder*, we perceive our present standpoint as "absolute" – that is, we cannot maintain an external distance towards it.

In other words, absolute historicism sublates itself: historicity consists in the very fact that, at every given historical moment, we speak from within a finite horizon that we perceive as absolute – every epoch experiences itself as the "end of history". And "absolute knowledge" is nothing other than the explication of this historically specified field that *absolutely limits our horizon*: as such, it is "finite", it can be contained in a finite book – in the works of the individual named Hegel, for example.[44] This is the reason why, at the very end of his system, on the last page of his *Lessons on the History of Philosophy*, Hegel says: "This is now the standpoint of our time, and the series of spiritual formations is thereby *for the time being* [*für jetzt*] completed."[45] – a proposition which is totally meaningless if we read it against the background of the standard notion of "absolute knowledge".

Here, we can risk a topological specification of the Kant–Hegel relationship. The structure of the Kantian transcendental field is that of a circle with a gap, since man as a finite being does not have access to the totality of beings:

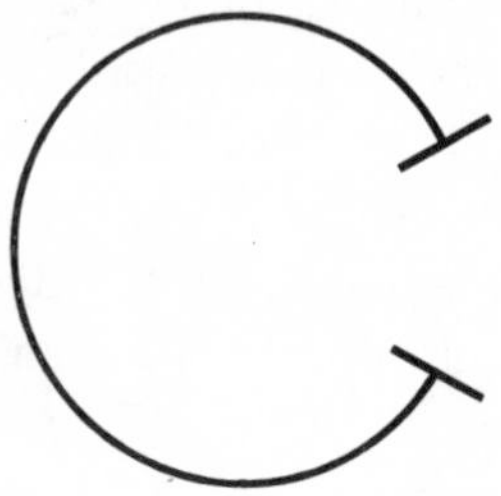

However, contrary to the common view, the passage from Kant to Hegel does *not* consist in closing the circle:

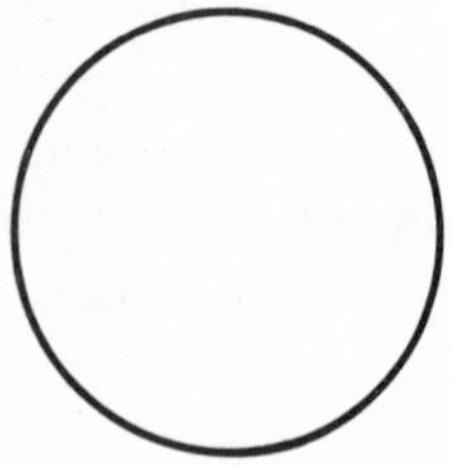

If this were the case, Hegel would simply return to pre-Kantian, pre-critical metaphysics. Hegel does indeed "close the circle", but this very closure introduces a supplementary loop transforming it into the "inner eight" of the Moebius band:

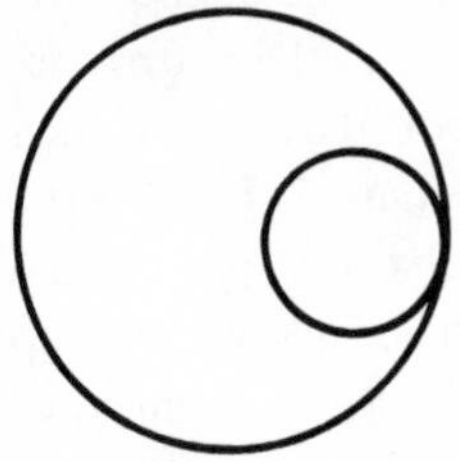

In other words, Hegel definitely *maintains* the gap around which the transcendental field is structured: the very retroactivity of the dialectical process (the "positing of presuppositions") attests to it. The point is just that he *displaces* it: the external limit preventing the closure of the circle changes into a curvature which makes the very closed circle vicious.

The Kantian Thing

The status of the "Thing-in-itself" is therefore strictly *ontic*: it is the part of the ontic (of "innerworldly" entities) that must fail to appear, must fall out from the ontological horizon, if the ontological constitution is take place – to use Heideggerian terms: if the ontological difference is to occur. Kant was deeply aware of this "ontological equivocality" of the relationship between the transcendental and the Thing-in-itself; it suffices to glance at the last paragraph of the first part of *Critique of Practical Reason*, where he expressly conceives the inaccessibility of the Thing (God, in this case) as a positive condition of our ethical activity: if God *qua* Thing were immediately to disclose Himself to us, our activity could no longer be ethical, since we would not do Good because of moral law itself but because of our direct insight into God's nature – out of immediate assurance that Evil would be punished. It is as if, at this point, Kant's famous ethical maxim "You can, because you must!" again reverses into "You cannot (know

God *qua* Thing), because you must not (because the consequences of this knowledge would be catastrophic for man *qua* moral being)!"

These catastrophic consequences of the encroachment upon the forbidden/impossible domain of the Thing are spelled out in the Gothic novel: it is by no means accidental that the Gothic novel, obsessed as it is with the motive of the Thing in its different embodiments (the "living dead", and so on), is contemporary to Kant's transcendental turn. We could even risk the hypothesis that the Gothic novel is a kind of critique *avant la lettre* of the Kantian insistence on the unsurmountable gap between phenomena and the transcendent Thing-in-itself: what are the spectres that appear in it if not *apparitions of the Thing*, if not points of a "short circuit" at which the transphenomenal Thing invades the phenomenal domain and disturbs its causal order?

Apropos of the "transcendental apperception", Kant points out the utter voidance of the "I" that thinks: "I" is the empty form of thoughts, we can never accomplish the step from it towards substance and attain the hypothetical X, "the Thing that thinks" – yet the apparitions in the Gothic novels are precisely this: *Things that think*. This Kantian background is most easily perceived in the vampire novels; when, in a typical scene, the hero endeavours to deliver the innocent girl who has become a vampire by finishing her off in the appropriate way (the wooden stake through the heart, and so on), the aim of this operation is to differentiate the Thing from the body, to drive out the Thing, this embodiment of perverse and traumatic enjoyment, from the body subordinated to the "normal" causal link. Let us just recall the scene from Bram Stoker's *Dracula* in which Arthur stakes Lucy, his ex-fiancée:

> The Thing in the coffin writhed; and a hideous, blood-curdling screech came from the opened red lips. The body shook and quivered and twisted in wild contortions, the sharp white teeth champed together till the lips were cut, and the mouth was smeared with a crimson foam.

– a desperate resistance of the Thing, of enjoyment fighting not to be evacuated from the body. When, finally, the Thing is driven out, the expression on Lucy's face changes back to normal, assuming again the features of innocent beatitude – the Thing within the body is dead. One of the usual phrases about the Thing in the Gothic novel is the horrified exclamation: "It's alive!" – that is to say, the substance of enjoyment is not yet mortified, quartered by the transcendental-symbolic network. The paradox of the vampires is that, precisely as "living dead", they are *far more alive* than us, mortified by the symbolic network. The usual Marxist vampire metaphor is that of capital sucking the blood of the workforce, embodiment of the rule of the dead over the living; perhaps the time has come to reverse it: the real "living dead" are we, common mortals, condemned to vegetate in the Symbolic.

It is precisely for this reason, however, that vampires are not part of our *reality*: they exist only as "returns of the Real"; as fantasy-formations filling out the gap, the radical discontinuity between the two perspectives (the "forward view" which perceives the situation as "open" and the "backward view" which perceives the past course of events as causally determined). The two perspectives can never be fully synchronized, since the gap separating them is another name for the *subject*. One cannot reduce one perspective to another by claiming, for example, that the "true" picture is that of necessity discovered by the "backward view", that freedom is just an illusion of the immediate agents who overlook how their activity is a mere wheel within the large causal mechanism; or, conversely, by embracing a kind of Sartreian existentialist perspective and affirming the subject's ultimate autonomy and freedom, conceiving the appearance of determinism as the later "pratico-inert" objectivization of the subject's spontaneous *praxis*. If we proceed in this way, we retain the ontological unity of the universe, whether in the form of substantial necessity pulling the strings behind the subject's back or in the form of the subject's autonomous activity "objectivizing" itself in the substantial unity – what gets lost in both cases is the *subject* in the Lacanian sense which is not an autonomous power "positing" the substance but precisely a name for the *gap* within substance, for the discontinuity which prevents us from conceiving the substance as a self-contained totality.

The ultimate consequence of this status of the subject *qua* discontinuity within the substance, its temporal non-synchronization, is, however, that it entails an additional "turn of the screw": a *reversal* of the above-described notion of historical process as "forwards open – backwards determined". Namely, when we spoke of the symbolic integration of a trauma, we omitted a crucial detail: the logic of Freud's notion of the "deferred action" does not consist in the subsequent "gentrification" of a traumatic encounter by means of its transformation into a normal component of our symbolic universe, but in the almost exact opposite of it – something which was *at first* perceived as a meaningless, neutral event changes *retroactively*, after the advent of a new symbolic network that determines the subject's place of enunciation, into a trauma that cannot be integrated into this network.

Let us just recall Freud's analysis of the Wolf Man: the paternal *coitus a tergo* was first perceived as something neutral, a trace without any libidinal weight, and it was only years later, with the further elaboration of the child's sexual "theories", that it acquired its traumatic status: only at this later stage did it become possible for the child to "do something with it", to fit it into a symbolic frame in the form of a traumatic wound. Here again, Hegel's proposition that what is lost comes to be through being lost receives its full value: an event is experienced as "traumatic" afterwards, with the advent of a symbolic space within which it cannot be fully integrated.

And is it ultimately not the same with the *act of freedom*? An act is never fully "present", the subjects are never fully aware that what they are doing "now" is the foundation of a new symbolic order – it is only afterwards that they take note of the true dimension of what they have already done. The common wisdom about how history *in actu* is experienced as the domain of freedom, whereas retroactively we are able to perceive its causal determination, is therefore idiotic after all and should be reversed: when we are caught in the flow of events, we act "automatically", as if under the impression that it is not possible to do otherwise, that there is really no choice; whereas the retrospective view displays how the events could have taken a radically different turn – how what we perceived as necessity was actually a free decision of ours. In other words, what we encounter here is another confirmation of the fact that the time of the subject is never "present" – the subject never "is", it only "will have been": we never *are* free, it is only afterwards that we discover how we *have been* free.[46] This is the ultimate meaning of the "missing link": it is never missing "now" – "now", in present time, the chain is always completed; it is only afterwards, when we endeavour to reconstruct the chain, that we discover how "something is missing".

Notes

1. *Hegel's Science of Logic*, London: Allen & Unwin 1969, p. 836.

2. Theodor W. Adorno, "Über einige Schwierigkeiten des Komponierens heute", in *Aspekte der Modernität*, ed. H. Steffen, Göttingen 1965, p. 133.

3. The complementary reverse of this paradox is of course that things must change if they are to remain the same: capitalism is forced to revolutionize its material conditions precisely in order to maintain the same fundamental relations of production.

4. Hence follows the ultimate incompatibility of Hegelian procedure with recent "post-modernist" attempts to oppose to "totalitarian", "monological", "repressive", "universalizing" Reason the contours of another plural, polycentric, dialogical, feminine, Baroque, etc., Reason (the "weak thought", for example). From the Hegelian perspective, such a move is simply superfluous: it is already the first ("monological") Reason which reveals itself as *its own opposite*, as soon as we endeavour to grasp it "in itself", "as such".

5. See Fredric Jameson, "The Vanishing Mediator; or, Max Weber as Storyteller", in *The Ideologies of Theory*, vol. 2, Minneapolis: University of Minnesota Press 1988.

6. What is unusual about Jameson's text is that it does not mention the role of *Weber himself* as the "vanishing mediator" between the traditional (pre-positivist) approach to society and twentieth-century sociology as "objective science". As Jameson points out, Weber's notion of *Wertfreiheit*, of a value-free stance, is *not yet* the later positivist "neutrality": it expresses a pre-positivist Nietzscheian attitude of distance towards values which enables us to accomplish a "transvaluation of values" and thus a more efficient intervention into social reality – in other words, *Wertfreiheit* implies a very "interested" attitude towards reality.

Incidentally, does not Wittgenstein play the same role in contemporary analytical philosophy: is he not even a *double* "vanishing mediator", in relation to classical logical positivism as well as in relation to speech-acts theory? A simple sensitivity to theoretical finesse tells us that the most valuable aspect of Wittgenstein's *Tractatus* gets lost with its systematization in logical positivism: that "surplus" with which Russell, Carnap and others did not know what to do and dismissed as confusion or mysticism (the problem of form as unspeakable and of silence which inscribes the subject of enunciation into the series of propositions, and so on). And it is similar with the codification of speech acts in Searle *et al.*: we lose a series of paradoxes and borderline questions, from the paradoxical status of "objective certainty" (which cannot be put in doubt, although it is not necessarily true) to the splitting of the subject of speech acts (the radical discontinuity between "I" and the proper name).

7. Alain Badiou, *L'être et l'événement*, Paris: Éditions du Seuil 1988.

8. G.W.F. Hegel, *Phenomenology of Spirit*, Oxford: Oxford University Press 1977, p. 10.

9. Joseph Stalin, *Selected Writings*, Westport: Greenwood Press 1942, p. 411.

10. John Forrester, *The Seductions of Psychoanalysis*, Cambridge: Cambridge University Press 1990, p. 189.

11. Jean-Claude Milner, *Les noms indistincts*, Paris: Éditions du Seuil 1983, p. 16.

12. G.K. Chesterton, "A Defence of Detective Stories", in H. Haycraft, ed., *The Art of the Mystery Story*, New York: The Universal Library 1946, p. 6.

13. In this precise sense we could say that the Lenin to be unearthed is *the one who was not yet a Leninist*; the same goes for Lacan's "return to Freud": by means of it Lacan endeavours to reinvent the "freshness" of Freud's act of discovery, of his subverting the field of doxa that precedes the establishment of psychoanalysis as a new scientific and ideological "commonplace".

The paradox of Lacan's "return to Freud", however, is to ascertain that the *Freud who was not yet a Freudian was already a Lacanian* – that he knew "in practice" what the "autonomy of the signifier" means. To persuade oneself of it, one has only to cast a brief look at one of Freud's numerous dream analyses – that of the badly tuned piano, for example:

> *Her husband asked her: "Don't you think we ought to have the piano tuned?" And she replied: "It's not worth while; the hammers need reconditioning in any case."* . . . the key to the solution was given by her words: "*It's not worth while.*" These were derived from a visit she had paid the day before to a woman friend. She had been invited to take off her jacket, but had refused with the words: "Thank you, but *it's not worth while*; I can only stop a minute." As she was telling me this, I recollected that during the previous day's analysis she had suddenly caught hold of her jacket, one of the buttons having come undone. Thus it was as though she were saying: "Please don't look; *it's not worth while.*" In the same way the "box" ["*Kasten*"] was a substitute for a "chest" ["*Brustkasten*"]; and the interpretation of the dream led us back at once to the time of her physical development at puberty . . . (Sigmund Freud, *The Interpretation of Dreams*, Harmondsworth: Penguin 1976, pp. 273–4)

How, exactly, does Freud proceed here? Far from searching for a possible meaning of the scene as a whole, he so to speak puts in parentheses its atmospheric weight; he also does not endeavour to discern the meaning of its individual components (piano "means" . . . , etc.) – instead, he looks for particular, radically contingent connections between the dream and its "repressed" (its "other scenes") *on the level of the pure signifier*. This way, he isolates the signifier's sequence "it's not worth while" which, by means of its double inscription ("it's not worth while – to tune the piano; to look at my breasts"), gives us access to the series of "repressed" associations which reach up to the domain of pre-genital, anal eroticism. (Note how even the apparent case of "symbolism" – the piano which is a substitute for chest – is founded in the autonomy of the signifier: the point is not that piano "symbolizes" chest but that the same *word* – *Kasten* – is doubly inscribed.) This "doubly inscribed" element of the dream sequence – "it's not worth while" – therefore plays a role strictly homologous to that of a *clue* in detective fiction: a detail "out of joint" which enables us to pass over into the "other scene".

14. Claude Lefort, *The Political Forms of Modern Society*, Cambridge: Polity Press 1986.

15. Ernesto Laclau, *New Reflections on the Revolution of Our Time*, London: Verso 1990.

16. In Heideggerian terms we could say that, among the different spheres of social life, politics is the only place where Truth can arrive: where a new way a community discloses itself to itself can be founded.

17. See Jean-Claude Milner.

18. As with Hegel, where words as such belong to the domain of abstract Understanding and are therefore incapable of giving expression to speculative truth: this truth can emerge only by means of particular contingencies of wordplay (the three meanings of *Aufhebung; zugrundegehen* (to fall to ruin) as *zu Grunde gehen* (to arrive at one's ground); etc.). See Chapter 1 above.

19. In the present ideological constellation, when the glorification of (post-modern) "culture" at the expense of (modern) "civilization" is again fashionable (the German culture against the allegedly superficial Anglo-Saxon or French civilization, etc.), it would be theoretically productive to arrange into a semiotic square the two oppositions of culture–primitivism and of civilization–barbarism:

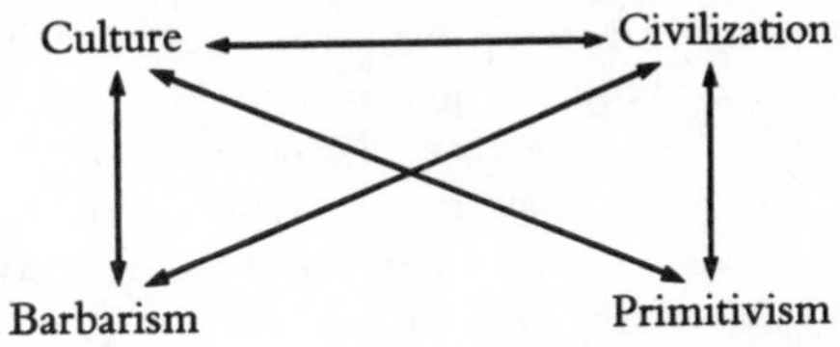

The crucial point not to be missed here is that culture and barbarism do *not* exclude each other: the opposite of barbarism is not culture but civilization (i.e. "non-civilized" equals "barbaric"); in other words, culture in itself, in so far as it is affirmed in its opposition to civilization, sets free an unmistakable barbaric potential – it was already Hegel who, apropos of the medieval culture of alienation, spoke of the "barbarism of pure culture" [*Barbarismus der reinen Kultur*]. The fact that the greatest *barbarism* of our century (Nazism) took place within the nation which glorified its *culture* against the superficial civilization of its neighbours (Germany) is by no means accidental: there is ultimately no contradiction between Heinrich Heydrich, who directed the Nazi terror in occupied Bohemia and planned the "final solution" of the Jewish question, and the same Heydrich who, in the evening after the hard day's work, played with friends Beethoven's string quartets, perhaps the supreme achievement of German culture. The first model of this German *Kulturbarbarismus* is Luther, whose Protestant refusal of Rome presents a reaction of pure, inner culture against the worldly Catholic civilization, and at the same time, by means of its savage, violent attitude, displays the latent barbarism proper to the German ideology.

20. The time paradox implied here emerges directly in a series of recent films centred around the motif of time travel (*Back to the Future*, *Terminator*, etc.): their matrix is always that of a subject who, by means of a voyage into the past, endeavours to witness his own conception, as in *Back to the Future*, in which the hero arranges the matching of his parents and thus provides for his own existence . . . . *Terminator*, on the contrary, stages an inverted situation: the cyborg arriving from the future is charged with a mission to *prevent* the conception of a future leader. See Chapter 7 ("Time Travel, Primal Scene, and the Critical Dystopia") of Constance Penley, *The Future of An Illusion: Film, Feminism and Psychoanalysis*, Minneapolis: University of Minnesota Press 1989.

21. Jean-Jacques Lecercle, *Frankenstein: mythe et philosophie*, Paris: PUF 1988, pp. 98–9. Incidentally, it should be remembered that the figure of the monster in *Franken-*

stein was conceived as a metaphor for the terrors of the French Revolution, i.e. of a human creation gone astray.

22. Jacques Lacan, *Le Séminaire, livre III: Les Psychoses*, Paris: Éditions du Seuil 1981, p. 48; translation quoted from John Forrester, *The Seductions of Psychoanalysis*, Cambridge: Cambridge University Press 1990, p. 138. What we have here is another case of how, in Lacanian definitions of crucial notions, opposites coincide. The "big Other" is simultaneously the presupposed Reason which confers meaning upon the meaningless contingency, *and* the pure appearance of Meaning to be maintained at any price. It is simultaneously another human being in its unfathomable singularity, beyond the "wall of language" – the "person" in its elusive abyss – *and* the "anonymous" symbolic mechanism which regulates intersubjective exchanges. The order of succession here is the same as that in Freud's dream of Irma's injection: at the very moment when we cast a look into the Other's throat, when we came across the Other (person) in its horrifying abyss beyond the imaginary mirror-relationship, the register changes and we find ourselves within a "symbolic beatitude" of a machine which delivers us from every responsibility, desubjectivizes us, since it "runs of itself".

23. See Donald Davidson, "On the Very Idea of a Conceptual Scheme", in John Rajchman and Cornel West, eds, *Post-Analytical Philosophy*, New York: Columbia University Press 1985.

24. The acceptance of this gap preventing us from "founding" language *qua* meaningful totality from the particular points of correspondence between individual propositions and "reality" led Davidson to a radical conclusion: a strict disjunction between the theory of truth (the status of which is purely semantic) and the epistemological problematic of ascertaining how we proclaim a proposition or theory to be "true". Thus, Davidson breaks up the circle of Cartesian epistemology which equates the theory of truth (i.e. the theory telling us what is truth) with the theory procuring (formal, transcendental, a priori) guarantees for the truth of our knowledge – a gesture which is strictly homologous to that of Louis Althusser.

25. Although some of Wittgenstein's formulations from *Philosophical Investigations* do allow of such a "behaviourist" reduction (those, for example, which reduce language to a form of "expressive behaviour" and conceive the verbal expression of pain as a form of new pain-behaviour: instead of crying, I say "I am in pain"), the most appropriate interpretation still seems to be that the very totality of "life-form" *qua* texture of language and non-language behaviour *is already overdetermined by language*: if "Wittgenstein's view is that anyone's certainty about anything presupposes a mass of knowledge and belief that is inherited from other human beings and taken on trust" (Norman Malcolm, *Wittgenstein: Nothing is Hidden*, Oxford: Blackwell 1986, p. 235), does this not imply that, as Lacan would put it, the "big Other", the guarantee of symbolic truth, is *always-already here*?

26. Jacques Lacan, *Écrits: A Selection*, London: Tavistock 1977, p. 48.

27. Blaise Pascal, *Pensées*, Harmondsworth: Penguin 1966, pp. 46–7.

28. *Kant's Political Writings*, ed. Hans Reiss, Cambridge: Cambridge University Press 1970, p. 143.

29. Ibid., p. 162.

30. In his *Perpetual Peace: A Philosophical Sketch*, Kant himself assumes that, at the dawn of history, savages concluded the first "social contract" because of "pathological" considerations (to survive, to insure their "egotistical" interests, etc.), not

because of their inherent moral stance.

31. *Kant on Education*, London: Kegan Paul, French, Truebner 1899, pp. 3–4.

32. Ibid., p. 5.

33. *Kant's Political Writings*, p. 146.

34. Ibid., p. 145.

35. Ibid.

36. Ibid., p. 146.

37. Ibid.

38. Karl Marx, *Capital*, vol. I, Harmondsworth: Penguin 1981, pp. 873–4.

39. *Hegel's Science of Logic*, p. 802.

40. See Dieter Hombach's perspicacious book *Die Drift der Erkenntnis* (Munich: Raben Verlag 1990), which detects outlines of the same "auto-poetic" logic in the Godelian logical paradoxes of self-relating inconsistent systems, in psychoanalysis and in Hegelian dialectic.

41. It is almost superfluous to recall that this trans-coding is just another name for the elementary signifying operation designated by Lacan as "quilting point" [*point de capiton*].

42. *Hegel's Science of Logic*, p. 842.

43. Although Heidegger himself would refuse such a use of the term "transcendental" (for him, its place is strictly within the metaphysics of subjectivity), it could be elucidated by means of his thesis that a great work of art founds a new disclosure of reality, a new "worlding of the world". The most famous example here is of course that of the Swiss Alps: for pre-Romantic Classicists, they were a chaotic, shocking deformity of Nature, to be crossed as quickly as possible in a veiled coach on the way to the harmonious beauty of Italy; whereas just a few decades later, these "same" Alps became the very embodiment of Nature's abysmal sublime Power and as such an object of art *par excellence*. The talk about "changed esthetic sensibility" falls short here: it overlooks the fact that the change is not simply "subjective" – with the Romantic notion of the Sublime, the Alps themselves, in their very "reality", were disclosed in a new way, i.e. offered themselves to us in a new dimension.

Perhaps we could risk the hypothesis that a similar "transcendental" break is at work in every artistic revolution: did not Arnold Schoenberg, for example, accomplish the same turn apropos of female hysteria? Did he not make hysterical outbursts a possible object of art? It is for the same reason that Raymond Chandler is effectively an "artist": he unearthed the poetic potential of what was up to that time looked down upon as the faceless, soulless universe of the megalopolis called "Los Angeles". In today's England, a similar achievement was wrought by Ruth Rendell: nobody who has read one of her detective novels can continue to view the suburbs of Greater London in the same way as before; she discovered the poetic potential of its overgrown gardens, abandoned railway tracks, decaying façades. After reading her novels, the very "real" London appears "the same as before, yet totally different" – a worn-out phrase which, however, renders quite accurately the shift in the transcendental horizon.

44. One of the standard ways to mock Hegel is to point out the patent absurdity of the fact that a miserable individual living in Berlin in the 1820s proclaimed that the Absolute was speaking through his mouth; yet those who are versed in dialectics can easily recognize in this what is perhaps the ultimate variation on the infinite judgement "The Spirit is a bone". Therefore it should also be read the same way: its "truth" is

precisely in the effect of absurdity it evokes in a naive reader, the effect which renders manifest the precarious status of rational totality, its dependence on some radically contingent "little piece of the real". This mocking attitude towards Hegel is unknowingly closer to the true spirit of the Hegelian dialectics than the attitude of reverent comprehension which endeavours to minimalize Hegel's "exuberant" claims, as if ashamed of the Master's megalomania.

45. G.W.F. Hegel, *Vorlesungen über die Geschichte der Philosophie* III, Leipzig: Verlag Philipp Reclam junior 1971, p. 628.

46. As to this problem of the temporality of freedom, see Slavoj Žižek, *The Sublime Object of Ideology*, London: Verso 1989, pp. 165–9.

6

Much Ado about a Thing

I The Variants of the Fetishism-Type

Why is Sade the truth of Kant?

It is of course a commonplace to ascertain that psychoanalysis arose as the final outcome of a long "incubation period". However, answers differ as to where and when, in the "history of ideas", the process was set in motion which finally gave birth to psychoanalysis. In his "Kant avec Sade", Lacan provides an unequivocal, albeit unexpected, answer to this question: Immanuel Kant's *Critique of Practical Reason*. The gist of Lacan's argument is that Kant was the first to outline the dimension of what Freud later designated as "beyond the pleasure principle".

Kant's starting point is the question: What is the impetus of our will, of our practical activity? His answer is: a representation [*Vorstellung*] which determines our will by means of the sentiment of pleasure or displeasure it brings about in the subject. We represent to ourselves an object and the pleasure or displeasure attached to its representation sets off our activity. Such a determinateness of our will is, however, always *empirical*, linked to contingent circumstances – that is to say: "pathological" in the Kantian sense of the term. Man as finite being is limited by his phenomenal, temporal–spatial experience; he has no access to the "Thing-in-itself" which transcends the horizon of his possible experience. This means that the Supreme Good – the a priori object which sustains itself on its inherent necessity and, consequently, does not depend on any external conditions – is irrepresentable, out of reach to our consciousness: if Kant did not formulate the notion of *A barré* (the barred big Other), he at least conceived of the barred G [*Good*].

Yet Kant is looking precisely for an impetus of our will which would be a priori – that is, unconditional and independent of our experience, of its contingent circumstances; since it cannot be found in the object, in the content of our practical activity, the only thing that remains is the very *form* of this activity: the form of universal legislation, independent of its particular, contingent content ("act only on that maxim through which you can at the same time will that it should become a universal law"). This way, we can test out every moral maxim: if it retains its consistency after assuming the form of universal law, then it is suitable to serve as the moral Ought [*Sollen*].

The paradox not to be missed here is that of the Freudian notion of *Vorstellungsrepräsentanz* – representative of some missing, "primordially repressed" representation: the representation which is "primordially repressed" in Kant is of course that of the Supreme Good, and the Law – the *form* of Law – emerges precisely in the place of this missing representation, filling out its void. That is to say, what should not pass unnoticed is that we run into the (form of) Law *at the precise point where the representation is lacking* (namely, the representation of an a priori object that could act as the impetus of our will). The form of moral Law is thus not simply the form of a certain content – its mediation with its content is far more paradoxical: it is so to speak the form *supplanting, holding the place of the missing content.* The structure is here again that of the Moebius band: form is not a simple reverse of content; we encounter it when we progress far enough on the side of content itself.

We can see, now, in what the link between Kant and Lacan consists: this "wiping out" of all pathological content is what Lacan calls "symbolic castration" – namely the renunciation of the incestuous object, of the Mother as Supreme Good – it is by way of this "wiping out" of the incestuous *content* that the paternal Law emerges as its *formal* metaphoric substitute. To resort to a rather worn-out wordplay, we attain the big Other (the symbolic Law) when we cross out M in M-Other and thereby hollow a gap around which the Other turns in its vicious circle. This is why Lacan rejects all usual attempts to account for the prohibition of incest: from utilitarianism to Lévi-Strauss, they all promise something in exchange for this radical renunciation; they all present it as a "reasonable" decision which provides a greater amount of long-term pleasure, a multitude of women, and so on – in short, they all refer to some Good as its ground, contrary to Lacan for whom the prohibition of incest is unconditional, since it is radically unaccountable. In it, I give *something in exchange for nothing* – or (and therein consists its fundamental paradox), in so far as the incestuous object is in itself impossible, I give *nothing in exchange for something* (the "permitted" non-incestuous object).

This paradox is at the root of what Freud called the "economic problem of masochism": the only way to explain the strange economy of our psychic apparatus is by means of the hypothesis of a certain "pure" loss which opens up the very field within which we can calculate gains and losses. This loss has an "ontological" function: the renunciation of the incestuous object changes the status, the mode of being, of all objects which appear in its place – they are all present *against the background of a radical absence* opened up by the "wiping out" of the incestuous Supreme Good. In other words, no later profit can recompense us for castration; since every possible profit appears within the space opened up by the very act of castration – since there is no neutral position from which we could "compare" gains and losses – the only possible field of their comparison is the empty space constituted by the "wiping out" of the Object. Or, to put it in the topological terms of the "logic of the signifier": castration introduces the distinction between an element and its (empty) place, more precisely: the *primacy* of the place over the element; it ensures that every positive element occupies a place which is not "consubstantial" to it, that it fills out a void which is not "its own".[1]

It is this paradoxical short circuit between form and content which confers upon Kantian ethics its "rigorist" features: since the field of Good is "barred", emptied of all "pathological" content, our activity can be considered truly moral only in so far as it is motivated by the form alone, to the exclusion of every "pathological" impetus, however "noble" it may be (compassion, etc.). Lacan's point in "Kant avec Sade" is, however, that this wiping out of all "pathological" objects, this reduction to the pure form, produces of itself a new, unheard-of kind of object; Lacan designates this "*non-pathological*" *object* – a paradox unthinkable for Kant – as *objet petit a*, the surplus-enjoyment, the object-cause of desire. What Lacan does is to repeat the inversion proper to the Moebius band on the level of the form itself: *if we progress far enough on the surface of the pure form, we come across a non-formal "stain" of enjoyment which smears the form* – the very renunciation of "pathological" enjoyment (the wiping out of all "pathological" content) brings about a certain surplus-enjoyment.

This stain of enjoyment that pertains to the Kantian categorical imperative is not difficult to discern: its very rigorist formalism assumes the tone of cruel, obscene "neutrality". Within the subject's psychic economy, the categorical imperative is experienced as an agency which bombards the subject with injunctions that are impossible to fulfil: it brooks no excuses ("You can because you must!") and observes with mocking, malevolent neutrality the subject's helpless struggle to live up to its "crazy" demands, secretly enjoying his failure. The imperative's categorical demand goes against the subject's well-being – more precisely, it is totally indifferent to it: from the viewpoint of the "pleasure principle" and its inherent prolongation, the "reality principle", the imperative is "non-economical", "unaccountable", senseless. The Freudian name for such an "irrational" injunction which prevents the subject from acting appropriately to present circumstances and thus organizes his failure is, of course, *superego*. According to Lacan, Kant fails to take into account this mischievous, superego reverse of the moral law, this obscene enjoyment that pertains to the very form of Law, in so far as he conceals the *split* of the subject into the subject of the enunciated and the subject of the enunciation, implicated in moral law – therein consists the emphasis of Lacan's criticism of the Kantian example of the depositary's moral dilemma:

> I have, for example, made it my maxim to increase my property by every safe means. Now I have in my possession a deposit, the owner of which has died without leaving any record of it. Naturally, this case falls under my maxim. Now I want to know whether this maxim can hold as a universal practical law. I apply it therefore to the present case and ask if it could take the form of a law, and consequently whether I could, by the maxim, make the law that every man is allowed to deny that a deposit has been made when no one can prove the contrary. I immediately realize that taking such a principle as a law would annihilate itself, because its result would be that no one would make a deposit.[2]

Lacan's commentary on this is that "the practice of a deposit being based on the two ears which, in order to constitute the depositary, must be plugged up against any condition which could be opposed to this fidelity. In other words, no deposit without a depositary equal to his charge."[3] In yet other words: the "subject of the enunciation" is here silently reduced to the "subject of the enunciated", the depositary to his function of depositary – Kant presupposes that we are dealing with a depositary "equal to his charge": with a subject who lets himself be taken without remaining in the abstract determination of being the depositary. Lacan's joke runs in the same direction: "My fiancée never misses a rendezvous, because as soon as she misses it, she would no longer be my fiancée" – here also, the fiancée is reduced to her symbolic function of fiancée.

Hegel pointed out the terrorist potential of this reduction of the subject to an abstract determination: the presupposition of revolutionary terror is indeed that the subject lets himself be reduced to his determination as Citizen who is "equal to his charge", which brings about the liquidation of subjects who are *not* equal to their charge – the Jacobinical terror is the consequent outcome of the Kantian ethic. One is dealing here with what Lacan, in his first seminars, called the "founding word" [*la parole fondatrice*] – namely, the conferring of a symbolic mandate ("you are my fiancée, my depositary, our citizen . . . ") which was later conceptualized as the Master-Signifier (S1): the point of Lacan's criticism of Kant is that there is in the subject who takes upon himself the symbolic mandate, who agrees to incarnate an S1, always an excess, a side which does not let itself be taken into the S1, in the place conferred on him by the socio-symbolic network. This excess is precisely the side of the *object*: the surplus in the "subject of the enunciation" which resists being reduced to the "subject of the enunciated" (embodiment of the symbolic mandate) is the object within the subject.

The "totalitarian object"

That, then, is the split between the "subject of the enunciated" and the "subject of the enunciation" as it is at work in the domain of the Law: behind the S1, the Law in its neutral, pacifying and solemn side, there is always a side of the object which announces an obscene mischievousness. Another well-known joke illustrates this split perfectly: in response to the question of explorers researching cannibalism, the native answers: "No, there are no longer cannibals in our region. We ate the last one yesterday." At the level of the subject of the enunciated, there are no more cannibals, whereas the subject of the enunciation is precisely this "we" who have eaten the last cannibal. Therein consists the intrusion of the "subject of the enunciation" avoided by Kant: the order of the Law prohibiting cannibalism can be ensured only by means of such an obscene agent who takes upon himself to eat the last cannibal. Kant's prohibition to probe into the origins of law, of legal power, concerns precisely this *object* of the Law in the sense of its "subject of the enunciation"; of the subject who assumes the role of its obscene agent–instrument.

And that is why Sade is to be taken as the truth of Kant: this object whose experience is avoided by Kant emerges in Sade's work, in the guise of the *executioner*, the agent who practises his "sadistic" activity on the victim. The Sadeian executioner has nothing whatsoever to do with pleasure: his activity is *stricto sensu* ethical, beyond any "pathological" motive, he only fulfils his duty – witness the lack of wit in Sade's work. The executioner works for the enjoyment of the Other, not for his own: he becomes a sole instrument of the Other's Will. And in so-called "totalitarianism", this illegal agent–instrument of the law, the Sadeian executioner, *appears as such* in the shape of the Party, agent–instrument of historical Will.[4] That is the meaning of Stalin's famous proposition: "we Communists are people of a special mould. We are made of special stuff."[5] This "special stuff" (the "right stuff", one could say) is precisely the incarnation, the apparition of the *objet petit a*.

Here, one should go back to the Lacanian determination of the structure of perversion as "an inverted effect of the fantasy. It is the subject who determines himself as object, in his encounter with the division of subjectivity."[6] The Lacanian formula for fantasy is written as $\$\Diamond a$: the crossed-out subject, divided in its encounter with the object-cause of his desire. The sadist pervert inverts this structure, which gives $a\Diamond\$$: by means of occupying himself the place of the object – of making himself the agent–executor of the Other's Will – he avoids the division constitutive of the subject and transposes his division upon his other – like the Stalinist, for example, confronted with the hysterical split petty-bourgeois "traitor" who did not want to give up his subjectivity completely and continued to "desire in vain". In the same passage Lacan goes back to his "Kant avec Sade" in order to recall that the sadist occupies the place of the object "to the benefit of another, for whose *jouissance* he exercises his action as sadistic pervert".[7]

The Other of Stalinism, the "inevitable necessity of laws of historical development" for which the Stalinist executor practises his act, could then be conceived as a new version of the "Supreme Being of Evilness", this Sadeian figure of the Other. It is this radical objectivization–instrumentalization of his own subjective position which confers upon the Stalinist, beyond the deceptive appearance of a cynical detachment, his unshakable conviction of only being the instrument of historical necessity. By making himself the transparent instrument of the Other's (History's) Will, the Stalinist avoids his constitutive division, for which he pays through the total alienation of his enjoyment: if the advent of the bourgeois subject is defined by his right to free enjoyment, the "totalitarian" subject shows this freedom to be that of the Other, of the "Supreme Being of Evilness" with reference to which his own will is totally instrumentalized.[8]

One could then conceptualize the difference between the classical Master and the "totalitarian" Leader as that between S1 (the unary Master-Signifier) and the object. The authority of the classical Master is that of a certain S1, signifier-without-signified, auto-referential signifier which embodies the performative function of the word. The Enlightenment wants to do without this instance of "irrational" authority; thereupon, the Master reappears in the guise of the "totalitarian" Leader: excluded as S1, he takes the shape of an object which embodies S2, the chain of knowledge (the "objective knowledge of the laws of history", for example), assuming the "responsibility" of carrying out the historical necessity in its cannibalistic cruelty.[9] The formula, the matheme, of the "totalitarian subject" would thus be

$$\frac{S2}{a}$$

– the semblance of a neutral "objective" knowledge, under which the obscene object–agent of a superegotistical Will hides.

The decisive point here is not to confuse the "irrational" authority of traditional Master with that of the modern "totalitarian" regime: the former is based on the gap of S1 in relation to S2, whereas "totalitarianism" makes resort to a bureaucratic "knowledge" (S2) which *lacks* support in a Master-Signifier (S1) that would "quilt" its field. This difference comes out when one considers the justification of obedience: the "totalitarian" Leader demands submission in the name of his alleged "effective" capacities (his wisdom, his courage, his adherence to the Cause, and so on); if, on the other hand, one says "I obey the king because he is wise and just", one already commits a crime of *lèse-majesté* – the only appropriate justification for it is the tautology "I obey the king *because he is King*". Kierkegaard has developed this point in a magnificent passage which extends, in a long arc, from divine authority, through the highest secular authority (the monarch), up to school and family authority (the father):

> To ask if Christ is profound is a blasphemy and an attempt to destroy him with ruse (either with consciousness or unconsciously) since the question contains doubt concerning his authority. . . . To ask if a king is a genius – for him to be obeyed in the case of a positive answer – is actually a *lèse-majesté* since the question contains the doubt in the sense of submission to his authority. To submit oneself to school on the condition that this place knows how to be inventive, really means that one makes a fool of it. To venerate one's father because he is smart is impiety.[10]

Horkheimer, who quotes these lines in his "Authority and Family", sees in them an indication of the passage of the liberal-bourgeois principle of "rational authority" in the post-liberal "totalitarian" principle of "irrational", unconditional authority. Against such a reading, one must insist that Kierkegaard moves here on the terrain of pre-liberal, traditional authority: he ascertains authority as S1, a charisma not founded in "effective" capacities.

The logic of "totalitarian" bureaucracy is, on the other hand, *its exact opposite* – namely: when, under what conditions, does state bureaucracy become "totalitarian"? Not where S1, the point of "irrational" authority, exerts a pressure "too strong", "excessive", on the bureaucratic *savoir(-faire)*, but, on the contrary, where this unary point which "quilts" the field of knowledge (S2) is wanting. In other words: when the bureaucratic knowledge loses its support in the Master-Signifier (S1) and is "left to itself", it "runs amok" and assumes the features of "mischievous neutrality" proper to *superego*. The theoretical point not to be missed here is that the apparently self-evident affinity between Master-Signifier (S1) and superego is misleading: the status of superego is that of a chain of knowledge (S2) and not that of a unary point of symbolic authority (S1).

The example which comes to mind immediately is (again) the discourse of the Stalinist bureaucracy – a discourse of knowledge if there is one: its position of enunciation, the place from which it claims to speak, is clearly that of pure, non-subjectivized knowledge (the infamous "objective knowledge of the laws of historical progress"). This position of neutral, "objective" knowledge – that is to say: of a knowledge not subjectivized by means of the intervention of some "quilting point", some Master-Signifier – is in itself mischievous, enjoying the subject's failure to live up to its impossible demands, impregnated by obscenity – in short: superegotistical. Lacan insists on the link between the superego and the so-called "sentiment of reality" – what we accept as "reality" is always sustained by a superego imperative: "When the sentiment of unreality bears on something, it is never on the side of the superego. It is always the ego that gets lost."[11] Does he not indicate thereby an answer to the question: Where do the confessions come from in the Stalinist trials? Since there was no "reality" for the accused outside the superego of the Party, outside its mischievous imperative, the only alternative to it being the abyss of the real, the confession demanded by the Party was indeed the only way for the accused to avoid the "loss of reality".

Lacan's fundamental thesis is that superego in its most fundamental dimension is an *injunction to enjoyment*: the various forms of superego commands are nothing but variations on the same motif: "Enjoy!"[12] Therein consists the opposition between Law and superego: Law is the agency of prohibition which regulates the distribution of enjoyment on the basis of a common, shared renunciation (the "symbolic castration"), whereas superego marks a point at which *permitted* enjoyment, freedom-to-enjoy, is reversed into *obligation* to enjoy – which, one must add, is the most effective way to block access to enjoyment.

One finds in Franz Kafka's work a perfect staging of bureaucracy under the aspect of an obscene, mischievous law which inflicts enjoyment. "The Court makes no claims upon you. It receives you when you come and it relinquishes you when you go."[13] How can one not recognize, in these lines with which the interview between Josef K. and the priest ends in Chapter IX of *The Trial*, the "mischievous neutrality" of the superego? Kafka's two great novels, *The Trial* and *The Castle*, start with the call of a superior bureaucratic instance (the Law, the Castle) to the subject – aren't we dealing here with a law which "appears to be giving the order, 'Enjoy!' [*Jouis!*], to which the subject can only reply 'I hear!' [*J'ouis!*], the enjoyment being no more than an innuendo"?[14] Is not the perplexity of the subject confronting this instance, precisely due to the fact that he misunderstands the imperative of enjoyment which resounds here and perspires through all the pores of its "neutral" surface? When Josef K., in the empty interrogation chamber, opened the first of the books the judges had read when the Court was in session, he

> found an indecent picture. A man and a woman were sitting naked on a sofa, the obscene intention of the draughtsman was evident enough . . . K. did not look at any of the other pages, but merely glanced at the title-page of the second book, it was a novel entitled: *How Grete was Plagued by her Husband Hans.*[15]

That is the superego: a solemn indifference impregnated in parts by obscenities. No wonder, then, that for Kafka, bureaucracy was "closer to original human nature than any other social institution" (letter to Oscar Baum, June 1922): what is this "original human nature" if not the fact that man is from the very beginning a "being-of-language" [*parlêtre*]? And what is superego – the functioning mode of bureaucratic knowledge – if not the purest, most radical embodiment of the signifier as the cause of the subject's division, of the signifier's injunction in its traumatic, senseless aspect?

The notion of superego as obscene reverse of law introduces a third element which perturbs the customary opposition of external social law (state and police regulations) and unwritten ethical "inner law" in whose name we (can) resist the external legal regulations – that is to say, the opposition of legality (the heteronomy of the social law) and legitimacy (the autonomous Law within us).[16] The way the Lacanian approach subverts this opposition is best exemplified by his critique of the following Kant fable intended to illustrate the moral law as *ratio cognoscendi* of our freedom:

> Suppose that someone says his lust is irresistible when the desired object and opportunity are present. Ask him whether he would not control his passion if, in front of the house where he has this opportunity, a gallows were erected on which he would be hanged immediately after gratifying his lust. We do not have to guess very long what his answer would be. But ask him whether he thinks it would be possible for him to overcome his love for life, however great it may be, if his sovereign threatened him with the same sudden death unless he made a false deposition against an honorable man whom the ruler wished to destroy under a plausible pretext. Whether he would or not he perhaps will not venture to say; but that it should be possible for him he would certainly admit without hesitation. He judges, therefore, that he can do something because he knows he ought, and he recognizes that he is free – a fact which, without the moral law, would have remained unknown to him.[17]

It seems that Lacan's commentary fully confirms the opposition of the external state law and the inner unwritten law – his reproach is precisely that, in the first part of his apologue, Kant implicitly equates them: "For the gallows is not the Law . . . the police may be the state, as is said, on the side of Hegel. But the Law is something else, as has been known since Antigone."[18] Lacan's point, however, is that a truly moral subject would resist the temptation to satisfy his lust not out of an inner moral stance, or because of the external threat represented by the gallows, but:

> it might happen that someone who holds to his passions, and would be blind enough to mix in a point of honour, could give Kant problems, forcing him to recognize that no occasion will more certainly precipitate some men towards their end, than to see it offered as a challenge to, or even in contempt of, the gallows.[19]

What Kant fails to take into account is that the subject's desire itself functions "beyond the pleasure principle" – beyond the "pathological" motivations of self-preservation, of pleasure and displeasure: the problem with Kant is not his moral idealism, his belief that man can act out of pure Duty independently of "pathological" utilitarian considerations of interests and pleasures, but – quite on the contrary – his ignorance of the fact that a certain "idealism" (disregard for the "pathological" considerations) is already at work in the domain of desire, of sexual "passion".[20] True "passion" is not only not hindered, but even encouraged and sustained by the prospect of the "gallows" – *in other words, true "passion" is uncannily close to the fulfilling of one's duty in spite of the external threat to it* (the second example from Kant's apologue). And it is precisely at this level that the opposition of pleasure and enjoyment is to be located: a simple illicit love affair without risk concerns mere *pleasure*, whereas an affair which is experienced as a "challenge to the gallows" – as an act of transgression – procures *enjoyment*; enjoyment is the "surplus" that comes from our knowledge that our pleasure involves the thrill of entering a forbidden domain – that is to say, that our pleasure involves a certain *displeasure*.

The uncanny excess that perturbs the simple opposition between external social law and unwritten inner law is therefore the "short circuit" between desire and law – that is to say, a point at which desire itself becomes Law, a point at which insistence upon one's desire equates to fulfilling one's duty, a point at which Duty itself is marked by a stain of (surplus-) enjoyment. And it is this "short circuit" which enables us to locate the paradox of the Kafkaesque bureaucratic machinery: far from being reducible to the external social law (the "gallows"), it epitomizes the perverse reverse of the "inner", "unwritten" law itself.

If the Kafkaesque bureaucracy were not embodied in an ex-timate perverse agency – a foreign body upon which the subject chances in his very heart, a kind of inner parasite which prevents the subject from achieving identity with itself – then it would be possible for the subject to assume a simple external distance towards it; bureaucracy would not be something "close[r] to original human nature". That is to say, what does the subject discover in himself after he renounces his "pathological" interests for the sake of the autonomous moral law? An unconditional injunction which exerts ferocious pressure upon him, disregarding his well-being. Psychoanalysis is here as far as possible from the standard utilitarian image of man according to which human psyche is thoroughly dominated by the pleasure principle and as such susceptible to control and direction: in this case, the social Good would be easy to realize, since egotism can by definition be manipulated and canalized in a socially desirable way. What works against the social Good is not egotistic pleasure-seeking but the superegotistical reverse of the moral law: the pressure of the "unwritten law" within myself, its obscene call to enjoyment that Freud baptized by the unfortunate name "primary masochism".[21]

The Kafkaesque bureaucracy therefore belongs indubitably to the inner, "unwritten" law: it epitomizes the "crazy" reverse of the Social that we encounter precisely when we escape contingent, external legal regulation. It functions as a strange body within ourselves, "what is in us more than ourselves", an obscene ex-timate agency which demands the impossible and mockingly observes our helpless attempts to comply with it. And the external law which regulates social exchange is perhaps here precisely in order to deliver us from the unbearable deadlock of the inner law run amok and to bring about a kind of pacification – perhaps "totalitarianism" is not so much the retreat of the inner "unwritten law" under the pressure of the external social law (the standard explanation according to which in "totalitarianism", the individual forfeits his moral autonomy and follows the law of the group) but rather a kind of "short circuit" entailing the loss of the distance between the two. Perhaps the usual opposition of the corrupted social law and the reliable inner moral sense is to be reversed: the pacifying intervention of the external social law enables us to elude the self-torture provoked by the obscene superegotistical "law of conscience".[22] The external law regulates *pleasures* in order to deliver us from the superegotistical imposition of *enjoyment* which threatens to overflow our daily life; *Carpe diem*, enjoy the day, consume the surplus-enjoyment procured by your daily sacrificing – there is the condensed formula of "totalitarianism".

We all know the worn-out phrase about free rational argumentation: it is completely powerless, there is no external force sustaining it – and yet, precisely as such, it is binding to such a degree that nobody can really escape it. When we are aware of the simple fact that somebody is right, all our rage against him is in a way helpless; he has a hold upon us stronger than any external compulsion. Free rational argumentation exerts no overt pressure upon us, we are free to use it or to shirk it – but the moment we accept it, our freedom has gone. In this precise sense, a convincing rational argumentation "makes no claims upon you. It receives you when you come and it relinquishes you when you go." Do not these words (quoted above) by means of which the priest from *The Trial* defines the mode of functioning of the Kafkaesque Court – that is, of the purest embodiment of bureaucracy in its superegotistical "irrational" dimension of the unfathomable, traumatic, perverse law – also offer the best possible definition of the mode of functioning of the free, non-compulsive rational argumentation? This is the way superego is at work in the very heart of the autonomous, free subject: the external social law is sustained by compulsion, whereas the superego shares with freedom its non-intrusive character: in itself, it is completely powerless, it is activated only in so far as the subject adresses it. Václav Havel's pathetic motto "the power of the powerless" suits perfectly the superego in its most obscene dimension – in it, the subject *stricto sensu* gets only what he wanted.

"I know, but nevertheless . . ."

This predominance of the superego over the law disturbs the relationship of knowledge and belief that determines our everyday ideological horizon: the gap between (real) *knowledge* and (symbolic) *belief*. We can illustrate it with the well-known psychological experience of when we say of something (as a rule terrible, traumatic) "I know that it is so, but nevertheless I can't believe it": the traumatic knowledge of

* we sacrifice our enjoyment to stability

reality remains outside the Symbolic, the symbolic articulation continues to operate as if we do not know, and the "time for understanding" is necessary for this knowledge to be integrated into our symbolic universe.[23] This kind of gap between knowledge and belief, in so far as both are "conscious", attests to a psychotic split, a "disavowal of reality"; propositions of this type are what linguistic analysis calls "pragmatic paradoxes".

Let us take, for example, the statement "I know that there is no mouse in the next room, but nevertheless I believe that there is a mouse there": this statement is not logically irreconcilable – since there is no logical contradiction between "there is no mouse in the next room" and "I believe there is a mouse in the next room" - the contradiction comes only on the pragmatic level, in so far as we take into account the position of the subject of the enunciation of this proposition: the subject who knows that there is no mouse in the next room cannot at the same time, without contradiction, believe that there is a mouse there. In other words, the subject who believes this is a split subject. The "normal" solution to this contradiction is of course that we repress the other moment, the belief, in our unconscious: in its place enters some spare moment which is not in contradiction to the first – this is the logic of so-called "rationalization".

Instead of the direct split "I know that the Jews are guilty of nothing, but nevertheless . . . (I believe that they are guilty)" comes the statement of the type "I know that the Jews are guilty of nothing; however, the fact is that in the development of capitalism, the Jews, as the representatives of financial and business capital, have usually profited from the productive labour of others"; instead of the direct split "I know that there is no God, but nevertheless . . . (I believe that there is)" appears a statement of the type "I know that there is no God, but I respect religious ritual and take part in it because this ritual supports ethical values and encourages brotherhood and love among people." Such statements are good examples of what might be called "lying by way of the truth": the second part of the statement, the claim which follows the syntagm "but nevertheless . . . ", can on a factual level be largely accurate but nevertheless operates as a lie because in the concrete symbolic context in which it appears it operates as a ratification of the unconscious belief that the Jews are nevertheless guilty, that God nevertheless exists, and so on – without taking into account these "investments" of the unconscious belief, the functioning of such statements remains totally incomprehensible.

One of the greatest masters of this was the Stalinist "dialectical materialism", the basic achievement of which, when it was necessary to legitimize some pragmatic political measure which violated theoretical principles, was "in principle it is of course so; nevertheless, in the concrete circumstances . . . ": the infamous "analysis of concrete circumstances" is basically nothing other than a search for rationalization which attempts to justify the violation of a principle.

This gap between (real) knowledge and (symbolic) belief determines our everyday ideological attitude: "I know that there is no God, but nevertheless, I operate as if (I believe that) he exists" – the part in brackets is repressed (belief in a God whom we witness through our activity is unconscious). Its inherent reversal is perhaps best seen in the work of de Sade: the most incisive analyses of his work (above all those by Pierre Klossowski) have long since demonstrated the way in which Sade's work is never simply atheistic, but in its internal economy presupposes the existence of God, only here the existence of God is affirmed not on the level of *belief* but on the level of *knowledge*. Sade's hero does not believe in God, he violates every ethical norm, and so on, yet he does this on the basis of knowledge that God exists: therein consists the force of fascination of Sade's hero, the fascination of his heroic–demonic position – we try in vain here to vindicate God, not because Sade's hero refuses to accept our evidence, but because he knows very well himself that God exists, but nevertheless heroically refuses to believe this, although he knows he will thus earn eternal damnation. His position is thus "(I know that God exists, but nevertheless) I act as though I believe that there is no God" – what he represses is the *knowledge* of the existence of God.[24]

Is not the same kind of self-distance at work in the so-called "totalitarian" ideologies in which individuals cynically maintain an "inner distance" towards the "external" ritual through which these ideologies reproduce themselves, and yet partake in it? This appearance, however, is deceptive: "totalitarian" ideology relies on a characteristically different, much more radical type of self-distance that was of course first revealed by George Orwell in *Nineteen Eighty-Four*.

The difficulty with Orwell is that the vocabulary of *Nineteen Eighty-Four* (Big Brother, the Thought Police, doublethink . . .) has already become a commonplace, which of course entailed a series of crucial simplifications; let us just recall the idea of "total manipulation": the idea that some hidden subject remains which oversees the entire social process, from which nothing escapes, which "takes all the threads in its hands", which sits in perfect judgement over the whole of society; such a presentation of the "totalitarian master" as the big Other who is not in himself "deceived", inscribed in a game which he does not command, *reproduces the myth propagated by "totalitarianism" itself*. . . . For all its defects, Orwell's vision of "1984" is far from this kind of naivety: he knows very well that we do not have on the one hand manipulated simpletons and on the other the non-deceived Manipulator, who could "lead the game" – the one who most believes in "totalitarianism", the one who really believes in the results of manipulation, is *the manipulator himself*:

> In our society, those who have the best knowledge of what is happening are also those who are furthest from seeing the world as it is. In general, the greater the understanding, the greater the delusion: the more intelligent, the less sane . . .

appears in "Goldstein's book", which is included in *Nineteen Eighty-Four.*[25] This paradox is the core of so-called doublethink: we must consciously manipulate the whole time, change the past, fabricate "objective reality", at the same time sincerely believing in the results of this manipulation. The "totalitarian" universe is a universe of psychotic split, disavowal of the obvious evidence, not a universe of "repressed secrets": the knowledge that we "deceive" in no way prevents us from believing in the result–effect of the deception.

In order to dispel the impression that these postulates of Orwell are only abstract, absurd possibilities, never fully realized, it suffices to read, for example, Hitler's *Mein Kampf*: even on first reading it displays all the weakness of the view that Hitler simply cheated, manipulated, consciously counted on "base instincts", and so on – the problem with such a reproach is not that it does not hold but, much more uncanny: it is shoving against an open door in painfully trying to demonstrate what Hitler himself openly admitted, since he wrote abundantly on the manipulation of the "psychology of the masses", on how it is necessary to hystericize the crowd, to lie and simplify problems, to find simple and understandable solutions for them, to hold them in obedience with a mixture of threat and promise . . . . However, here we are faced with the crucial trap: the fallacious conclusion that it is not therefore necessary to take Nazi theory seriously, that it does not warrant serious theoretical criticism, since it does not actually take itself seriously – that we are concerned with simple means of manipulation without inherent claims to truth; with an external instrument towards which the Nazis themselves maintained a cynical distance: a trap in which even such a perspicacious critical intellect as Adorno is caught.

Such a perception misses the key fact: notwithstanding his awareness of manipulation, Hitler basically believed in its results. For example, he knows that the image of the Jew as enemy who takes "all the threads into his hands" is only a means by which to channel the aggressive energy of the masses, to frustrate its radicalization in the direction of the class struggle, and so on, yet at the same time he "*really believes*" that the Jews are the primordial enemy. The uncanny dimension of this split, of this simultaneous coexistence of the ultimate cynicism and the ultimate fanaticism, is what we avoid as soon as we interpret it as the cynicism of manipulation – as soon as we see the moment of truth only in the manipulation (the popular concept of the Nazis as heedless cynical authority who manipulate everything); this avoidance enables us to reduce the Nazi subject to the traditional utilitarian-egotistic bourgeois subject.

Traditional, manipulative, totalitarian power

We could thus say that the formula of fetishism is "I know, but nevertheless . . . " ("I know that Mother doesn't have a penis, but nevertheless . . . [I believe that she has]"); however, this formula in its generality proves too abstract to enable a concrete analysis of different ideological formations. So it is necessary to complicate matters somewhat, to articulate three modes, three ways of working of the logic "I know, but nevertheless . . . ", three modes of disavowal of castration, which could be called "normal", "manipulative" and "fetishistic" *stricto sensu*. Octave Mannoni (on whom we draw here heavily[26]), illustrates the first mode with a story about initiation among the Hopi Indians; it is based on a book by Talayesva, *The Sun Hopi*:[27]

> We see here very clearly belief in the mask and how this belief is transfigured. The Hopi masks are called Katchin. Each year at a predetermined time, they are displayed in the pueblo, like Father Christmas with us, and like Father Christmas, they are of great interest to children. The second similarity: the children are deceived with the agreement of the parents. The deception is very strictly organized and none is allowed to

> reveal the secret. Unlike Father Christmas, who is an uncertain but friendly figure, the Katchin inspire terror since what fascinates the children is that they might be eaten by them. The mother of course relieves the children's fear by offering the Katchin pieces of meat . . . [28]

This is thus the first stage, when children believe naively that they are really faced with a terrible apparition. Those who break the charm of this naive belief are the parents themselves or relatives – when the children reach a predetermined age, they arrange an initiation ritual and in the course of this ritual, which directly evokes castration, the masks are paraded before the children and they are shown who is really hidden behind them – that it is only their fathers and uncles. The key question is how the children react to this revelation:

> "When the Katchin . . . step in front of the masks, writes Talayesva, it was a great shock to me: these were not therefore spirits. I knew them all and felt very unhappy since all my life they had told me that the Katchin were gods. Above all I was disappointed and angry when I saw that my father and all my uncles in the clan danced dressed up as Katchin. The worst was to see my own father."
>
> Really, in what can we believe if authority is an impostor? However . . . this ritual of demystification and breaking of belief in the Katchin became the institutional basis for a new belief in the Katchin, which formed an essential part of the Hopi religion. We must reject reality – the Katchin are fathers and uncles – with the aid of a transformation of belief . . . . Now, say the children, now we know that the real Katchin will no longer, as before, dance in the pueblo. They will only come in an invisible way, they will dwell in a mystical way in the masks for the day of the dance . . . . The Hopi divorce the deception with which they mislead the children from the mystic truth into which they are initiated. And the Hopi can say in all sincerity: "I know that the Katchin are not spirits, that they are fathers and uncles, but nevertheless, the Katchin are here when the fathers and uncles dance in the masks." This story of Talayesva is a story of everyone, normal or neurotic, Hopi or not. In the end we can see how we ourselves, when we can find no trace of God in the heavens, with the aid of some transformation which is analogous to that of the Hopi, can say that God dwells in the heavens.[29]

Mannoni rightly stresses that here we are concerned with the passage from the imaginary to the symbolic register: "belief abandons its imaginary form and is symbolized in such a way as to open faith, or commitment",[30] – that is, while the children's belief in the Katchin before initiation is imaginary, afterwards it is transformed into symbolic faith. It is essential that we do not miss how, with this passage, the relationship changes between the mask and what is hidden behind it, the face which is behind it. As soon as we enter the Symbolic, the real secret is no longer what is hidden behind the mask but the "efficacy" of the mask as such: the fathers or uncles can be ordinary everyday people, with nothing magic in them, but as soon as they "adopt" the mask, things are no longer the same, the spirit is what governs their movements, what speaks through them. So the spirit is not something which is hidden behind the mask, the spirit dwells in the mask itself: the symbolic function, the ritual form, thus has more weight than its bearer, than that which is hidden behind the ritual form.

We can conceive of the passage from naive belief in the mask into symbolic faith in its significance as an "internalization": we no longer believe in the direct reality of the mask, we know that the mask is only a mask – the mask is only a signifier which expresses an internal, invisible spirit, a mystical preserve. However, we must not forget that this mystical spirit, invisible Beyond, *is not what is hidden behind the mask* – behind the mask is the everyday image in which there is nothing holy or magic. All the magic, all the invisible mystical spirit, is *in the mask as such* – therein consists the basic feature of the symbolic order: there is more truth in the mask, in the symbolic form, than in what is hidden behind it, than in its bearer. If we "tear away the mask" we will not encounter the hidden truth; on the contrary, we will lose the invisible "truth" which dwells in the mask.[31]

Mannoni illustrates the second mode with an entertaining adventure of Casanova: Casanova wanted to trick some naive young country wench into seduction. In order to make a suitable impression on her, he played the role of a wizard, a master of occult knowledge – he knew very well that it was all a trick, that he was only an impostor exploiting the credulity of the country girl. So during the night he dressed himself in flamboyant "wizard's" outfit, marked a large circle on the ground with paper, which he designated the magic field, and began to prattle wizard's spells in this circle. Immediately something unexpected happened: a terrible storm raged, thunder and lightning started, and Casanova was terrified:

> I knew very well [of course] that this storm was natural, there was no

> reason for it, that it was unexpected. However despite that [nevertheless] I started to become so afraid that I longed to be back in my own room .[32]

Despite knowing very well that it was a natural phenomenon, he believed all the same that the celestial forces were punishing him for his profane playing with magic – and what did he do but step quickly into his own paper circle, where he felt completely safe!:

> In the fear which seized me, I was convinced that the lightning could not strike me since it could not enter the ring. Without that false belief, I could not have remained in that place even for a minute.[33]

The ring was thus, as Mannoni remarks, despite everything – despite being a completely conscious deception – nevertheless "magic"! This "I know, but nevertheless . . . " of Casanova, as we can see, is radically different from the "I know, but nevertheless . . . " of the Hopi: in the case of Casanova we have on the one hand the simpletons, the suckers, on the other a manipulator, an impostor who exploits the superstition of fools. The manipulator "knows very well" that all magic ritual is only deception – the moment of belief ("but nevertheless") is displaced, projected into the other, into the simpleton, into the object of his manipulation; he always needs the credulity of the other and if the deception is "too successful", if – as the story of Casanova's adventure shows – a fortuitous harmonization between the intended manipulation and reality occurs, if it seems as though the real "answered" the manipulation, the distance between manipulator and manipulated is destroyed and *the manipulator himself falls into credulity*, begins to believe in his own deception.

Casanova is thus basically incapable of performing *Aufhebung*, the sublation of naive belief into symbolic faith; he is incapable of experiencing the mystic "presence of the spirit" in the mask at the time of the symbolic ritual; the mask (ritual appearance) *remains for him simply a mask*. On the one hand, we have a credulous fool who directly believes in it and, on the other, the manipulator who exploits the credulity of the simpleton; when the manipulator loses the external distance, he does not achieve the level of symbolic faith but simply falls into the same naive-imaginary belief that characterizes the object of his manipulation.

Only with the third mode do we attain fetishism *stricto sensu*: here, as Mannoni demonstrates, we are not at all concerned with belief; the fetishist only "knows very well"; the second moment, the belief contained in "but nevertheless", *is directly incarnated in the fetishistic object*:

> the reinstatement of the fetish abolishes the problem of belief, magic or not, at least in the terms in which we set it: the fetishist does not seek any kind of credulity; for him the others are in ignorance and he is content to leave them in it . . . the place of credulity, the place of the other, is now occupied by the fetish itself.[34]

For the fetishist, therefore, his other, "ordinary people", are not simpletons, suckers whom it is necessary to exploit, but simply ignorant: the fetishist has privileged access to the Object, the significance of which "ordinary people" overlook; his position is thus in some sense the very opposite to that of the manipulator Casanova, since he is primarily himself that which appears in the eyes of "ordinary people" a simpleton, convinced of the exceptional value of the chosen Object.

These three modes of "disavowing castration", of working the logic of "I know, but nevertheless . . . ", can be interpreted as three elementary structures of the exercise of authority:

First, traditional authority is based on what we could call the *mystique of the Institution*. Authority bases its charismatic power on symbolic ritual, on the form of the Institution as such. The king, the judge, the president,and so on, can be personally dishonest, rotten, but when they adopt the insignia of Authority, they experience a kind of mystic transubstantiation; the judge no longer speaks as a person, it is Law itself which speaks through him. Such was the view of Socrates before the court which condemned him to death: in view of content, the judgement was undoubtedly faulty, it was conditioned by the vindictive nature of the judge, but Socrates did not want to flee since the form of the Law itself, which must remain inviolate, meant more than the empirical, fortuitous content of the judgement. Socrates' argument could thus actually be linked to the phrase "I know, but nevertheless . . . ": "I know that the verdict which condemned me to death is faulty, but nevertheless we must respect the form of the Law as such . . . " "The spirit of the Law" thus dwells in the symbolic ritual, in the form as such, not in the rottenness of its momentary bearer: constitutional Authority is better, however faulty in its content, than authority which is fortuitously "fair", yet without support in an Institution.

The specific mode of this symbolic authority epitomized by the Name-of-the-Father can best be exemplified by the version of the "*je sais bien, mais quand même . . .* " contained in the "wise saying" of the Philosopher from Mozart's *Così fan tutte*: although women's matrimonial fidelity is to be trusted, we must nevertheless avoid putting this trust to the test by exposing them to too much temptation. Far from being reducible to vulgar misogynous cynicism, these words enable us to grasp why Lacan determined Woman as one of the Names-of-the-Father. The Name-of-the-Father designates the phallic metaphor (the phallic signifier), so the key to this enigma is to be sought in the phallic dimension – it is this dimension which constitutes a link between the Philosopher's "wise saying" about women and the paternal symbolic authority. That is to say, the same thing that goes for women goes also for the Father as symbolic authority: Father's authority is to be fully trusted, yet one should not put it to the test too often since, sooner or later, one is bound to discover that Father is an impostor and his authority a pure semblance . . . . And it is the same with the King: his wisdom, justice and power are to be trusted, yet not too severely tested.

Therein consists the logic of the "phallic" power: to aggravate its paradox, it is *actual* (i.e. effective) only as *potential* – its full deployment lays bare its imposture. Every authority, in so far as it is symbolic – and every intersubjective authority *is* a symbolic one; is ultimately founded in the power of the signifier, not in the immediate force of coercion - implies a certain surplus of trust, a certain "if He knew about it (about the wrongdoings carried out in His name, about the injustices we have to suffer), He would set things right without delay" which, on account of a structural necessity, must remain a pure possibility. Perhaps this paradox enables us to account for *economy* as such: we possess power, we are "in" it, only in so far as we do not put it to use thoroughly, in so far as we keep it in reserve, as a threat – in short: in so far as we *economize*.

The Lacanian "plus-One" [*le plus-Un*] is precisely this necessary surplus: every signifying set contains an element which is "empty", whose value is accepted on trust, yet which precisely as such guarantees the "full" validity of all other elements. Strictly speaking it comes in excess, yet the moment we take it away, the very consistency of the other elements disintegrates. And is not this eventually the logic of all "reserves": monetary, military, food? Piles of gold have to lie around uselessly at Fort Knox so that the so-called monetary balance is maintained; weapons not meant to be used have been accumulated to guarantee the "balance of fear"; mountains of wheat and corn must rot in silos to secure our food reserves – how can one not apprehend that the logic at work here is senseless from the viewpoint of "reality"; that in order to explain its efficacy, one has to take into account a purely symbolic function?[35]

The second mode corresponds to what might be called *manipulative authority*: authority which is no longer based on the mystique of the Institution – on the performative power of symbolic ritual – but directly on the manipulation of its subjects. This kind of logic corresponds to a late-bourgeois society of "pathological Narcissism", constituted of individuals who take part in the social game externally, without "internal identification" – they "wear (social) masks", "play (their) roles", "not taking them seriously": the basic aim of the "social game" is to deceive the other, to exploit his naivety and credulity; the social role or the mask is directly experienced as manipulative imposture; the whole aim of the mask is to "make an impression on the other".

The basic attitude of manipulative authority is consequently cynical, in so far as we understand cynicism in the strict Lacanian sense: the cynic, from the fact that "the Other does not exist" – that the Other (the symbolic order) is only a fiction, that it does not pertain to the Real – erroneously concludes that the Other does not function, is not effectual. What is meant by the fact that the Other, despite being a fiction, is "effective" can actually best be illustrated precisely with the above-mentioned mystique of the Institution proper to traditional power: we know that Authority is a fiction, but nevertheless this fiction regulates our actual, real behaviour; we regulate social reality itself *as though* the fiction were real. But the cynic – who believes only in the Real of enjoyment – preserves an external distance towards the symbolic fiction; he does not really accept its symbolic efficacy, he merely uses it as means of manipulation. The efficacy of the fiction takes its revenge on him when a coincidence of the fiction with reality occurs: he then performs as "his own sucker".

The third mode, fetishism *stricto sensu*, would be the matrix of *totalitarian authority*: the point is no longer that the other ("ordinary people") would be deceived manipulatively but that we are ourselves those who – although "we know very well" that we are people like others – at the same time consider ourselves to be "people of a special mould, made of special stuff" – as individuals who participate in the fetish of the Object-Party, direct embodiment of the Will of History.

The breach between cynicism and totalitarian logic can be well illustrated by the different attitude to the experience that "the Emperor has no clothes". A variation on this theme is typical cynical "wisdom": "phrases about values, honour, honesty are all empty words, they serve only to deceive the suckers; what counts is only the Real (money, power, influence)." . . . The cynic overlooks here that *we are naked only beneath our clothes*: a cynical kind of demystification is itself still all too naive in that it fails to notice how the "naked Real" is sustained by the symbolic fiction. The totalitarian, too, does not believe in the symbolic fiction, in his version of the Emperor's clothes; he knows very well that the Emperor is naked (in the case of the Communist totalitarian, that the system is actually corrupt, that talk about socialist democracy is just empty verbiage, and so on). Yet in contrast to traditional authority, what he adds is not "but nevertheless" but "just because": *just because* the Emperor is naked we must hold together the more, work for the Good, our Cause is all the more necessary . . .

There is a point in *Nineteen Eighty-Four* at which Orwell "produces his own symptom", says more than he is aware of saying: it is an insertion which in its form already operates as something exceptional, an extrusion – namely, the so-called "Goldstein's book", the theoretical treatise of a "dissident" which clarifies the "real nature" of totalitarian society: that it is concerned with power for its own sake, and so on. What is its place in the universe of "1984"? Towards the end of *Nineteen Eighty-Four* we learn that this book was not written by Goldstein at all, but fabricated by the Party itself – why? The first answer is, of course, that it is an old, regular tactic of a totalitarian Party in power: if there is no opposition it must be invented, since the Party needs external and internal enemies so that, in the name of this danger, it can maintain the state of emergency and total unity; "Goldstein's book" is intended to encourage the formation of opposition groups and thus create the excuse for incessant purges, the settling of internal accounts. However, this answer, although valid, is not enough: in "Goldstein's book" there is "something more": it contains primarily a truth about the working of a totalitarian system – from where does this "compulsion" of the Party come, to produce a Text which expresses its own truth?

Nineteen Eighty-Four belongs to the so-called "last-man novels" (it should not be forgotten that one of its provisional titles was *The Last Man*): novels which describe some catastrophic situation in which "the last living beings" exert all their force to tell others – posterity – the truth of what happened. This catastrophic situation can be of the most varied nature: from natural catastrophes which destroy some group, to concentration camps (where, as is well known, a number of prisoners held on to life only by the desire to pass on to posterity the truth of their experiences) and similar social catastrophes, like the emergence of a totalitarian society as perceived by the "last man" who still resists its closure. If this paradigm is applied to *Nineteen Eighty-Four*, then a paradoxical result is achieved: the "last man" is not so much the unhappy Winston Smith with his diary as primarily *the Party itself with its "Goldstein's book"*. This book "settles acounts" with the big Other, the guarantor of truth: it lays out the "real state of things" as for the "Last Judgement". It is for this that the Party needs "dissidents", for this that it needs "Goldstein": it cannot express its truth in the first person – even in the "innermost circle" it can never come to the point at which "the Party knows how matters actually stand", at which it would recognize the tautological truth that the aim of its power is just power itself – so it can achieve it only as a construction imputed to someone else. The circle of totalitarian ideology is thus never closed – it necessarily contains what Edgar Allan Poe would call its "imp of perversity" compelling it to confess the truth about itself.

II "The King is a Thing"

The King's two bodies

According to Saint-Just's famous motto, Revolution has established happiness as a political factor. What Saint-Just meant by "happiness" has of course little to do with enjoyment: it implies revolutionary

Virtue, a radical renunciation of the decadent pleasures of the *ancien régime*. In the Jacobinical universe, this surplus of enjoyment corrupting the sound body of the People is incarnated in the person of the King: it is as if the very body of the King condenses in itself the secret cause of the People's enslavement to the forces of corruption and tyranny. The Jacobins effectuated here a kind of anamorphotic reversal: what appeared in the traditional perspective as the charismatic embodiment of the People, as the point at which the People's "life-substance" acquired immediate existence, changes now, when viewed from another perspective, into a cancerous protuberance contaminating the body of the People – which is why the purification of the People demands that this protuberance be cut off. To paraphrase Saint-Just: if the Republic is to survive, this man – the King – must be put to death, because his very existence poses a threat to the Republic.

It is a commonplace that with this logic of the King's necessary execution, the Jacobins reached an impasse; however, this impasse is more sophisticated than it may seem. At first sight, it appears that the Jacobins succumbed to the illusion indicated, among others, by Marx in a note to Chapter 1 of *Capital*: they overlooked that "to be a king" is not an immediate natural property of the person of a king but a "determination-of-reflection" – that a king is a king because his subjects treat him like one, and not the reverse. The proper way to get rid of this illusion is thus not the murder of the king but the dissolution of the network of social relations within which a certain person acquires the status of a king – as soon as this symbolic network loses its performative power, we suddenly see how the person who previously provoked such fascination is really an individual like others; we are confronted with the material remainder which was stuck on the symbolic function.[36] It is true that we thus reach the comforting conclusion that the greatest punishment for the king is to let him live outside his symbolic function, as an ordinary citizen, which is at the same time supposed to be the most successful way to dispense with the symbolic efficiency of the function "king"; however, such a distinction between king as a symbolic function and its empirical bearer misses a paradox that we could designate by the term "chiasmic exchange of properties" introduced by Andrzej Warminski.[37]

Claude Lefort has already articulated this paradox apropos of his criticism of the classical thesis of Ernst Kantorowicz concerning "the king's two bodies": his sublime, immaterial, sacred body and his terrestrial body subjected to the cycle of generation and corruption.[38]

The point is not simply that his transient material body serves as a support, symbol, incarnation of his sublime body; it consists rather in the curious fact that as soon as a certain person functions as "king", his everyday, ordinary properties undergo a kind of "transubstantiation" and become an object of fascination:

> . . . it is the natural body which, because it is combined with the supernatural body, exercises the charm that delights the people. It is insofar as it is a sexed body, a body capable of procreation and of physical love, and a fallible body, that it effects an unconscious mediation between the human and divine.[39]

The wisdom of royal families to this very day has therefore been not only to tolerate, but even to incite rumours about their intrigues, small human frailties, love escapades, and so on – all of which have served precisely to enforce the charisma of the royal figures. The more we represent the king as an ordinary man, caught in the same passions, victim of the same pettinesses as we – that is, the more we accentuate his "pathological" features (in the Kantian meaning of the term) – *the more he remains "king"*. Because of this paradoxical exchange of properties, we cannot deprive the king of his charisma simply by treating him as our equal. At the very moment of his greatest abasement, he arouses absolute compassion and fascination – witness the trial of "citizen Louis Capet".

What is at stake is thus not simply the split between the empirical person of the king and his symbolic function. The point is rather that this symbolic function *redoubles his very body*, introducing a split between the visible, material, transient body and another, sublime body, a body made of a special, immaterial stuff. In his seminar on *Desire and its Interpretation* (1958–9) Lacan proposes a similar reading of the well-known dialogue from *Hamlet*: "The body is with the king, but the king is not with the body. The king is a thing. – A thing, my Lord? – Of nothing." The distinction body/thing coincides here with the difference between the material and the sublime body: the "thing" is what Lacan calls *objet petit a*, a sublime, evasive body which is a "thing of nothing", a pure semblance without substance. According to Lacan, it is here that we must look for the reason behind Hamlet's hesitation and prevarication: he wants to strike Claudius in such a way that by striking a blow to his material body, he would hit the "thing" in it, the king's sublime body. At the same time, he knows that in so far as this sublime body is a pure semblance, it would forever slip out of his reach – his blow would always strike empty:

> . . . one cannot strike the phallus, because the phallus, even the real phallus, is a *semblance*.
>
> We were troubled at the time by the question of why, after all, no one assassinated Hitler – Hitler, who is very much this object that is not like the others, this object *x* whose function in the homogenization of the crowd by means of identification is demonstrated by Freud. Doesn't this lead back to what we're discussing here?
>
> . . . What stays Hamlet's arm? It's not fear – he has nothing but contempt for the guy – it's because he knows that he must strike something other than what's there.[40]

The impasse of the Jacobins apropos of the king should be located at the same level. They were guided by the right intuition that with the king we cannot simply distinguish the empirical person from his symbolic mandate – the more we isolate the person, the more this remainder remains a king. For all that, their regicide cannot but strike us as misdirected, as an impotent *acting out* which was simultaneously excessive and empty. In other words, we cannot elude the paradoxical, contradictory impression that the decapitation of the king was fundamentally superfluous *and* a terrifying sacrilege confirming the king's charisma by very means of his physical destruction. The same impression is at work in all similar cases, including the execution of Ceausescu: when confronted with the picture of his bloodstained body, even the greatest enemies of his regime shrank back, as if they were witness to excessive cruelty, but at the same time a strange fear flashed across their mind, mixed with incredulity: is this really *him*? Or, to use the terms from *Hamlet*: is the thing really with this body? Did it really die with it?

Lenin's two bodies

This mention of Ceausescu is by no means accidental. Within the post-revolutionary "totalitarian" order, we have witnessed a re-emergence of the sublime political body in the shape of Leader and/or Party. The tragic greatness of the Jacobins consists precisely in the fact that they refused to accomplish this step: they preferred to lose their head physically, rather than to take upon themselves the passage to personal dictatorship (to assist at the Napoleonic Thermidor). They did not want to pass a certain threshold beyond which they could again "rule innocently" by means of assuming the position of a pure instrument of the Other's will. It was of course again Saint-Just, the "purest" among them, who had a kind of presentiment of this threshold, when he imputed to the waverers who dared not assume the burden of Terror the implicit reasoning "We are not sufficiently virtuous to be so terrible".

The Jacobins lacked the absolute certainty that they were nothing but an instrument fulfilling the Will of the big Other (God, Virtue, Reason, Cause). They were always tormented by the possibility that behind the façade of the executor of the Terror on behalf of revolutionary Virtue, some "pathological" private interest might be hiding – or, to quote a concise formulation by Lefort:

> The fact is that the organization of the Terror was never such that its agents could free themselves from their own will or imprint themselves on a body whose cohesion was ensured by the existence of its head. In short, they could not act as bureaucrats.[41]

As such they were, so to speak, *ontologically guilty*, and it was only a matter of time before the guillotine would cut off their heads. It is precisely for this reason, however, that their Terror was democratic, not yet "totalitarian", in contrast to post-democratic totalitarianism, in which the revolutionaries fully assume the role of an instrument of the big Other, whereby their very body again redoubles itself and assumes sublime quality. It is against this background that we must conceive, for example, Stalin's famous "vow of the Bolshevik Party to its leader Lenin": "We, the Communists, are people of a special mould. We are made of special stuff" – it is quite easy to recognize the Lacanian name for this "special stuff": *object petit a*, the sublime object, the Thing within a body.

In the first chapter of the first edition of *Capital*, Marx conceived money, in its relation to all other commodities, as a paradoxical element which immediately, in its very singularity, embodies the universality of all commodities – as a "singular reality which comprises in itself all effectively existing species of the same kind".[42] The same paradoxical logic also distinguishes the functioning of the "totalitarian" Party: it is as if, alongside classes, strata, groups and sub-groups, their economic, political and ideological structures, which together constitute the different parts of the sociohistorical universe governed by the objective laws of social development, there existed *the* Party, an immediate individual incarnation of these objective laws, a point of paradoxical short circuit between subjective will and objective laws. Therein consists the "special mould" of the Communists: they are the "objective Reason of History" incarnated, and in so far as the stuff they are made of is ultimately their body, this body again undergoes a kind of transubstantiation; it changes into a bearer of *another* body within the transient material envelopment.

It would be interesting to reread, on the basis of this logic of the sublime body of the Communists, Lenin's letters to Maxim Gorky, above all those from 1913 which concern the debate on the "construction of God" [*bogograditel 'stvo*], a revisionist current of Russian social democracy supported by Gorky. The first thing that strikes the eye is a feature without any apparent theoretical weight: Lenin is literally obsessed with Gorky's good health – here are a few samples of Lenin's final words:

> – Let me know how you are. / Yours, *Lenin*.
> – Are you in good health? / Yours, *Lenin*.
> – *Take care of yourself*. Send me a word. *Repose yourself* better. / Yours, *Lenin*.

When, in autumn 1913, Lenin heard that a fellow-Bolshevik was treating Gorky for his pneumonia, he wrote to him promptly:

> When a "Bolshevik" – true, an old one – treats you with a new method, I must confess that this disquiets me terribly! God save us from doctors-friends in general and from doctors-Bolsheviks in particular! . . . I assure you that you must undergo a cure *only* with the best specialists (with the exception of benign cases). It is simply horrible to experiment on yourself the inventions of a Bolshevik doctor!! At least take a check-up with the professors in Naples . . . [at that time, Gorky lived on Capri] . . . if these professors really know their job . . . . I'm telling you that if you leave [Capri] this winter, you must visit *without further ceremony* some first-class doctors *in Switzerland* and *in Vienna* – it would be unpardonable not to do so!

Let us pass over the associations that a retroactive reading of this passage inevitably evokes today (twenty years later, the whole of Russia tried out on itself the new methods of a certain Bolshevik); let us rather raise the question of the *horizon of meaning* of Lenin's concern for Gorky's health. At first sight, the reasons seem clear and innocent enough: Gorky was a precious ally and as such deserved great care . . . . However, the subsequent letter already throws a different light on this whole affair: Lenin is alarmed by Gorky's positive attitude towards the "construction of God" which, according to Gorky, should be only "postponed", put aside "for the moment", definitely not "rejected". Such an attitude is incomprehensible to Lenin, an extremely unpleasant surprise – here are the beginning and the end of this letter:

> Dear Alexei Maximovitch, / what are you doing, then? Really, it is terrible, simply terrible! // Why are you doing this? It is terribly painful. / Yours, *V.I.*

And here is, in addition, the postscript:

> P.S. *Take care of yourself* more seriously, really, so that you will be able to travel in winter *without catching cold* (in winter, it is dangerous).

What is really at stake here emerges even more clearly at the end of the subsequent letter, posted together with the preceding one:

> I enclose yesterday's letter: don't mind my being carried away. Perhaps I didn't understand you *well*? Perhaps *you* were *joking* when you wrote "for the moment"? Concerning the "construction of God", perhaps you didn't write that seriously? / Good Heavens, take care of yourself a little bit better. / Yours, *Lenin*.

Here, the thing is finally said in a formal and explicit way: basically, Lenin conceives Gorky's ideological confusion and his hesitations as a sign of his illness and physical exhaustion. This is why he does not take Gorky's counter-arguments seriously – in the last resort, his answer consists in repeating "Relax, take better care of yourself . . . ".

This attitude of Lenin, however, has nothing whatsoever to do with any kind of vulgar materialism, with an immediate reduction of

Gorky's reasoning to physiological processes; on the contrary, it implies a notion of the Communist as a man of "special mould": when a Communist speaks and acts as a Communist, it is the objective necessity of History itself which speaks and acts through him. In other words, the mind of a true Communist cannot deviate because it is the immediate self-consciousness of historical necessity – consequently, the only thing that can go wrong and introduce disorder is his body, this fragile materiality charged with a mandate to serve as a transient support of *another* body, "made of special stuff". Is not the ultimate proof of this special attitude of Leninist Communists towards the body the fact of the *mausoleum* – their obsessive compulsion to preserve intact the body of the dead Leader (Lenin, Stalin, Ho Chi Minh, Mao Zedong)? How can we explain this obsessive care if not by reference to the fact that in their symbolic universe, the body of the Leader is not just an ordinary transient body but a body redoubled in itself, an envelopment of the sublime Thing?

How to extract the People from within the people?

The emergence of this sublime body is clearly linked to the illegal violence that founds the reign of law: once the reign of law is established, it rotates in its vicious circle, "posits its presuppositions", by means of foreclosing its origins; yet for the synchronous order of law to function, *it must be supported by some "little piece of the real" which, within the space of law, holds the place of its founding/foreclosed violence* – the sublime body is precisely this "little piece of the real" which "stops up" and thus conceals the void of the law's vicious circle. The logic of the "totalitarian" Leader's sublime body, however, is not the same as the traditional logic of the "king's two bodies" – how do they differ? One has to look for the answer via an unexpected detour: in the Marquis de Sade.

Lacan – not to mention Adorno and Horkheimer – has already demonstrated the inner connection between de Sade and Kantian ethics – has asserted that the Sadeian universe offers us the truth of Kantian ethical formalism. The structural homology between Kant and the democratic Terror is likewise a classical topos: in both cases, the point of departure consists in an act of radical emptying, evacuation. With Kant, what is evacuated and left empty is the locus of the

Supreme Good: every positive object which would occupy this place is by definition "pathological", marked with empirical contingency, which is why the moral law must be reduced to the pure Form bestowing on our acts the character of universality. The elementary operation of the Jacobinical democratic Terror is also the evacuation of the locus of Power: every pretender to this place is by definition a "pathological" usurper – "nobody can rule innocently", to quote Saint-Just again. The conclusion to be drawn is that there must also be a parallel between de Sade and Saint-Just.

Let us begin with the fundamental Sadeian fantasy formulated by the Pope in Book V of *Juliette*. The Sadeian vision of Nature articulated here is an effective forerunner of Stalinist "dialectical materialism": Nature is conceived as an eternal circuit of generation and corruption in which, following iron laws, the old withers and the new is born. Why, then, does de Sade give a clear preference to destruction before giving birth to the new? According to his view, Nature is a slave of its own laws, caught in the implacable necessity of its circular movement; the only way to enable it to create something effectively new is therefore an absolute Crime – that is to say, a crime whose destructive force exceeds the circular movement of generation and corruption, a crime which interrupts this very circuit and, so to speak, liberates Nature from its own laws, rendering it possible to create new forms of life *ex nihilo*, from the zero-point. It is therein that Lacan locates the link between sublimation and the death-drive: sublimation equates to creation *ex nihilo*, on the basis of annihilation of the preceding Tradition. It is not difficult to see how all radical revolutionary projects, Khmer Rouge included, rely on this same fantasy of a radical annihilation of Tradition and of the creation *ex nihilo* of a new (sublime) Man, delivered from the corruption of previous history. The same fantasy also inspired the Jacobinical revolutionary Terror: Revolution must erase the body of the people corrupted by the long reign of tyranny and extract from it a new, sublime body. To quote from Billaud-Varenne's speech to the Convention on 20 April 1794:

> The French people have set you a task which is as vast as it is difficult to carry out. The establishment of a democracy in a nation that has languished in chains for so long might be compared to the efforts made by nature during the astonishing transition from nothingness to existence, and those efforts were no doubt greater than those involved in the transition from

> life to annihilation. We must, so to speak, recreate the people we wish to restore to freedom.[43]

The contours of the Sadeian fantasy are easy to discern here: like the Sadeian agent in regard to nature, the revolutionary has to deliver the People from the chains of the old society, enabling it to cast away its corrupted body and to (re)create itself *ex nihilo*, i.e. to repeat the "astonishing transition from nothingness to existence": "As the People must be extracted from within the people, the only means to extract them from themselves is to make a distinction between being and nothingness."[44] This "extraction of the People from within the people" equates to the extraction of the sublime, pure object (Thing) from the corrupted Body. Its logic could be illustrated perfectly by a well-known paradox from cartoons: in a moment of panic or fight, a wolf or a cat strips off its animal skin, and beneath it we catch sight of ordinary human skin – in the cartoon universe, the hairy animal skin has thus the status of clothing; animals are really humans dressed up as animals. To be convinced, we have only to scrape off their fallacious wrapper . . . . The aim of revolutionary Terror is likewise to arrive at such an undressing: to flay off the animal, barbaric skin of the People, in hopes that its true, virtuous human nature will thus appear and assert itself freely.

All the paradoxes detected by Lefort in the passage quoted from Billaud-Varenne follow the same matrix of time-paradox. The People charges the Convention – that is to say, its delegates – with the mandate to give birth to it, to create it anew from nothingness . . . . How can somebody who does not yet exist deputize the mission to create himself? How can somebody who still waits to be created precede his own conception? Here Lacanian theory offers us a precise answer: this paradoxical presence is that of a pure object, voice or gaze. Before its proper birth, the Nation is present as a superego voice charging the Convention with the task of giving birth to it. Lefort is quite justified in designating this condition by the term "fantasy". The structure of this time-paradox also allows us to articulate the logic of the Leader's sublime body. By conceiving of himself as an agency through which the People gives birth to itself, the Leader assumes the role of a *deputy from (of) the future*; he acts as a medium through which the future, not yet existing People organizes its own conception. What was a retroactive projection in the case of the myth of "primitive accumulation" now becomes a self-legitimization of an actual political agent.

The "Hypothesis of the Master"

The general conclusion to be drawn from what we have elaborated hitherto is that to grasp the functioning of a given ideological field, reference to the symbolic order (the Lacanian "big Other") and its different mechanisms (overdetermination, condensation, displacement, and so on) is not sufficient. Within this field, there is always at work a remainder of an object which resists symbolization, the remainder which condenses, materializes pure enjoyment and which, in our case, assumes the form of the King's or Leader's other, sublime body. This remainder of the sublime body of Power is what allures the subject to "give way as to his desire" and thus entangle himself in the paradoxes of *servitude volontaire*, as it was clear already to La Boétie:

> Your oppressor has but two eyes, two hands, one body, and has nothing that the least of your infinite number of citizens does not have – except the advantage you give him, which is the power to destroy you. Where did he get those eyes which spy on you, if you did not give him them? Would he have all those hands to strike you with, if he did not get them from you? Those feet which trample upon your cities, where did he get them if they are not your own? What power has he over you, if it is not the power you give him?[45]

La Boétie's answer is therefore ultimately that of Pascal and Marx: it is the subject himself who, by behaving towards the Master in a subject-like way, *makes* him a Master. The secret of the Master, what is "in Master more than himself", that unfathomable X which confers upon him the charismatic aura, is nothing but the reverse image of the "custom", the subject's symbolic rite – whence La Boétie's advice: there is nothing easier than to get rid of the Master; one just has to stop treating him like one and, automatically, he will cease to be one:

> . . . you can deliver yourselves if you make the effort - not an effort to deliver yourselves, but an effort to want to do so! Resolve to be slaves no more, and you are free! I am not asking you to push him out of your way, to topple him: just stop propping him up and, like a great colossus whose

> plinth has been taken from under him, he will crumble and be shattered under his own weight.[46]

Note La Boétie's precise formulation: to deliver himself from the Master's yoke, the subject is *not* obliged to make an effort to deliver himself, just an effort to *want to do so*! In other words, the gesture which constitutes a Master is a gesture in which there is no gap between "will" and its accomplishment: the moment we "want" something, it is done. Why, then, do the subjects remain servants at all? Why do they treat their Master in a master-like way? There is only one possible answer: because the same paradox also defines the status of freedom:

> Freedom is the one thing which men have no desire for, and it seems as though the only reason this is so is that if they desired it, they would have it.[47]

"Freedom" is therefore the impossible point of pure "performativity" where intention coincides immediately with its fulfilment: to have it, I just have to desire it – such a saturation, of course, completely blocks the space of desire. And the "Hypothesis of the Master" is precisely one of the possible issues enabling us to save our desire from this saturation: we "externalize" the impediment, the inherent impasse of desire, transforming it into a "repressive" force which opposes it from outside. The logic of this "externalization" appears in its purest apropos of the Despot, this exemplary figure of the "Other's whim": to elude the disquieting fact that the Other itself is ultimately impotent, impeded, unable to provide "it" (the object-cause of our desire), we construct a figure of the Other who *could have* satisfied us, provide "it", but does not do so because of his purely arbitrary *whim*.[48]

In short, the trick here is the same as that of "courtly love": "A very refined manner to supplant the absence of the sexual relationship by feigning that it is us who put the obstacle in its way."[49] We elude the inherent impossibility of the sexual relationship by positing an external hindrance to it, thus preserving the illusion that without this hindrance, we would be able to enjoy it fully – no wonder, then, that the Lady in courtly love acts as the very embodiment of a whimsical Despot, submitting her knight to the most arbitrary and nonsensical ordeals. Here, we should recall the crucial passage from "The Subversion of the Subject and the Dialectic of Desire" where Lacan articulates how law "bridles" desire: the desire to be "checked" by the law is not the subject's desire but the desire of its Other, of Mother as "primordial Other"; before the intervention of the Law, the subject is at the mercy of the "whim" of the Other, the all-powerful Mother:

> . . . it is this whim that introduces the phantom of the Omnipotence, not of the subject, but of the Other in which his demand is installed . . . and with this phantom the need for it to be checked by the Law. . . . [the desire] reverses the unconditional nature of the demand for love, in which the subject remains in subjection to the Other, and raises it to the power of absolute condition (in which "absolute" also implies "detachment").[50]

Before the reign of Law, Mother (the "primordial Other") appears as the "phantom of the Omnipotence"; the subject depends totally on its "whim", on its arbitrary (self-)will, for the satisfaction of its needs; in these conditions of total dependence on the Other, the subject's desire is reduced to the demand for the Other's love – to the endeavour to comply with the Other's demand and thus gain its love. The subject identifies its desire with the desire of the Other–Mother, assuming a position of complete alienation: it finds itself totally submitted to the Other-without-lack, non-subjected to any kind of law, which, according to its momentary whim, can satisfy or not satisfy the subject's demand.

The advent of symbolic Law breaks this closed circle of alienation: the subject experiences how the Other–Mother itself obeys a certain Law (the paternal Word); the omnipotence and self-will of the Other are thereby "checked", subordinated to an "absolute condition". Consequently, the advent of Law entails a kind of "disalienation": in so far as the Other itself appears submitted to the "absolute condition" of Law, the subject is no more at the mercy of the Other's whim, its desire is no more totally alienated in the Other's desire – that is to say, the subject succeeds in establishing a kind of distance towards the Mother's desire; its desire is no longer reduced to the demand for the Mother's love. In contrast to the "post-structuralist" notion of a Law checking, canalizing, alienating, oppressing, "Oedipianizing" some previous "flux of desire", Law is here conceived as an agency of "disalienation" and "liberation": it opens our access to desire by enabling us to disengage ourselves from the rule of the Other's whim.

All these are, of course, Lacanian commonplaces; what is usually overlooked here, however, is the way this "checking" of the Other's desire by means of Law follows the structure of the "negation of negation"; of the self-relating negation. The subject "liberates" itself not by "overcoming" the negative power of the Other to which it is submitted, but by experiencing its *self-referential* character: the negativity which the Other directed against the subject is actually directed against the Other itself, which means that this Other is already in itself split, marked by a self-referring negative relationship, submitted to its own negativity. The relationship of the subject to the Other thus ceases to be that of direct subordination, since the Other is no longer a figure of full omnipotence: what the subject obeys is no longer the Other's will but a Law which regulates its relationship to the Other – the Law imposed by the Other is simultaneously the Law which the Other itself must obey.

The "Other's whim" – the fantasy-image of an omnipotent Other upon the self-will of which our satisfaction depends – is therefore nothing but *a way to avoid the lack in the Other*: the Other *could have* procured the object of full satisfaction; the fact that it did *not* do so depends simply upon its inscrutable self-will. It is almost superfluous to point out the theological and political implications of this logic of the "Other's whim": one needs only to recall on the one hand the Calvinist theory of predestination – the idea of an omnipotent and free God who, unsubordinated to any law, determines in advance, according to His inscrutable "whim", who will be damned for ever and who will be saved; and, on the other hand, the already-mentioned fantasy of the Despot, of a power which is absolute, omnipotent, and simultaneously at the mercy of the absolute self-will: where the only law is the Despot's whim.

It is in this precise sense that we should also conceive Lacan's thesis according to which *Father itself* (as agency of prohibition) *is a symptom*; a "compromise-formation" which attests to the fact that the subject "gave way as to its desire". Desire in its purity is of course "death-drive", it occurs when the subject assumes without restraint its "being-towards-death", the ultimate annihilation of its symbolic identity – that is, when it endures confrontation with the Real, with the impossibility constitutive of desire. The so-called "normal" resolution of the Oedipus complex – the symbolic identification with the paternal metaphor: that is to say, with the agency of prohibition – is ultimately nothing but a way for the subject to avoid the impasse constitutive of desire by transforming the inherent *impossibility* of its satisfaction into *prohibition*: as if desire would be *possible* to fulfil if it were not for the prohibition impeding its free rein . . . . Psychoanalysis, however, does not "bet on Father", the aim of the psychoanalytic process is in no way to bring about "successful" identification with the Name-of-the-Father: its aim is, on the contrary, to induce the analysand to choose "the worst" in the alternative "the Father or the worst" [*le père ou le pire*] – that is to say, to dissolve Father *qua* symptom by choosing the desire's impasse, by fully assuming the impossibility constitutive of desire.[51]

The King as a place-holder of the void

The ultimate paradox of the Master's sublime body, however, is that its role cannot be reduced to that of a "symptom" enabling the subject to avoid the Real of its desire: one should also *reverse* the perspective by exhibiting how the King's body could also function as the very *guarantee* of the non-closure of the Social the acceptance of which characterizes democracy. What we have in mind, of course, is Hegel's deduction of monarchy from his *Philosophy of Right*.

The paradox of the Hegelian monarch becomes manifest if we locate it against the background of what Claude Lefort called the "democratic invention": the radical break in the very mode of the performing of Power introduced by the emergence of democratic political discourse. Lefort's fundamental thesis – which has today already acquired the status of a commonplace – is that with the advent of the "democratic invention", the locus of Power becomes *an empty place*; what was before the anguish of interregnum, a period of transition to be surmounted as soon as possible – the fact that "the Throne is empty" – is now the only "normal" state. In pre-democratic societies, there is always a legitimate pretender to the place of Power, somebody who is fully entitled to occupy it, and the one who violently overthrows him has simply the status of an usurper, whereas within the democratic horizon, *everyone* who occupies the locus of Power is by definition a usurper.[52]

All that is allowed within this horizon is that by means of electoral legitimation, a political subject temporarily exerts Power, whereat his status is thoroughly that of a *proxy*: we are constantly aware of the distance separating the locus of Power as such from those exerting Power at a given moment. Democracy is defined precisely by this untrespassable limit preventing any political subject from becoming consubstantial with the locus of Power, and what is of special significance to us here is that Lefort designates this limit by means of the Lacanian notions of the Real and the Symbolic. With the advent of democratic discourse, the locus of Power changes into a purely symbolic construction that cannot be occupied by any real political agency.

Bearing in mind the homology between Lefort's thesis on the empty locus of power and Saint-Just's famous motto "Nobody can reign innocently!" which served as the immediate legitimization of the Terror, the crucial fact becomes evident: the Jacobinical Terror was not a simple aberration or betrayal of the democratic project but, on the contrary, of a strictly democratic nature. The Jacobinical Terror differs from the post-democratic "totalitarian" terror in that it is not the terror of those who claim the right to "reign innocently" in the name of their "historical (class, race, religious . . .) mission"; the very notion of the Party as the embodiment of the "historical interest" is alien to the universe of Jacobinism. The Jacobins, on the contrary, perceived themselves as *protectors of the empty locus of Power*, as a safeguard against false pretenders to this place: "The Terror is revolutionary in that it forbids anyone to occupy the place of Power; and in that sense, it has a democratic character."[53]

This is why, for example, Robespierre's argument against Danton does not consist in any positive evidence of his guilt. It is enough to recall the obvious, purely formal fact that Danton is a revolutionary hero and as such elevated above the mass of ordinary citizens – that is, claiming a special status for himself. In the Jacobinical universe, the hero of the Revolution is separated from its traitor by a thin, often indefinable line. The very *form* of hero can turn into a traitor one who, as to deeds, is a revolutionary hero; this form raises him over ordinary citizens and so exposes him to the danger and lure of tyranny. Robespierre himself was quite aware of this paradox, and his tragic greatness expresses itself in his stoic acceptance of the prospect of being decapitated in the service of the Revolution.

This deadlock of the Jacobinical position of protector of the empty locus of Power could be precisely articulated by reference to the Lacanian distinction between the subject of the enunciated and the subject of the enunciation. On the level of the enunciated, the Jacobin safeguards the emptiness of the locus of Power; he prevents anybody from occupying this place – but does he not thus reserve for himself a privileged place, does he not function as a kind of King-in-reverse –

that is to say, is not the very position of enunciation from which he acts and speaks the position of absolute Power? Is not safeguarding the empty locus of Power the most cunning and at the same time the most brutal, unconditional way of occupying it?

Far from entailing any kind of return to the pre-democratic political order with a legitimate "natural" pretender to the locus of Power, the Hegelian defence of monarchy presents us with a speculative solution to this Jacobinical impasse. The function of the Hegelian monarch corresponds exactly to that of the Jacobinical Terrorist: to serve as a protector of the empty locus of Power. That is to say, his function is ultimately of a purely negative nature; he is an empty, formal agency whose task is simply to prevent the current performer of Power (executive) from "glueing" on to the locus of Power – that is, from identifying immediately with it. The "monarch" is nothing but a positivization, a materialization of the *distance* separating the locus of Power from those who exert it. It is for this reason – because his function is purely negative – that the question of "who should reign" could be, even *must* be, left to the contingency of biological lineage – only thus is the *utter insignificance* of the positivity of the monarch effectively asserted.

We can now see why the monarch, precisely as the point which guarantees and personifies the *identity* of the State *qua* rational totality, is a pure "reflective determination". The impasse, the short circuit, of the Jacobinical position is dissolved by means of a "reflection-into-itself" of the negative barrier which, within the democratic universe, prevents political subjects from occupying the locus of Power – this very barrier is anew materialized in a subject in which pure, empty Name coincides with the immediacy of nature's "last residue". In other words, the only way effectively to bar political subjects from becoming "glued" to the locus of Power is to subjectivize anew this very barrier in the person of monarch. The vicious circle of Terror – of democrats cutting off each other's heads indefinitely – is thus interrupted. So the monarch is a kind of inversion of the Jacobinical paradox. If, in the Jacobin, his position of enunciation (executor of Power) belies his enunciated (that of being a protector of the empty locus of Power, i.e. of its democratic character), the monarch, on the contrary, succeeds in functioning, on the level of enunciation, as an effective protector of the empty locus of Power precisely by assuming, on the level of enunciated, the shape of an unitary, positive Person, that of a Sovereign, guarantor and embodiment of the State's identity with itself.[54]

Is today's Left therefore condemned to pledge all its forces to the victory of democracy? The irony here is unmistakable: up till recently, the Left displayed all its dialectical virtuosity in demonstrating how liberal-democratic freedom is not yet "actual freedom", how an inherent antagonism pertains to it that will ultimately dig its own grave, how all phenomena which appear to liberal-democratic ideology as mere excesses, degenerations, aberrations – in short: signs that the liberal-democratic project is not yet fully realized – are *stricto sensu* its symptoms, points at which its hidden truth emerges. Should today's Left therefore resign itself to accept the pseudo-Hegelian thesis on the "End of History" and – to paraphrase Hegel's Preface to *The Philosophy of Right*[55] – recognize reason as the rose of the only possible freedom in the cross of the late-capitalist present? Should it shamefacedly become speechless or indulge in the masochistic ritual of denouncing the "totalitarian potential" of its own past – to the great satisfaction of conformist dwarfs whose self-complacency triumphs in today's scoundrel time over the Leftist "utopiansm"?

In the face of the apparent worldwide triumph of liberal-capitalist ideology, it would be far more productive to recall Hegel's dictum that a political movement gains victory when it *splits*. The moment of liberal democracy's triumph, the moment when its *external* adversary, incarnated in the Communist "Evil Empire", disintegrated, is in itself (and will soon become also "for itself") the moment of confrontation with its *immanent* limit: its own weaknesses can no longer be exculpated by means of a comparison with "Them". In the West as well as in the East, we are already witnessing new political movements which are "events" in the sense elaborated by Alain Badiou: emergences of something that cannot be integrated into the existing ideological frameworks, signs of the New the pathbreaking character of which is attested by the very fact that they do not know what they are signs of and therefore often take refuge in the language of the past; it suffices to mention the Green movement.

This New can be recognized by the diverse forms of refusal to follow the updated formula of the categorical imperative: "Act so that your activity in no way impedes the free circulation and reproduction of capital!" Today, when the cracks in the façade of the worldwide greening of democracy render more and more visible its grey flesh of capital; when – exemplarily the former GDR – democratic enthusiasm proves to be nothing more than a prelude to the integration of a new territory into the flux of capital, this effective force of deterritorialization which undermines all fixed local identities, this veritable *rhizome* of our time, psychoanalysis is more than ever charged with the task of delimiting the space of possible resistance to this circulation: new forms of hysterical refusal of the subject to assume the preordained place in this circulation, new forms of the hysterical question addressed to capital.

To find proper names for this New is the task ahead for Left thought. In fulfilling this task, the Left has no need to renounce its past: how symptomatic is today's forgetfulness about the fact that the Left was the "vanishing mediator" which gained most of the rights and freedoms today appropriated by liberal democracy, starting with the common right to vote; how symptomatic is the forgetfulness about the fact that the very language by means of which even the mass media perceive Stalinism ("Big Brother", "Ministry of Truth", and so on) was the product of a *leftist* criticism of the Communist experience. Today more than ever, in the midst of the scoundrel time we live in, the duty of the Left is to keep alive the memory of all lost causes, of all shattered and perverted dreams and hopes attached to leftist projects. The ethics which we have in mind here, apropos of this duty, is the ethics of Cause *qua* Thing, the ethics of the Real which, as Lacan puts it, "always returns to its place".

Psychoanalysis knows many kinds of ethics; we could almost say that every "pathology" implies its own ethical attitude. The *hysterical* ethical imperative is to keep the *desire* alive at any price: apropos of every object which could satisfy it and thus threatens to extinguish it, the hysterical reaction is a "This is not *that*!" which sets the desire again in motion. The object of the *obsessional* desire is the Other's *demand*: his imperative is to guess it and comply with it at any price. The obsessional is completely at a loss if the Other poses no demands on him, if he cannot in any way be "useful" to the Other; since this lack of a demand throws him face to face with the abyss of the Other's desire beyond his demand – the obsessional sacrifices himself, works all the time for the Other, in order to prevent the appearance of the Other's desire. The imperative of a *pervert*, on the contrary, is to work for the Other's *enjoyment*, to become an object-instrument of it. And it seems as if the Left has until now vacillated between these three positions:

from the anarchist radical Left dominated by the "Narcissism of a lost Cause", which feels good when far from power where it can remain unsatisfied and maintain its distance towards the existing social order, over the traditional social-democratic obsessional ethics of compulsive satisfying the Other's (voter's) demands – "let us forget about great Goals, let us concentrate on what people really want and endeavour to provide it within the limits of the possible" – to the Stalinist pervert position of an instrument serving the enjoyment of the big Other of History (the "iron Laws of historical Progress", etc.).

Beside these three ethics of hysterical desire, obsessional demand and pervert enjoyment there is, however, a fourth ethical attitude, that of the *drive*. Lacan's thesis is here sharpened to a point: it is not just that the subject must not "give way as to his drive"; *the status of the drive itself is inherently ethical*. We are at the exact opposite of vitalist biologism: the image that most appropriately exemplifies drive is not "blind animal thriving" but the ethical compulsion which compels us to mark repeatedly the memory of a lost Cause. The point is *not* to remember the past trauma as exactly as possible: such "documentation" is a priori false, it transforms the trauma into a neutral, objective fact, whereas the essence of the trauma is precisely that it is too horrible to be remembered, to be integrated into our symbolic universe. All we have to do is to mark repeatedly the trauma as such, in its very "impossibility", in its non-integrated horror, by means of some "empty" symbolic gesture.

A deeply affecting case of such a gesture was the evidence of a Polish Jew who survived Auschwitz and, despite the pressure of Communist power, refused to leave for the West. Asked by journalists about the reasons for his insistence, he answered that every time he makes a visit to the site of the camp, he notices a concrete block, a remainder of some camp building – he is himself like this mute concrete block, the only important thing is that he returns, that he is there. On another level, Claude Lanzmann did the same in his holocaust documentary *Shoah*: he renounced in advance every attempt to reconstruct the "reality" of the Holocaust; by means of numerous interviews with survivors, with peasants who today live on the site of Auschwitz, by means of shots of desolated remnants of the camp, he *encircled* the impossible place of the Catastrophe. And this is how Lacan defines drive: the compulsion to *encircle* again and again the site of the lost Thing, to *mark* it in its very impossibility – as exemplified by the embodiment of the drive in its zero degree, in its most elementary, the *tombstone* which just marks the site of the dead.

This, then, is the point where the Left must not "give way": it must preserve the traces of all historical traumas, dreams and catastrophes which the ruling ideology of the "End of History" would prefer to obliterate – it must become itself their living monument, so that as long as the Left is here, these traumas will remain marked. Such an attitude, far from confining the Left within a nostalgic infatuation with the past, is the only possibility for attaining a distance on the present, a distance which will enable us to discern signs of the New.

Notes

1. See Joan Copjec, "The Sartorial Superego", *October* 50, New York: MIT 1989.

2. Immanuel Kant, *Critique of Practical Reason*, Indianapolis: Bobbs-Merrill 1957, pp. 26–7.

3. Jacques Lacan, *Écrits*, Paris: Éditions du Seuil 1966, p. 767.

4. Stalinist Communism is therefore in a way more straightforward than the "normal" civil order: it openly acknowledges the violence in its foundation. The Party is like an indigene who would say: "Our aim is to outlaw cannibalism – and our task is to eat the last of them in order to achieve it." The conclusion to be drawn from it, perhaps, is that what we call "democracy" implies a certain fundamental naivety, a certain resolve to leave some things unspoken and to act *as if* we do not know them.

5. J.V. Stalin, *Works*, vol. 6, Moscow: Foreign Languages Publishing House 1953, p. 47.

6. Jacques Lacan, *The Four Fundamental Concepts of Psycho-Analysis*, London: Hogarth 1977, p. 185.

7. Ibid.

8. There is a telling detail in Bertolucci's otherwise dull and pretentious film epic *The Last Emperor*: the imprisoned ex-emperor complains to his benevolent supervisor of how the Communists keep him alive and treat him (comparatively) well only because he is of use to them, to which the supervisor replies, with disarming candour: "And what is so bad about being useful?" Here we have at its purest the opposition of the *hysteric* apprehensive of being "used" by the others as object (witness Dora, Freud's analysand, resisting her role of an object of exchange between her father and Mr K) and of the *pervert* voluntarily assuming and enjoying his position of an instrument-object useful to the Other. By the same token it becomes clear why the modern form of hysteria depends upon the predominance of the utilitarian capitalist ideology: it is precisely a rebellion of the subject against being reduced to his/her "usefulness".

9. One remembers how in the Stalinist hagiography the Leader is described as somebody who, although privately a kind and gentle person (Lenin liked cats and

children, etc.), nevertheless carries out without delay radical and cruel decisions when the Other (History) demands it.

10. Søren Kierkegaard, "The Notion of the Chosen One", quoted from Max Horkheimer, *Traditionnelle und kritische Theorie*, Frankfurt: Fischer Verlag 1970, p. 210.

11. Jacques Lacan, *Le Séminaire, livre III: Les Psychoses*, Paris: Éditions du Seuil 1981.

12. In his first seminars from the early 1950s, Lacan elaborates the thesis that superego is a Law (an injunction) in so far as it is experienced by the subject as traumatic, meaningless – as something that cannot be integrated in his symbolic universe; it is only in the 1970s, however, in the last years of his teaching, that Lacan provides the ground for this resistance of the superego to being integrated in the Symbolic: the ultimate trauma that resists symbolization is that of *enjoyment*, so the superego remains a foreign body that cannot be integrated into the subject's horizon of meaning precisely in so far as it commands enjoyment.

13. Franz Kafka, *The Trial*, Harmondsworth: Penguin 1985, p. 244.

14. Jacques Lacan, *Écrits: A Selection*, London: Tavistock 1977, p. 319.

15. Kafka, p. 61.

16. This opposition played a crucial role in the last years of "actually existing socialism", since it articulated the spontaneous ideological self-perception of the dissidents: the authority in whose name they refused to comply with the "totalitarian" legal order was that of the Antigonesque "unwritten laws" of human dignity and decency, etc.

17. Kant, p. 30.

18. Lacan, *Écrits*, p. 782.

19. Ibid.

20. Note how Lacan's procedure here is the exact opposite of what one usually imputes to psychoanalysis, namely the idea that every ethical act is actually regulated by "pathological" considerations (lust for power, esteem, etc.): his point is, on the contrary, that desire itself is ethical in the strictest Kantian sense.

21. See Mladen Dolar, "Foucault and the Enlightenment", *New Formations* 14, London 1991.

22. This is why law's intervention is sometimes experienced as a kind of relief: "The anxiety had always been within himself, a battle of himself against himself, so tortuous he might have welcomed the law's intervention. Society's law was lax compared to the law of conscience. He might go to the law and confess, but confession seemed a minor point, a mere gesture, even an easy way out, an avoidance of truth. If the law executed him, it would be a mere gesture." (Patricia Highsmith, *Strangers on a Train*, Baltimore, MD: Penguin 1974, p. 161)

23. The opposite distinction is of course more widespread: "I know that it is not so, but nevertheless I believe it" – the formula of the fetishistic disavowal ("I know that my mother hasn't got a penis, but nevertheless I believe that . . . [she has one]"), which is generally well known in the form of so-called racial "prejudice" ("I know that the Jews are not guilty, but nevertheless . . . ").

24. In the kind of relation between (real) knowledge and (symbolic) belief it is of course not difficult to recognize the characteristic Hegelian distinction of the relation between object and knowledge of it which are both "for the consciousness", only here, in place of the object, we have (real) knowledge, and instead of knowledge, (symbolic) belief: both moments, "objective" knowledge of reality as well as "subjective"

symbolic belief, "fall within the subject": we *believe* in God, yet at the same time we could, so to speak, "step on our own shoulders" and *know* that there is no God.

25. George Orwell, *Nineteen Eighty-Four*, Harmondsworth: Penguin 1982, p. 174.

26. See Octave Mannoni, "Je sais bien, mais quand même . . . ", in *Clefs pour l'Imaginaire,* Paris: Éditions du Seuil 1968.

27. Talayesva, *le Soleil Hopi*, Paris: Éditions du Seuil 1959.

28. Mannoni, *Clefs pour l'Imaginaire*, pp. 14–15.

29. Ibid., pp. 16–17.

30. Ibid., p. 17.

31. The author of the present book could illustrate the meaning of this radically non-psychological character of the big Other (the symbolic order) with an experience from his own pedagogic practice: in order to block the students' customary reaction at the exams, which consists in pretending that it is *really just this* question which has unpleasantly surprised them, struck them on their weak point, he allowed them to *ask themselves a question* they had to answer – the apparent liberalism had of course an underhand repressive motive: he wanted thus to bar the possibility of the students' flight – they had to stay for their own question; here there is no excuse left for them. However, this strategy did not block the aforementioned ritual mechanism: the students themselves put up the question *and then calmly behaved according to the same ritual*: they started to moan pitiously, rolling their eyes – how unlucky it was; that this was *the* unpleasant question; how could it have happened to me? . . . Far from being an insincere pretence, the symbolic disposition which operates directly was thereby confirmed, notwithstanding the constraints on the psychological level: surprise at the question is a ritual which flies in the face of the psychological facts.

32. Mannoni, *Clefs pour l'Imaginaire*, p. 27.

33. Ibid.

34. Ibid., p. 32.

35. This function of the "plus-One" is often staged in cleverly plotted "whodunits" (some of the best Erle Stanley Gardners, etc.): in a closed locale (liner, isolated hotel . . .) murder or suicide is staged (i.e. one of the persons seen before disappears without trace under suspicious circumstances); the solution is of course that the death never occurred – the same subject was impersonating two individuals never seen together, so that after the disappearance of one of them, he simply assumes the identity of the other, while the police rack their brains about the mysterious disappearance . . . . A variation on this motif is when, after a violent scene, person A is found dead and person B disappears; here, the solution is also that the two of them are one and the same person – that the corpse is really that of the person presumed to disappear (while, of course, the murderer is the one whose corpse was seemingly found). What these cases have in common is *the presence of a supplementary, empty symbolic place lacking its bearer*: the jigsaw puzzle falls together the moment we become aware of the non-correspondence between the number of symbolic places and the number of "real" persons – i.e. of the surplus, the "plus-One", on the side of the symbolic network.

36. In short, the Jacobins were caught in the following paradox: is the King effectively a king or just an impostor? If he is effectively a king, then there is no sense in killing him because he does not cheat – i.e. he is what he claims to be; if, on the contrary, he is an impostor, then there is again no reason to kill him because he does not present any real danger – it is enough to unmask his imposture . . . . The Jacobins'

solution is that the King is a deceptive semblance which ontologically does not exist, *and it is precisely for that reason that it is so dangerous* – i.e. it is precisely because of its ontological delusiveness (a nothing claiming to be something, a "thing of nothing") that it must be fought by every means. In other words, the real mystery of the King's charisma is that of *servitude volontaire*: how was it possible for a pure impostor without any substance to fascinate and dominate people for such a long time?

37. Andrzej Warminski, *Readings in Interpretation*, Minneapolis: University of Minnesota Press 1987, pp. 110–11.

38. Ernst Kantorowicz, *The King's Two Bodies*, Princeton, NJ: Princeton University Press 1959.

39. Claude Lefort, *Democracy and Political Theory*, Minneapolis: University of Minnesota Press 1988, p. 244.

40. Jacques Lacan, "Death and the Interpretation of Desire in *Hamlet*", in S. Felman, ed., *Literature and Psychoanalysis*, Baltimore, MD and London: Johns Hopkins University Press 1982, pp. 50–51. The term "phallus" should not mislead us here: in 1959, Lacan had not yet elaborated the difference between phallus and *objet a*; from the later articulation of his theory it is clear, however, that the phallic "thing" mentioned here is *objet petit a*.

41. Lefort, p. 87.

42. Quoted from Paul-Dominique Dognin, *Les "sentiers escarpés" de Karl Marx* I, Paris: CERF 1977, p. 72.

43. Lefort, p. 79.

44. Ibid.

45. Étienne La Boétie, *Slaves by Choice*, Egham: Runnymede Books 1988, p. 43.

46. Ibid., p. 44.

47. Ibid., p. 43.

48. See Alain Grosrichard, *La Structure du sérail*, Paris: Éditions du Seuil 1979.

49. Jacques Lacan, *Le Séminaire, livre XX: Encore, Paris: Éditions du Seuil* 1975, p. 65.

50. Lacan, *Écrits: A Selection*, p. 311.

51. This is also the reason why, as Lacan puts it, Woman [*la Femme*] is "one of the Names-of-the-Father": the figure of Woman, its fascinating presence, simultaneously embodies and conceals a certain fundamental impossibility (that of the sexual relationship). Woman and Father are two ways for the subject to "give way as to its desire" by transforming its constitutive deadlock into an external agency of prohibition or into an inaccessible Ideal.

52. Here we can see how the "democratic invention" accomplishes the operation which Lacan calls "*point de capiton*" (quilting point). What was at one moment a terrifying defect, a catastrophe for the social edifice – the fact that "the throne is empty" – turns into a crucial prerogative. The fundamental operation of the "democratic invention" is thus of a purely symbolic nature: it is misleading to say that the "democratic invention" *finds* the locus of Power empty – the point is rather that it *constitutes, constructs* it as empty; that it reinterprets the "empirical" fact of interregnum into a "transcendental" condition of the legitimate exercise of Power.

And, incidentally, herein consists another argument for the structural homology between "democratic invention" and Kant's philosophy, in so far as Kant's "transcendental turn" also changes into the subject's constitutive *power* what the previous metaphysics had perceived as the subject's crucial *weakness* (its limitation to the finite, sensual experience). As Heidegger pointed out in his *Kant and the Problem of Metaphysics* (Bloomington: Indiana University Press 1962), Kant was the first in the history of philosophy to confer ontologically constitutive power upon finitude as such and not to grasp it as simply an obstacle on our way to the supra-empirical Truth.

53. Lefort, p. 86.

54. A *prima facie* argument against the purely formal status of the Hegelian monarch is that he still presents the point of decision, i.e. the agency which, by means of his "Such is my will!", cuts short the indeterminate weighing of arguments and transforms his counsellors' proposals into a formal decree. What we should bear in mind at this point, however, is the groundless, non-founded, "abyssal" character of the monarch's decision. This decision does not simply follow the calculus of justified reasons – ultimately, it is founded in itself; it *interrupts* the chain of reasons by an act of pure will ("It is so because I say so!").

Here, we could refer to Jon Elster's *Solomonic Judgements* (Cambridge: Cambridge University Press 1989), where the author, by means of a series of ingenious examples, demonstrates the inherent limitation of rational deciding. If we apply the theory of rational choice to the dilemmas of concrete interpersonal relations, sooner or later we reach the point of "undecidability" at which it is not possible to foresee in a rational way the entire chain of consequences of different decisions. For that reason, the most adequate decision, from the standpoint of rationality itself, is to leave the choice to chance (to draw lots, etc.). Elster's main example is child custody disputes. It is often not only impossible to predict the long-term gains and losses of different options – the point is rather that this very procedure of finding out what would be in the best interests of the child can be counterproductive (it puts the child in extremely embarrassing situations where, by stating his/her preference for one of the parents, s/he can irreparably damage his/her relations with them, etc.), so that the optimal solution is sometimes equivalent to tossing a coin.

The role of the Hegelian monarch is to be conceived on the basis of this inherent limitation of deciding founded upon a series of positive reasons. The monarch effectively "decides", makes a choice, only when the best solution, from the rational standpoint, is to leave the decision to chance. He thus prevents an endless weighing of pros and cons. Here Hegel is quite explicit: in his *Philosophy of Right*, he compares the role of the modern monarch with the way the Greek Republic looked for a reference that would help it to reach a decision in natural "signs" (the entrails of ritually slaughtered animals; the direction of the flight of birds, etc.) With modern monarchy, this principle of decision no longer needs an external support; it can assume the shape of pure subjectivity. The very agency of the monarch thus attests the inherent limitation of Reason – let this be a reminder to those who still prattle about Hegel's "panlogicism", his presumed belief in the infinite power of Reason . . .

55. G.W.F. Hegel, *The Philosophy of Right*, London: Clarendon Press 1942, p. 12.

Index